Black Religion / Womani:
Series Editors Dwight N. Hc
Published by Palgrave Macmillan

"How Long This Road": Race, Religion, and the Legacy of C. Eric Lincoln
Edited by Alton B. Pollard, III and Love Henry Whelchel, Jr.

African American Humanist Principles: Living and Thinking Like the Children of Nimrod
By Anthony B. Pinn

White Theology: Outing Supremacy in Modernity
By James W. Perkinson

The Myth of Ham in Nineteenth-Century American Christianity: Race, Heathens, and the People of God
By Sylvester Johnson

Loving the Body: Black Religious Studies and the Erotic
Edited by Anthony B. Pinn and Dwight N. Hopkins

Transformative Pastoral Leadership in the Black Church
By Jeffery L. Tribble Sr.

Shamanism, Racism, and Hip Hop Culture: Essays on White Supremacy and Black Subversion
By James W. Perkinson

Women, Ethics, and Inequality in U.S. Healthcare: "To Count Among the Living"
By Aana Marie Vigen

Black Theology in Transatlantic Dialogue: Inside Looking Out, Outside Looking In
By Anthony G. Reddie

Womanist Ethics and the Cultural Production of Evil
By Emilie M. Townes

Whiteness and Morality: Pursuing Racial Justice through Reparations and Sovereignty
By Jennifer Harvey

The Theology of Martin Luther King Jr. and Desmond Mpilo Tutu
By Johnny B. Hill

Conceptions of God, Freedom, and Ethics in African American and Jewish Theology
By Kurt Buhring

Black Theology and Pedagogy
By Noel Leo Erskine

The Origins of Black Humanism in America: Reverend Ethelred Brown and the Unitarian Church
By Juan M. Floyd-Thomas

Black Religion and the Imagination of Matter in the Atlantic World
By James A. Noel

Bible Witness in Black Churches
By Garth Kasimu Baker-Fletcher

Enslaved Women and the Art of Resistance in Antebellum America
By Renee K. Harrison

Ethical Complications of Lynching: Ida B. Wells's Interrogation of American Terror
By Angela D. Sims

Representations of Homosexuality: Black Liberation Theology and Cultural Criticism
By Roger A. Sneed

The Tragic Vision of African American Religion
By Matthew V. Johnson

Beyond Slavery: Overcoming Its Religious and Sexual Legacies
Edited by Bernadette J. Brooten with the editorial assistance of Jacqueline L. Hazelton

Gifts of Virtue, Alice Walker, and Womanist Ethics
By Melanie Harris

Racism and the Image of God
By Karen Teel

Self, Culture, and Others in Womanist Practical Theology
By Phillis Isabella Sheppard

Sherman's March and the Emergence of the Independent Black Church Movement
By Love Henry Whelchel

Black Men Worshipping: Intersecting Anxieties of Race, Gender, and Christian Embodiment
By Stacy C. Boyd

Womanism Against Socially Constructed Matriarchal Images: A Theoretical Model Towards A Therapeutic Goal
By MarKeva Gwendolyn Hill

Indigenous Black Theology: Toward an African-Centered Theology of the African American Religious
By Jawanza Eric Clark

Black Bodies and the Black Church: A Blues Slant
By Kelly Brown Douglas

A Theological Account of Nat Turner: Christianity, Violence, and Theology
By Karl Lampley

African American Female Mysticism: Nineteenth-Century Religious Activism
By Joy R. Bostic

A Queering of Black Theology: James Baldwin's Blues Project and Gospel Prose
By E. L. Kornegay Jr.

Formation of the African Methodist Episcopal Church in the Nineteenth Century: Rhetoric of Identification
A. Nevell Owens

Toward a Womanist Ethic of Incarnation: Black Bodies, the Black Church, and the Council of Chalcedon
Eboni Marshall Turman

Religio-Political Narratives: From Martin Luther King Jr. to Jeremiah Wright
Angela D. Sims, F. Douglas Powe Jr., and Johnny Bernard Hill

Churches, Blackness, and Contested Multiculturalism: Europe, Africa, and North America
Edited by R. Drew Smith, William Ackah, & Anthony G. Reddie

Womanist and Black Feminist Responses to Tyler Perry's Productions
LeRhonda S. Manigault-Bryant, Tamura A. Lomax, and Carol B. Duncan

James Baldwin's Understanding of God: Overwhelming Desire and Joy
Josiah Ulysses Young III

A Womanist Pastoral Theology Against Intimate and Cultural Violence: A Narrative Approach to Self-Recovery
Stephanie M. Crumpton

Black Bodies and the Black Church

A Blues Slant

Kelly Brown Douglas

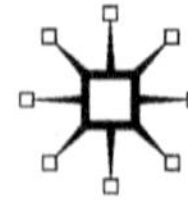

BLACK BODIES AND THE BLACK CHURCH

First published in hardcover in 2012 by PALGRAVE MACMILLAN® in the United States—a division of St. Martin's Press LLC, 175 Fifth Avenue, New York, NY 10010.

Where this book is distributed in the UK, Europe and the rest of the world, this is by Palgrave Macmillan, a division of Macmillan Publishers Limited, registered in England, company number 785998, of Houndmills, Basingstoke, Hampshire RG21 6XS.

Palgrave Macmillan is the global academic imprint of the above companies and has companies and representatives throughout the world.

ISBN: 978–1–137–44154–6

The Library of Congress has cataloged the hardcover edition as follows:

Douglas, Kelly Brown.
Black bodies and the Black church : a blues slant /
Kelly Brown Douglas.
p. cm.—(Black religion/womanist thought/social justice)
ISBN 978–0–230–11681–8
1. African American churches. 2. Black theology.
3. African Americans—Religion. 4. Blacks—Religion.
5. Discrimination—Religious aspects—Christianity.
6. Blues (Music)—Religious aspects. I. Title.

BR563.N4D67 2012
277.30089'96073—dc23 2012011548

A catalogue record of the book is available from the British Library.

Design by Newgen Knowledge Works (P) Ltd., Chennai, India.

First PALGRAVE MACMILLAN paperback edition: November 2014

10 9 8 7 6 5 4 3 2 1

In Loving Memory of My Parents
William Lewis Brown Sr. and Mary Elizabeth Brown

Contents

Acknowledgments

While writing is often a solitary process, no book is done alone. This book is no exception. My journey through blues would not have been possible without the support of many. This book would not have been possible without the support I received from Goucher College as the Elizabeth Conolly Todd Distinguished Professor. I am also indebted to my students in the course, Religion 240: Sex, Race, and God in Blues Literature. They offered invaluable insights and fueled my passion for blues. I am especially grateful to my colleague Ann Duncan who worked doubly hard so that I could bring this project to completion.

Many individuals have supported me along this journey, providing just the right thing at just the right time. I cannot possibly name them all, but I must mention a few. I thank Kaylan Connally, Burke Gerstenschalger, and the staff of Palgrave Macmillan for their support of this project I am exceedingly grateful to Linda E. Thomas for believing in and encouraging this project and making its publication possible. I thank her also for her abiding sisterhood throughout my blues journey. This project would absolutely not have been possible without the time, energy, support, and insights of Angelo Robinson, Kimberly Huff, Seble Dawit, Ronald Hopson, Isaac Lawson, and Nydia Coleman. To each of them I am forever grateful. Thanks for giving of your selves.

As always, nothing would have been possible without the support of my family. I am most appreciative for my church family of Holy Comforter Episcopal Church. I am blessed to be a part of such a loving and giving community.I am most thankful for being a witness to what it means to be a church. I am also thankful beyond words for the immeasurable support of the Reverend Dr. D. H. Kortright Davis. Then there is my own family. I must thank my sisters Karen Fallings and Kendall Lash. They are the blues women in my life. The motherhood, sisterhood and friendship we share is my daily joy. Last, but not least, I am grateful beyond words to the two most important people in my life, my husband Lamont and son Desmond. Their love, patience, laughter and belief in me keeps my blues spirit alive. They are my inspiration.

Introduction: *Black Body/Black Church: A Blues Slant*

Blues Call

Ooh, Ooh there's something going all wrong[1]

A Personal Call

"There's something going all wrong" in the black church. This became most apparent during the 2008 presidential campaign. During this campaign, as a result of a sermon preached by Dr. Jeremiah Wright on September 16, 2001 in response to the September 11, 2001 terrorist attacks on America, the media spotlight was turned on the black church. At the time of the sermon, presidential candidate Barack Obama was a member of Dr. Wright's church. In that sermon, Wright proclaimed that "the chickens had come home to roost." These words became the sound bite repeatedly played across various media outlets. Though shamefully taken out of context in relation to the wider message preached in the sermon, this sound bite became political fodder. It was used as a springboard for an attack against not only candidate Barack Obama but also the black church. This black religious institution, which had long been "invisible in and invisible to the eyes of the dominant culture," thereby garnered headline attention and intense public scrutiny.[2] Media pundits, journalist, and politicians alike variously accused the black church of being a platform for racist diatribes and home to a theology of hate. Just as Mr. Obama was put on the defensive, so too was the black church. While presidential candidate Obama hastened to renounce his membership in Dr. Wright's congregation, the black church community scrambled to support Dr. Wright and to situate him within the prophetic strand of the black religious tradition. More significantly, black clergy and black religious scholars seized the media attention to articulate the meaning of the black church and its role in the black struggle for freedom. They explained the nature of black liberation theology. In general, black church leadership attempted to present the black church in a manner more reflective of its "rich history, incredible legacy and multiple meanings."[3]

It was as I listened to black church leaders tell the story of the black church, and especially as I sat in the National Press Club on the April 28, 2008 Monday morning listening to Dr. Wright's impassioned and careful analysis of the black church and black liberation theology, that I began to gain clarity concerning what was "going all wrong." "Something was going all wrong" in the black church, something beyond what I had previously recognized. Before, I thought it was a matter of sexuality. Now I was beginning to understand that it was about more than black sexuality and the LGBTQ body—even as it was precisely about sexuality and LGBTQ bodies.

In reflecting on Dr. Wright's speech and the other responses to the attacks on the black church, I realized that these spokespersons were doing more than protecting the integrity of the black church, as they claimed. Intentionally or not, they were offering an "apologetic defense." The church that emerged in slavery and asserted itself in protest to "slaveholding" versions of Christianity was now on the defensive, seeking at least a favorable reception within mainstream society and dominant religious culture. Of course, there was much at stake. Inasmuch as the black church was seen as unacceptable to white society, so too would candidate Barack Obama. Perhaps in an effort to further black social and political well-being, the black church community took advantage of the unusual media interest to enter a Faustian pact with the white electorate—if the white electorate could accept the black church, then maybe it could accept one of its members as president. However, even if this apologetic defense was reflective of a shrewd Faustian pact, it revealed another troubling narrative within the black church, one that I identify as a *narrative of civility*.

Generally unarticulated and unrecognized, this narrative of civility is a persistent and controlling narrative within the black church. It presumes that the way black people are perceived by wider society is related to the way in which the black church is perceived. It, therefore, protects the image of the black church and strives to present this church as an institutionalized embodiment of black civility. By encouraging a certain degree of decorum within the black church itself, it projects black men and women as civilized and cultured people. Essentially, this narrative aims to maintain the centrality and respect of the black church within greater civil society to elevate the social, cultural, and even political status of black women and men.

Without a doubt, the narrative of civility is inspired by a commitment to black people's life, freedom, and overall social well-being. However, it does not always function to the benefit of all black bodies. It lends itself to several paradoxical and troubling tendencies. For instance, while it emphasizes the uniqueness of black church history and culture, it exalts white church culture. At the same time that it insist on the moral advantage of the black oppressed, it easily incorporates white socialcultural ideas and values. This narrative further asserts god's preferential option for the outsider, yet it also legitimates a white god. Finally, and perhaps most hurtful, while it presents the black church as a refuge for black life, it repeatedly alienates various black bodies. Overall, the narrative of civility is far too compatible with the very culture, systems, and ideologies that have disrespected black bodies. Consequently, even with its good intentions, this narrative leads to an uncertain relationship with the very bodies for whom the black church exists. Instead of safeguarding the well-being of black people, the narrative of civility fosters a hostile culture and sustains a rejected class within the black church community. It literally drives the black church to "cast off" and "look down" on various bodies. This brings us to what is going wrong in the black church. Given the existence of a narrative of civility, the black church has a body problem. This problem has led it to "cast off" certain bodies, which I designate as blues bodies.

A Communal Call

The blackness of the black church is more than a matter of color or culture. The blackness of this church depends upon its morally active commitment to advance the life, freedom, and dignity of all black bodies. When this church, for whatever reasons, becomes alienated from certain bodies, its very blackness is threatened. At stake is the black church itself. Can the black church "last long" if it "casts off" or "looks down upon" any black body?[4] My answer to this is "no." This brings me to the purpose of this discussion.

If the black church is to maintain its unique identity and its singular relevance in the lives of black people, then it must have the capacity to accept all black bodies, regardless. In order for this to occur, several things must be done: a careful examination of what is going wrong between the black church and those it deems blues bodies, an exploration of the prospects for righting that wrong, and an approach for doing so. This book will attempt to tackle these tasks. It will do so by untangling the web of socialhistorical and religious narratives that inform the black church's relationship to blues bodies. Primary attention will be given to understanding the complexity and implications of the narrative of civility. As suggested above, this is the controlling narrative. It, however, does not stand alone. It interacts with other narratives, such as an evangelical religious narrative, to achieve its end. Essentially, the way in which the black church treats blues bodies is important to its very existence. As long as the black church is not a safe and affirming space for those it renders blues bodies, then its very authority within the black community is undercut and its integrity within wider society is subverted, and most important, its very black faith identity is betrayed.

A Passionate Resolve

During the 2008 presidential campaign, even though I was proud of the black church for asserting itself, I was also disheartened. This campaign exposed troubling dimensions of the church that penetrated its core identity. It raised questions as to whether the black church was actually what it claimed to be, an advocate for oppressed bodies, or if its apologetic defense was the truth of what it was, a bourgeois institution concerned with its status in mainstream society. Has the black church moved beyond its historical significance and become just another black bourgeois institution? In the end, this book is being written because of my deep love for the black church, my appreciation for the valuable historical role that it has played in the lives of black men and women, including my own, and my belief that it is, at its core, what it claims to be. I believe that the concern to be accepted within the mainstream, even if it is an ongoing concern, is a gross aberration of the black church's true historical and cultural identity. The anxiety to be seen as "up to standards," so that black people are well received in wider society, can be addressed in a way that does not compromise the black church's very commitment to the black people's well-being. I believe that the black church can be a reliable advocate for justice and provide for black people to progress within civil society at the same time that it maintains its original integrity. But for this to happen, it must examine its attitudes toward blues bodies. Understanding the complicated dynamics that sustain blues bodies is key to the black church maintaining its credibility in both the black community and wider society. This book is an attempt to understand these dynamics. Fittingly, there is no tradition more suitable for doing this than the blues tradition itself.

Blues Interpretations

Oh blues, oh blues, oh blues[5]

While it is important not to fetishize or romanticize blues as if it is a pure reflection of black life and culture, it does capture a profound side of black existence that other forms of black expressive culture do not. In so doing, blues provides an informal, yet incisive, perspective on the relationship between the black church and blues bodies and, correspondingly, the depth of the wrong in the black church. It also suggests a crossroads-inspired blue(s)print for correcting that wrong.

I am not the first to appreciate the insight blues provides into the black church tradition. Various scholars have recognized the theological and religious implications of blues. One of the earliest to do so was Rod Gruver in his 1970 essay, "The Blues as Secular Religion." In this essay Gruver describes blues as "religious poetry" that triumphs over "the moral prison of [America's] Puritan ethos."[6] He describes the blues poets as "prophets of lower class Negros"seeking revenge "against white America and the blacks who had accepted its Puritan ethos."[7] According to Gruver, therefore, blues reflects an existentialist secular religion that maintains a unified worldview, that is, one that does not distinguish between the realm of the gods and that of humans. It is in this way that Gruver says blues is liberated from "organized religion," namely, black Christianity.

Similar to Gruver, James Cone has also asserted that blues rejects polarizing distinctions such as that between the body and soul. Unlike Gruver, however, Cone sees a strong relationship between blues and the black religious tradition. In *Spirituals and the Blues*, Cone provides a compelling and rich analysis of blues as "secular spirituals." These secular spirituals, Cone argues, "flow from the same bedrock of [black] experience" as do the (religious) spirituals.[8] He calls blues secular, however, because it embraces issues of body and sexuality in a way that the spirituals simply do not. Nevertheless, Cone identifies blues as spirituals because "they are impelled by the same search for the truth" as the spirituals. Blues, like the spirituals, witnessed "the

God of Israel...[who is] involved in black history" as a liberator of the black oppressed.[9]

Others have noted the significance of blues for the black church by highlighting the ways in which this music is antireligious, most notable for doing so is Paul Garon. In his book *Blues and the Poetic Spirit*, Garon says that those who suggest blues engage theology "miss the point" entirely. He says that blues "does not intervene on the theological plane."[10] He further suggests that the blues performer revels in the role of being antireligious by embracing evil. Blues, Garon continues, "enters the fray wholeheartedly *on the side of Evil*." He concludes that "the 'Devil's music' is the denunciation of everything religion stands for and the glorification of everything religion condemns."[11]

In his book *Blues and Evil*, Jon Michael Spencer responds to the notion of blues as irreligious "devil's music." To counter such claims, Spencer puts forth what he calls a "theomusicological" analysis of blues. In it he suggests that blues actually contains a strong theodicy, and thus an answer to the question of "why evil." The blues' answer, he says, rejects "otherworldly solutions to black suffering." Instead, blues theodicy provides "provisional philosophical solutions to render evil and suffering comprehensible."[12] In this way Spencer suggests, similar to Gruver and Cone, that blues maintains a unified view of the world.

Other interpreters of blues have noted the similarities between the blues singer and the black preacher. Charles Keil provides one of the earliest and most extensive comparisons. In his book *Urban Blues*, Keil draws attention to the stylistic and ritualistic commonalities that "underlie the performance" of the bluesman and the preacher. He notes how the same experiences of black life inform both. However, Keil views blues as a decidedly secular, if not "profane," form of black expression. While he acknowledges the fact that many bluesmen were very religious, he concludes that the "Bluesman and preacher [should] be considered Negro prototypes of the no-good and good man respectively."[13] In Keil's view, a person cannot be at once a blues performer and a preacher. He must be one or the other. He, therefore, labels bluesmen who return to the church after a blues career "prodigal sons."[14]

Catholic theologian Shawn Copeland provides one of the most recent interpretations of blues. In her essay "Theology at the Crossroads," Copeland highlights the role of the crossroads imagery in African mythology and in blues lore. Drawing upon the notion of the crossroads as a place where divine and earthly realms interact, mysterious things happen, and the blues people reside, Copeland argues that a black catholic theology must embrace the blues crossroads. By doing so, Copeland says this theology will be accountable to the tribulations and triumphs of the black dispossessed as well as the cross of Jesus.[15]

Building upon this important foundation for examining blues through a religious lens, I will continue to let blues speak for itself. The depth of the blues meaning for the black church community begins to surface only when the integrity of the lore, rhythm, and language of blues is maintained. While it is not possible to listen to blues with unbiased ears—free from various theological paradigms and assumptions—in the least, the blues interpreters must listen with a suspicious ear. That is, they must always question how much their particular theological interests are influencing their interpretations of blues. Essentially, one must listen for what various blues have to offer without projecting certain expectations upon them. This means entering the context of blues not simply historically but also mythologically. To do so is to be open to the "truths" about the world and god found in blues. Such openness might lead to new ways for understanding life, god, and for defining knowledge and theology itself.

In this discussion I will attempt to listen to blues with such openness. Throughout this book I try to appreciate the historical and mythical context of blues and blues singers. I will try to listen to them from the ground up and from the inside out to see what they might offer the black church in terms of its blackness and its faith. This discussion is not intended to be a thorough musical analysis or theological analysis of blues. It is meant to be one blues listener's appreciation of blues meaning for the black church, especially as that church continues to struggle with issues concerning certain bodies, such as Lesbian Gay Bisexual Transgender Queer (LGBTQ) bodies and black female bodies. If nothing else, I hope this book can provide a source of empowerment for those who have been rendered blues bodies within the black church community. This book progresses as discussed below.

A Blues Slant: Sequence of the Book

Blue, blue, I got a tale to tell you, I'm blue[16]

In an effort to echo the soul, emotion, and integrity of blues rhythm, this book takes a "blues slant" approach.[17] Each section and chapter will be framed by a particular blues lyric. The chapters will open with a personal reflection from a blues performer. Both will inform on what is to follow, though other blues lyrics and blues reflections will be engaged throughout. This book will be organized according to blues musical form.

Blues is a 12-bar, 3-line musical form. Typically, the 3-line structure follows an AAB call-and-response pattern. The first two lines of a stanza repeat a problem while the third line resolves that problem. Various blues sometimes improvise, with the performer engaged in conversation. As will be shown below, there are three main parts to this book, with the second part representing a blues conversation. The first part examines the cultural, social, and religious context of blues. Part II explores blues meanings for the church. The third part responds with a blues-informed theology. With the exception of the blues conversation in chapter 4 which is part II, the remaining two parts have three chapters each. These chapters will also reflect the blues AAB call-and-response pattern. It is important to note, however, that improvisation is important to blues. Blues is dynamic. Its rhythms are driven by the message that is being conveyed, not by a static structure. This book will reflect blues improvisation. It will not always follow a precise AAB call-and-response pattern if, in my listening to blues, I discover improvisation is needed.

Language is another important characteristic of blues. Blues is not filled with "high sounding" words. The language of blues is down-to-earth and straightforward. Blues uses the lingo and jargon of blues people in an attempt to convey their experiences. The language of this book will reflect the integrity of blues language. I will strive to use language appropriate to the experiences of the blues people that sit in the pews of black churches. The aim of this book is to do as blues do—provide smart and thoughtful theological insight in a manner recognizable to blues people.

Blues is also not afraid of the personal. The story of a people is disclosed through personal experiences. Because of this, one cannot listen to blues without being touched. As bluesman John Lee Hooker says, blues "hit somethin' that have happened in your life...[blues] is 'touchable.'"[18] This book will not be afraid of the personal. In response to the personal side of blues, I will share the way various blues have touched me.

During the 2008 presidential campaign, as I pondered the reality of the black church, Robert Johnson's lyrics, "down at the crossroads," kept playing in my head. Though intellectually I have appreciated the role of music in black culture and in black lives, music has not been an integral part of my daily life. I am not a musical person. While I was familiar with Robert Johnson and his "infamous" crossroads blues, neither held special meaning for me. Therefore, when I could not get those words out my head, I knew something unusual was going on. Blues was "talkin' to me." I traveled to Robert Johnson's crossroads. I began to listen to various blues in a way I had not listened to them before. The organization of this book reflects that listening.

Part I: Blues Note

In 1903, while waiting for a train in Tutwiller, Mississippi, W. C. Handy was struck by the guitar-playing of a "lean, loose-jointed Negro." The lyrics and the sound led Handy to describe the tune "as the weirdest music I had ever heard." What W. C. Handy no doubt heard that afternoon as the "loose-jointed Negro" made a wailing sound on his guitar was the blues note.[19] The distinct sound of this note suggests the distinctive nature of blues and the people who have given life to this note. Part I of this book looks behind the blues note. This part clarifies why blues is indispensable for any serious assessment of the black church.

Chapter 1: Crazy Blues

Some consider blues the "unconscious and naïve creations of primitive folk."[20] It is not. The blues note signals blues as a self-aware and thoughtful form of black conversation. Chapter 1 will highlight four aspects of blues: blues as "sound communication," blues as signifyin' communication, blues as signifyin' laments, and blues as radical faith testimony. This chapter will discuss the meaning of a blues bond as well as blues hope. In the end, the significance of blues for the black community and church will become clear.

Chapter 2: Somebody's Angel Child

Behind the blues note are the people who bring blues to life. Blues-singing women are the focus of this chapter. These women are highlighted throughout this book for three reasons: their singular contribution to the blues tradition, their importance to understanding the meaning of blues bodies, and the insights they provide into a radical black faith. This chapter will explore what it means for these women to be wild, wicked, and sensuous. In the end, this chapter clarifies the meaning of blues people, blues bodies, and suggests blues meanings for the black church.

Chapter 3: The Devil's Gonna Get You

The blues note strikes an ominous tone for the black church community. Chapter 3 will explore the black church's historical response to blues as "devil's music." While it will recognize the role that blues lore, instrumentation, and lyrics have played in establishing such a reputation within the black church, major emphasis will be placed on the church's attitude toward blues people. The chapter explores the relationship between a narrative of civility and an evangelical faith narrative that leads to the demonizing of blues and blues people. In the end, this chapter clarifies why blues came to be known as "the devil's music."

Part II: Blues Truth

W. C. Handy says, "We look for truth in [blues] as in everything else. It won't always take shape as we think it will. There will always be some surprises."[21] Part II of this book represents improvised blues talk; as such, it has only one chapter. In this part, one listens to the surprising ways in which blues reveals the truth about the black church community. This part exposes the systems and values that inform the black church's disregard for certain black bodies. In the end, this part explores the complicated and disruptive reality of the narrative of civility for the black church.

Chapter 4: Hear Me Talkin' to Ya

Blues discloses the raw truth concerning class arrogance, color bias, discomfort with sexuality, and black church hypocrisy. Chapter 4 will explore blues signifyin' laments and their implications for the black church community. In the end, this chapter will clarify the dangers of the narrative of civility and the narratives of the evangelical faith for the black church.

Part III: Blues Crossroad

When recounting how his brother Tommy Johnson learned to play the guitar, Ledell Johnson said, "if you want to learn how to play anything…you take your guitar and you go to where a crossroad is."[22] The crossroad is the subject of many blues songs and the site of many blues legends. Bluesmen have sung about the crossroad where the Southern railroad crossed the Yazoo Delta. The crossroad at Highway 61 in the Mississippi Delta is where Robert Johnson reportedly sold his soul to the Devil. This same crossroad also marks the highway that took Bessie Smith's life. Crossroads and blues are bound together. Blues is nothing less than a crossroad music. Part III of this book explores the meaning of the crossroad within the blues tradition. The crossroad is explored as the place where the black church and the blues body can come together. In the end, this part puts forth a crossroads theology as an essential step toward the black church becoming a "home" for all black bodies, and thus reclaiming its own black Christian integrity.

Chapter 5: Down at the Crossroads

The story of what happens to Robert Johnson at the crossroad in Mississippi begins in Africa. The crossroads reveals the gods of Africa as well as an African worldview. Chapter 5 will explore various African cultural and theological understandings of the crossroad. Such understandings shape crossroad lore within the blues tradition. These African meanings also provide the foundation for an authentically black church and theology. In the end, this chapter will suggest a crossroad theology for the black church.

Chapter 6: A Crossroad God

Drawing upon African crossroad meanings found in blues and the significance of a crossroads theology, chapter 6 will explore the meanings of the god of Jesus Christ as a crossroads god. This chapter will place the gospel narratives and blues in dialogue. In the end, the gospels as blues discourse about a blues god will be clear.

Chapter 7: Black and Blues Church

Chapter 7 discusses the practical implications of a crossroads theology. It puts forth a model of the black church as at once black and blue. In the end the chapter argues that if the black church is to survive its crisis of relevance and remain a protagonist of that which denies any black body life and freedom, then it must indeed become a church that is black and blue.

Blues Coda: Back to the Crossroads

As I stood at the Highway 61 crossroad in Mississippi, trying to imagine Robert Johnson standing there, I realized that I was standing at my own life's crossroad. This coda will share my final response to my journey through blues.

1

Blues Note

1

Crazy Blues

Now I've got the crazy blues
Since my baby went away.[1]

From 9:30 a.m. to 5:30 p.m. on August 10, 1920, Perry Bradford was in "a pleasant dream that came from heaven."[2] After walking "out two pairs of shoes," "bow [ing] and scrap [ing]...with a perpetual-lasting watermelon grin,"[3] what to many was a preposterous fantasy had become a reality. Bradford's peers did not believe that he could convince anyone in a racist music industry to record a black woman singing blues. Yet, he did. He convinced Fred Hager, the recording manager of Okeh Records, to "take a chance" on a "Negro girl." Okeh reluctantly took that chance on a cold February 1920 morning when it recorded Mamie Smith singing "This Thing Called Love." The success of this song paved the way for Bradford's dreamlike August day. With "tears of gladness" in his eyes, he spent eight hours that day listening to Smith record "Crazy Blues."[4] This was the first time that blues was officially recorded. Within a month of its November release, *Crazy Blues* sold over 75,000 copies. Within a year, hundreds of thousands of copies were sold nationally. Pullman Car Porters unofficially boosted the sales of Smith's record as they bought and then resold it in rural areas across the country. "You couldn't walk down the street in a colored neighborhood and not hear that record. It was everywhere," said Alberta Hunter.[5] Victoria Spivey exclaimed, "By heaven, I was singing it long before I left Texas."[6] Black men and women were singing it from New York to Texas. The "prejudiced door" of the music industry had been "pried open."[7] The race record market in America was born.

Recording companies that had previously turned Bradford away were falling over themselves to record blues. They were sending scouts throughout the South to find blues artists, especially black women. Between 1920 and 1930, as many as 5 million blues records were sold annually, mostly to black people, which was "phenomenal" given the fact that the black population at that time was no more than 15 million.[8]

What was this blues craze all about? Why were black women and men willing to spend their hard-earned meager wages to buy blues? What was it about this music that gripped "colored neighborhoods" in a way that perhaps no other music had while at the same time repulsed a significant segment of the black church community?

Blues awakened black people's African soul and told the story of their American bodies with a passionate authenticity that no other musical form possessed. Through blues, black men and women encountered themselves. This music laid bare the everydayness of their lives—the good and bad times. It was in fact the way in which blues affirmed black bodies that seemingly compromised the black church's concern to save black souls as well as to free black bodies from the binds of white racism.

True to the life of black bodies, blues is not one-dimensional music. They are "sad-happy songs that laugh and weep all in one breath."[9] Precisely because they convey the "raw facts" of black life, bluesman Boogie Woogie Red says blues contains "so much good feeling" that they "relax" black peoples' "nerves" and help them to get through the trials of their living.[10] Henry Townsend, also a blues artist, remarks that he doesn't know how, but blues "kinda helps" black people to make it.[11] To be sure, as blues tells the stories of their living, they have enabled black people to affirm their somebodiness and to cling to their dreams. Essentially, the truth of black life, the depth of black emotions, and the inventiveness of black culture are all captured in blues' unique twelve-bar, three-line rhythmic structure, peculiar sounding note, and "matter of fact" lyrics. The significance of blues for black women and men reflects a vital longstanding relationship between the sounds of music and the rhythms of life for African peoples.

Blues as Sound Communication

African Beginnings "Where there is no music the Spirit will not come" (West African Proverb).

There is no singular African cultural tradition. Africa is home to over 50 nations and 3,000 different ethnic groups, and hence to a multitude of distinct political arrangements, languages, traditions, customs, beliefs, and values. Nigeria alone has at least 455 different ethnic groups and 250 distinct languages with additional dialects. Each of these languages and dialects reflects a particular way of navigating the world. To use the term "African" to connote a singular identity is to disrespect the immense array of African peoples and the ways of engaging life that they have crafted. Simply put, Africa is not a nation. It is a vast and diverse multinational, multiethnic continent. Given the complex richness of Africa, generalizing about anything African is problematic. Nevertheless, there are certain understandings, traditions, and practices that are common across various African peoples, even if they are expressed in culturally unique ways. Such is the case when it comes to the significance of sound, especially for West Africa.

Traditional West African cultures—the cultural origins for most African Americans—are typically sound-centered. As aptly noted by black cultural scholar Lawrence Levine, "The Africans from whom the slaves had descended lived in a world of sound."[12] Within this cultural world, sound and life are inextricably linked. Without sound there can be no life, and where there is life there must be sound. If it is the natural sound of the heart that signals life, it is the deliberate sounds of music that communicate the multidimensional meanings of life. For African peoples, music traditionally involves a call and response.[13] The dancing, the hand-clapping, foot-tapping, head-nodding, talking back, and any other reply that the initial musical sound prompts are all a part of the musical moment. African music simultaneously involves speaking, listening, and moving. It is about more than notes and beats. It is a fundamental language form. It is, for both human and divine beings, a way of communicating through performance.

Musical sound is a vehicle for women and men of African descent to express the meaning of their existence. Through call and response, they have told their stories, commented on life events, and conveyed the sacred value of life itself. With musical ingenuity the gatekeepers of African traditions, such as the griots or gewels, have passed on the history of their people, transmitted community news, and provided sociopolitical commentary. Through the medium of music, particularly through the sounds of drums, African gods spoke to their people and made their divine presence known in various life happenings.

Within an African worldview there are no profane dimensions of living; all of living is sacred and all of life is valued by the gods. It is for this reason that typically every aspect of African living—from routine activities of work and play to momentous rites of passage, such as birth, initiation, and death—is accompanied by an appropriate sound of music. Music reflects at once the spirit of the people and the spirit of the gods.

African cultural regard for music does not signal a prerational or illiterate people. Nor does it suggest a people so fixated on sound that they have little appreciation for literary traditions. Rather, the reverence for music indicates a profound awareness of the inability of words alone to convey the fullness of the human experience. Words reflect human efforts to order and understand the immediate world. They are the language form for rational, sensate experiences, those that involve the mind and the five senses. Yet, there are dimensions of human living that are extrarational and extrasensory. These are the sensual, affectional, and spiritual experiences, those that "make you want to holler," that move you to tears, or that touch your soul, but these are experiences that "you cannot put into words." Hence, many African cultures are non-logos-centered. The spoken word is a form of communication, but not the only and perhaps not the most important form. West African cultures tend to utilize various art forms, in this instance, music, as a means to express the richness of the human experience. As many have pointed out, "The aim of African music has always been to translate the experiences of life and of the spiritual world into sound."[14]

The value of musical communication to African life was heightened when Africans were forcibly brought across the Middle Passage. Not only did music retain its role as a way to communicate with life and about life, but it also became an essential tool for daily survival. Practically speaking, music allowed the captured and enslaved Africans to talk to one another across the barriers of their indigenous languages and dialects, which their captors did not respect. It also became a cultural/historical/religious living library, allowing various traditions to be preserved and then passed on to generations of enslaved blacks, especially to those who were born away from the African homeland. Moreover, music remained the medium through which the gods spoke. The gods traveled across the Middle Passage through the sounds of music and, thus, continued to be present in their people's lives—even in a strange land. Most significantly, music provided a "safe space" for enslaved Africans to talk honestly about their life circumstances and to share their secrets, even when white ears were listening. For while their masters and mistresses considered them ignorant "happy go lucky darkeys" with an instinct for singing and dancing; through the sounds of music the enslaved exchanged valuable information about survival and escape while also passing on cunning insights regarding the "ways of white folks." But, of course, it should never be forgotten that music was a source of entertainment—it allowed enslaved women and men to laugh and play through the hardships and toil of their bondage. Through musical play, the enslaved contested any notion that they were merely nonhuman beasts for labor. The music the Africans made, even under the vile conditions of slavery, signaled their vibrant protest against structural or ideological systems that denied their divine humanity.

Historically, the role of music in the African diaspora has been immense. It has provided continuity to a free African past as well as a means to navigate an unfree American present. As such, the persistent sounds of music throughout the black journey testify to the sacred status of black peoples in the universe. To enter into the musical tradition of African peoples, therefore, is to enter a compelling tradition of sound that tells the story of a people as they move from freedom robbed toward freedom reclaimed. Blues is a part of this tradition of sound.

> *Sounds of Blues*: "[put] into sound the feelings that are beyond words."[15]

Blues comprises the songs of blues people. These are the individuals who exist on the fringes of life: they are the black underclass. As such, their life circumstances are defined by both the ordeal of white racism and the deprivations of crushing poverty. When blues first emerged during the late nineteenth and early twentieth centuries, these were sharecropping, tenant-farming, migrating, "hand-to-mouth" black people. They were the black women and men who provided the back-bending hand-to-soil labor for the southern plantation/farm economy and the mind-numbing hands-on labor for the northern factory industry. As blues developed through the 1920s, and as throngs of blacks fled the rural South and crowded into northern cities, more and more of these songs told stories about the uncertain realities of urban existence. They told personal yet communal stories of lives that for the most part no longer depended on "the soil, the sun, the rain, or the wind," but instead on "the grace of jobs and the brutal logic of jobs."[16] These were stories of "check to check" black living. They were stories of black bodies propped up at the front door waiting for government checks. Blues told of black lives put at risk when the "pink slip" arrived saying that "Uncle Sam done put [them] on the shelf," but still finding a way to "go for [themselves]."[17] Blues stories, therefore, told of a people who were all too familiar with the reality of "House Rent Blues," "Washwoman Blues," or even "Workhouse Blues," all blues that reflect the various ways in which black men and women found a way to go for themselves when they "ain got a dime," to deal with the "starvation in [their] kitchen [or] rent sign's on [their] do.'"[18] Blues also told stories of the devastating and disproportionate impact that natural disasters ("Flood Blues,") or disease ("T.B. Blues") or unjust legal systems ("Cell Bound Blues)" had on vulnerable black lives. And, of course, blues characteristically tells intimate stories of love, longing, heartbreak, and betrayal. Also typical, but often overlooked, are the stories blues tells of hope.

This is a *blues hope*. It is not naïve. It is realistic about the harsh facts of black living. Nevertheless, it is optimistic about life's possibilities. It reminds black people that there is more to their lives than trials and tribulations. Such a hope is captured in the lyrics of Chippie Hill's "Trouble in Mind," where she proclaims that although she has the blues, "the sun will shine in my back door someday."[19] Moreover, blues hope does not give into self-pity, as seen in Bill Broonzy's lyrics "I'm laughing to keep from cryin."[20] Essentially, blues stories reveal the deep anguish and resilient spirit of "humble and unassuming" black men and women who live and celebrate life in a world that mocks their existence and exploits their bodies.[21]

As popular as blues became during the 1920s, not all black people appreciated them. There were those who were embarrassed if not repelled by the music and its people. During this time period, class divisions began to really take shape within the black community. As educational and social opportunities increased, class divides grew. There was a middle class of businesspeople, teachers, ministers, and others who had relatively stable employment. There was also an upper class of dentists, doctors, lawyers, and other professionals. While the middle class aspired to become a part of the upper class, both classes considered themselves "respectable" blacks and strove to distinguish themselves from those blacks they considered "the reverse element" or "unwashed lower class blacks"—blues people.[22] Yet, even as these middle and upper classes of blacks may have considered themselves distinct from the black masses, they realized that their acceptance into mainstream white society depended upon the "uplift" of the very blacks they looked down upon. They thus promoted a "*narrative of civility*" aimed toward refining the ways of black folks. Manuals such as Elias Woods's *The Gospel of Civility* became popular supplements to school texts to ensure that black students were properly educated in how to present themselves, especially among the white public.[23] These manuals covered everything from proper dress and speech, to table manners and appropriate gait. The narrative of civility basically "aped" white/puritan standards of decency and decorum. Whether or not these manuals contributed to the social or economic advancement of the black masses was not the fundamental concern of the self-proclaimed "respectable" blacks. Their first priority was to make sure that "lower class" blacks were not the public face of black America and that their "uncivilized" ways did not have a "demoralizing influence" on the wider black community. Indeed, for some, class divisions were a sign of black progress. Inasmuch as these divisions created a segregated class space, thus separating the disreputable blacks from the respectable ones, they were considered a "necessary aspect of racial evolution that would provide evidence to skeptical whites of African Americans' progress."[24] Thus invested with class consciousness and fueled by white approval, these "leading colored citizens" rejected anything they thought might corrupt black morals or give "the whole race an evil reputation."[25] This meant, for them, a rejection of blues.

In the minds of the class-conscious and status-seeking blacks, blues encouraged dissolute behavior and reinforced images of black people as irrepressible, irresponsible, and irredeemable animals. Blues was an affront to the narrative of civility. No one made this clearer than sociologist Charles S. Johnson when he said, "People who create the 'blues' and secular songs of the demimonde" are outside of "socially sanctioned class categories," and are "'worthless,' and 'undeserving poor' who are satisfied with their status, the 'outcasts,' the 'bad niggers,' prostitutes, gamblers, outlaws, renegades, and 'free' people...They are the ones who have in greatest measure a sense of irresponsibility."[26]

While much more will be said about this narrative of civility later, for now it is important to establish its emergence within the black community as contributing to certain black people's attitudes toward blues. With that said, though there were black respectables who were successful in fostering a narrative of civility and thus criticizing blues, there were other black people who were not in the first instance blues people but still strongly appreciated blues. Though blues may not have reflected their actual experiences, they believed that blues symbolized what it meant to be black in a white-dominated society. What, in fact, did it mean during the heyday of blues to be black in America?

To be black in a society defined by slavery, lynching, and Jim Crow meant that one's life was always at risk. To be black in a society determined to make sure black people did not "go beyond prescribed boundaries" meant that one's circumstances could "turn on a dime" and, in an instant, "Homeless Blues, "Traveling Blues," or even "Jail House Blues" could be one's life story. To be black meant that, on any given morning, one could "wake up with the blues" and have "no place to go."[27] Essentially, blues stories point to the precariousness of black living, regardless of class status. Hence, blues stories are a metaphor for black life, as many in the black community recognized. These songs "express both the profundities and trivialities of the black experience in America."[28] They are virtually musical *mascons*. As defined by literary scholar Stephen Henderson, mascons contain "a massive concentration of Black experiential energy…[and] cut across areas of experiences usually thought of as separate, but [whose] meanings overlap and wash into each other on some undifferentiated level of common experience."[29] In the second instance, then, blues people are those black women and men who are not necessarily downtrodden but who hear in blues stories the truths of their own black existence. Consequently, blues stories allow black people who otherwise maintain separate lives to connect with one another through the common experience of blackness.

Through the call and response of blues, black people are able to forge a *blues bond*. This is a bond that overcomes the kinds of social distinctions that foster divisions, if not animosity, within the black community. A blues bond emphasizes the shared predicament of being black in a white world and establishes a mutual commitment to the welfare of all black bodies. It is, for instance, the kind of bond that was seen during the many Depression-era rent parties where poor black people would cobble together their pennies around food, booze, and blues to help one another stay in their apartment one more month. A blues bond is fundamentally a bond built on an unapologetic black consciousness. This is a consciousness that is grounded in the reality of the least of these, for it recognizes that the plight of the social and economic bottom of the black community is a marker of black progress, but not in the way suggested by the elite. Rather, a black consciousness born of a blues bond understands that the value of black life in wider society is measured by the treatment of those at the bottom. Put another way, "Whatever is done to the least of black bodies is a warning of what can be done to all black bodies." It is in the way in which blues are suggestive of a certain black consciousness that they point to another dimension of sound communication within the African diaspora, one that reveals the depth of a people's struggle for identity.

The call and response of blues allow black people "to assert themselves and their feelings and their values."[30] Simply put, blues is a vehicle for black women and men to express through sound that which may be hard for them to otherwise articulate: their innermost feelings concerning what it means to be black. The initial sound of blues evokes responses (positive and/or negative) from black women and men that become the basis for communication between them concerning the complexity of their thoughts regarding their very blackness. Through the interactive nature of the blues performance, black people are able to indicate their connection to their own black reality as well as their connections to the black reality of others. In many respects, one can read from black peoples' responses to blues their thinking about their black identity and the "place" of black people in the world. These responses go beyond musical taste. That is, it is not about whether one is a connoisseur of blues sounds. The fact that one may not like blues as a musical form is not a measure of one's blackness. It is rather one's appreciation of what blues stories represent, in terms of speaking a truth about black existence, and how one views the significance of that truth in relation to one's own sense of self that is perhaps suggestive of a certain black consciousness. The relevance of blues to overall black life and identity becomes even clearer when appreciating an African-informed way in which blues communicates the messages intended for its black listeners.

If the peculiar sound of the blues note signals a culturally unique blues rhythm, then it also suggests a culturally unique way of communicating. This is a way that goes beyond the intrinsic paradoxical nature of blues, as well as beyond the sexual innuendo and double entendre typical of blues lyrics. Hidden within the matter-of-fact, sometimes paradoxical, and sometimes ambiguous blues lyrics are sharp truths on the "ways of black folk." These hidden truths go back to the African tradition of signifyin'. While not all blues signify, to overlook the signifyin' nature of various blues is to miss the full significance of blues communication for black people, and especially for the black church.

Blues as Signifyin' Communication

I got the world in a jug, the stopper's in my hand.[31]

Signifyin' can be traced back to African trickster myths, particularly those related to the ultimate African trickster Esu, also known as Legba or Esu-Elegbara (about whom much more will be said later). These trickster myths translated across the middle passage into a tale about a signifyin' monkey. In this tale the monkey's playful acidic wit—its signifyin'—embarrasses a lion, yet in the end places the very signifyin' monkey's life in jeopardy. Black culture has kept alive the monkey's signifyin' playfulness. While signifyin' has taken many forms, with each generation adding its own nuances, two characteristics stand out in this tradition: "double-speak" and non-heady/wise commentary.

Double-speak itself may take a variety of forms. It may employ word-play, performative or verbal sarcasm, mocking repetition, indirection, or mimicking behavior. Discerning the presence of double-speak typically requires an awareness of the signifyin' tradition within African informed cultures, as well as knowledge of certain cultural codes, so that the signifyin' message itself can be decoded. In other words, if one is not aware of the signifyin' tradition then s/he will not know to listen for it. This was in fact the predicament of the lion in the signifyin' monkey tale. "Mr. Lion" does not realize the monkey's signifyin' intent and thus acts on the literal meaning of the monkey's words. Even when one does recognize the art of signifyin' at play, it is still not easy to decode the message behind the signifyin' words or actions.

Discerning the intended message requires hearing beyond the words and reading between the lines of the words' performance. In order to do this, one must be versed, to some degree, in certain cultural protocols, symbols, gestures, conventions, and habits. Put simply, in order to get the point being made in the signifyin' moment, one must be able to pick up on certain cultural cues and codes. This is in fact why signifyin' has become such a persistent part of black culture. It makes it possible for black people to speak the truth of who they are as well as the truth of those who would do them harm, without jeopardizing their very lives. Signifyin' communication becomes a way to send a public yet concealed message. In so doing, it turns the dynamics of power upside down. Power lies with the signifyin' community, that is, with those who hear the message beyond the words. This is the case in the monkey tale. The little monkey has power over the big lion, as long as the lion remains unaware of the monkey's signifyin' intent.

While there are signifyin' moments that are simply meant to be playful, as perhaps was the case with the monkey, more often than not signifyin' provides essential knowledge about black existence. Such signifyin' knowledge is not abstract. It is, in this regard, nonheady because it does not originate in the "head." It is embodied knowledge. It is born from the raw, everyday living of black bodies. Hence, as we will soon see, it is a fitting aspect of a music that also springs from the experiences of ordinary black bodies. Signifyin' knowledge, perhaps not considered "scholarly" by some, is profoundly wise as it provides valuable insight into a given situation or predicament, even as it takes into account the point of view of both the powerless and the powerful (whomever they may be) in its assessments. Moreover, because it does not pretend to be objective or universal, signifyin' provides a passionate analysis of any given black condition. The very truth and authenticity of signifyin' commentary comes from its unapologetic standpoint—which in the case of blues is dogged, gritty black living. In this regard, signifyin' is an example of the "taken-for-granted" knowledge that black feminist sociologist Patricia Hill Collins identifies as central to black well-being. This is knowledge born from "ordinary" black women and men who do what they can to make it through the up-and-down circumstances of black living. It reflects the knowing that comes from "everyday thoughts and actions."[32] Taken-for-granted knowledge is a part of the wisdom tradition that is handed down from one generation to another on how to navigate an inhospitable world. Signifyin' is a part of this wisdom tradition. Again, that which gives signifyin' its validity is that it resonates with the "shared" experiences of black men and women.

Blues reflects the signifyin' tradition at its best. Black cultural scholar Henry Gates has led the way in highlighting the signifyin' quality of blues. Gates establishes signifyin' as "the black trope of tropes." It is a technique, he argues, used within various black art forms to comment on that which has gone before as well as to create something new. He describes it as "repetition with a difference."[33] For instance, Gates notes how various black literary artists signify upon one another's works as they "play upon" one another's methodology or allude to various symbols and rhetorical devices in each other's work. Gates, along with other scholars, observes this tradition within black music.

Musicologist Floyd says that "Musical Signifyin(g) is the rhetorical use of preexisting material as a means of demonstrating respect for or poking fun at a musical style, process or practice through parody, pastiche, implication, indirection, humor, tone play or word play, the illusion of speech or narration or other troping [signifyin'] mechanisms."[34] Various musicians signify on other musicians by commenting through their own musical style and performance on the style and performance of another. New musical forms often signify on previous musical forms. For instance, blues signify on spirituals and ballads, jazz on blues, and gospel on jazz, blues, and spirituals. Not only does music signify on other music, but various music forms themselves are signifyin' forms. For instance, the characteristic riffs and vamps of jazz are nothing less than signifyin' at play. Jazz is a signifyin' music form, and so too is the music it signifies upon: blues.

As a genre of music, blues employs a variety of the signifyin' double-speak techniques mentioned above. In so doing, blues signifies in at least two ways: through its musical style and patterns and through its lyrics. For purposes of understanding the importance of blues for the black church, I will primarily focus on blues signifyin' lyrics.

While blues lyrics certainly render perceptive judgments on the "ways of white folks," blues signifyin' is principally directed to black people, the intended audience for blues themselves. When white people are addressed in blues it is from the perspective of black concerns. As signifyin' communication, blues speaks in a way that is meant to be "decipherable by knowers of [black] culture but inaccessible to those outside it."[35] Through the art of blues signifyin', black people speak frankly to one another about difficult black truths without "airing their dirty laundry" to those outside of the community.

To appreciate the fullness of the signifyin' message, one needs to witness blues performance, with its nuanced movements, gestures, facial expressions, humor as well as the call-and-response banter between the performer and the audience. Blues songs are meant to be heard not read. Nevertheless, the lyrics themselves can provide adequate signifyin' commentary, which the performance of course enhances. Such is the case with Bessie Smith's " 'Down Hearted Blues.' "

Smith's 1923 rendering of "Down Hearted Blues" with Columbia Studios marked her recording debut. Alberta Hunter initially recorded this song which she co-wrote with Lovie Austin. Because of its successful run with Hunter and numerous other renderings of it by other blues artists, "Down Hearted Blues" was thought to have run its course by the time Smith recorded it. Columbia Records believed it would be secondary to "Gulf Coast Blues" which was on the flipside of Smith's first record. The black community, however, felt differently.

Black women and men responded to Smith's "Down Hearted Blues" in a way that Columbia's white music moguls had not anticipated. They did not realize the signifyin' message this song had for black people. This message was captured in one line, "I've got the world in a jug, the stopper's in my hand." Though he may not have comprehended fully what black people heard in this line, Frank Walker, the Columbia producer of Smith's work, realized that it was this line "that did it...it made that record a hit."[36] What was the signifyin' message beneath this lyric that spoke a deep truth to black women and men?

"Down Hearted Blues" tells of a heartbroken woman whose love for a man is answered with indifference. In the end, this woman claims her power and refuses to allow the man's betrayal to ruin her life. She further asserts that any man that enters her life must be committed solely to her, and if he betrays that commitment, then revenge will be visited upon him. The song concludes with the woman asserting, "I've got the world in a jug, the stopper's in my hand" and further declaring that she will not let go of it until "men come under my command."

On the most literal level, this song calls out to black women who experience the trauma of a bad relationship. Yet, even on this level the song is about more than one woman's love gone wrong; it is also a poignant commentary concerning the inherent difficulty of maintaining black relationships in a world hostile to black life. As the song moves from speaking specifically about love troubles in verse one to referencing generic troubles in verse two, the song connects the specific troubled black relationship to the broad troubles that black people endure every day. With this abrupt shift from the particular to the general, a shift that can be detected in Smith's vocal performance, "Down Hearted Blues" signifies on the ever-present oppressive realities of black existence that impose themselves on black bodies in such a way that it becomes virtually impossible for black people to maintain intimate relationships, let alone healthy ones. Inasmuch as verse three provides a response to the heartbreak described in the first two verses, it replies that black relationships are strained by the "troubles" of black living. This point is reinforced in verse four when the woman says that her only male relationships have been with her father, brother, and the lover who betrayed her, hence enunciating the fact black love is just hard to come by. Essentially, in moving from a troubled love story, to a general notion of black troubles, "Down Hearted Blues" places the blame of the bad relationship not on the black man alone, but also on the white society that makes all aspects of black life difficult. "Down Hearted Blues" is thus no longer just a story about one woman's relationship. Rather, it is an insightful story about the pressures that overwhelm black love—a story that most black people, women and men, are able to relate to. This point is brought home in the lyric that captured the attention of black women and men. It is in this lyric that the personal man problems are explicitly connected to the wider world of troubles as the climatic line, "I've got the world in a jug the stoppers in my hand," prefaces the proclamation, "I'm gonna hold it until you men come under my command." The final message is clear: it is when black women can bring the racist world under control that they will then have more command over their men, implying of course that black people will have more control over their relationships. There is, however, an even more profound message that is embedded in this lyric. To appreciate this, one must explore further the meaning of the lyrics' central image, the "jug." It would seem that the mention of the jug is not incidental, and thus, speaks to black people in a way that is perhaps not immediately obvious.

Within black culture, jugs have had special value, if not transcending powers. The first indication of the significance of jugs was seen in the making of face jugs. As far as can be determined, face jugs came into prominence around 1800 in the Edgeville, South Carolina, community of about 150 mostly enslaved people. This community began to make these jugs in response to the need for lead-free pottery. One prominent jug maker was an enslaved man named Dave. While making these face jugs, Dave also made jugs with various rebellious sayings carved onto them. Dave's use of the jugs suggested that there may have been a more purposeful if not clandestine use of jugs within enslaved communities. The fact that jug shards have been found on the grave sites of the enslaved and along underground railroad routes further supported the notion that jugs carried special significance within these communities. African American oral tradition further suggested that face jugs were placed at graves to serve as makeshift headstones and as totems to ward off the devil and other evil spirits. The special power of jugs is also referenced in an African American folktale where the jug is mentioned as a conjuring tool. As the tale goes, if persons want to put an end to their enemy they should get "some of his old dirty clothes and corking them up tightly in a brown jug. Bury this jug in the graveyard on the breast of the grave. In nine days your enemy will be dead."[37]

Whatever the precise origins of face jugs or the importance of jugs found along the Underground Railroad or at graves of the enslaved, that there are unique meanings associated with jugs within African American culture is clear. If nothing else, jugs symbolize a power that is not defined by historical circumstances or social status. It is an inexplicable and confounding power that sets things straight in the universe. It is the power to subdue evil. Evil, within African worldviews, is generally considered that which creates disharmony within and between human and divine relationships. Jugs thus become a vehicle for restoring harmony, by "corking evil" and making right that which was wrong. As a grave marker, face jugs affirm, make right, the sacredness of the black dead, contesting any notion that they are less than human. As a surreptitious means for communication, jugs testify to a restless spirit for freedom within the black community, foiling, setting straight, white lies of the content and "happy slave." As a conjuring tool, the jug witnesses a force greater than human authority, thus discrediting, again setting straight, white claims over black bodies. Essentially, as the jug represents the power of good over evil, it establishes the power the subjugated weak have over the tyrannical strong.

Against this backdrop of understanding, the signifyin' meaning behind the jug image in "Downhearted Blues" is deepened. First, the mere mention of the jug alerts the culturally astute listener about the signifyin' nature of the song. For, the jug is virtually a signifyin' symbol as it allows for a reversal of power where the little (the jug) "corks" the big (the world). Second, inasmuch as the jug is considered a tool to combat evil, its use in the song serves to name black male infidelity as evil, especially since it disrupts the harmony of a loving relationship. And of course, made profoundly clear is that the world that strains black relationships in the first place is evil, and so it is this world that must be put in a jug for things to be made right again. It is worth noting that the song does not mention putting black men in the jug, only the world, once again stressing the white world's responsibility for troubling black relationships.

Overall, with the clever mention of a jug, layers of meaning can be found in this seemingly straightforward line. Those with ears to hear would no doubt hear a message about any pretensions to divisive power they might claim over one another, be it claims of class, color, gender, or any other form. The warning is clear: such power is impotent and it is evil. It is impotent because it cannot contend with the force in the cosmos that surpasses human control. It is evil because it disrupts the harmony of the community. Most significantly, this seemingly innocuous line about a jug is a bold assertion of agency for black women in particular and black people in general as it scoffs at any human claims over black bodies. It suggests a force that overcomes the evil of human power that black people have the ability to access. It is no wonder then that the black community responded with enthusiasm to "Down Hearted Blues." Even as this song delivered a caustic reply to black male betrayals, it also provided an empowering message of hope to the black community. The image of the world in a jug virtually made a joke of white people's authority over black bodies. It reminded black people that white power was no match for the ultimate power in their hands—the power of a jug. It confirmed to black people that, regardless of how bad things were, the world would be set right: the weak would prevail, evil would be defeated, and harmony would be restored. Such an understanding fended off despair and fueled hope for blues people; "that's what did it" for black people in the lyric about a jug.

Bessie Smith's performance of "Down Hearted Blues" only reinforced the signifyin' appeal of this lyric. She delivers the first two verses with a deep pathos that certainly reflects the depth of her heartbreak. As she moves to verse three, for even a casual listener like myself, there is a discernible change in her tone; it is as assertive as that used in the first two verses, but seemingly filled with more matter-of-fact boldness and less emotional angst. This pattern repeats itself in the next three verses. When she reaches the last verse, there is a stress on the words "world" and "jug" as she makes the connection to men. In listening to Smith's version of the song, it seems quite clear that she is speaking about more than simply a personal story of love gone bad. By most reports, it was indeed Bessie Smith's "masterful blend of pathos and defiance" that gave the signature line its timeless, signifyin' significance in the black community.[38] In fact, this very line would become a signifyin' trope within the black literary tradition. For instance, in her novel *Their Eyes Were Watching God*, Zora Neale Hurston utilizes this line to indicate her protagonist Janie's recognition of her power as that which comes from her "inside" relationship with herself and not from an outside relationship to men.[39] Ralph Ellison actually signified upon this line when he titled an essay "The World and a Jug." In this essay he discusses white scholars' "interpretation of black work." He rejects a white view of segregation as an "opaque steel jug" with black people corked inside waiting for a black messiah to get them out. He responds that if black people are in a jug, the jug is transparent, allowing black people to "read" what is really going on in the white world, without the white world being able to read what is going on with them.[40] Again, the jug is used to suggest a power that comes from an "underside" position, with those at the bottom actually having more power, in this instance, insight, than those on the top.

The way in which "Down Hearted Blues" uses the image of a jug is just one example of the signifyin' character of blues. Later we will explore the various other ways in which blues signify on the ways of black folks. What is most important to understand for now is that signifyin' becomes a means through which blues speaks raw truth to the black community, and most especially to the black church. In fact, when speaking to the black church, blues often combines signifyin' with another tradition that makes the message to the church even sharper. This is the tradition of lament.

Blues as Signifyin' Lament

"Religion turns you inside out Moan you moaners."[41]

Within black faith, the Bible holds primary authority when it comes to black people's understanding of how god is present for them. Lament is prominent within the biblical tradition. It plays a critical role in the story of the Israelites, whose story about their struggle for freedom is the paradigmatic biblical story that allowed the black enslaved to know that god was with black people in their struggle against slavery, and a story that would remain central to black people throughout their sojourn toward freedom. For the Israelites, lament was a means to stay true to their identity as a "chosen people," especially after their Exodus from Egyptian bondage into the promised land of freedom. Through lament, they "rend their hearts" and recognized the ways in which they had betrayed their own covenantal relationship with the god who freed them. As such, lament was both a "pastoral" and "prophetic" activity.[42] It was pastoral as it provided a way for the Israelites to give voice to their suffering. It was prophetic in that it allowed them to not simply name the crisis they were facing but also to own any responsibility they may have had in producing the named crisis. Through the process of lament the Israelites engaged in a stirring self-reflection that compelled them to do their part in remedying the situation they found themselves in, and thus to make right their relationship with god. In short, among the many positive aspects of lament, it most notably served the Israelites as a vehicle for self-critique and a call for accountability to their religious covenant.

Ironically, blues—which, as we shall see later, was deemed by the black church to be devil's music—echoes the biblical tradition of lament. Blues laments are both pastoral and prophetic. They, like the Israelite laments, allow black women and men to "rend their hearts," as they identify particular crises that beset the community, and, in so doing, compel black people to recognize their role in perpetuating some of these crises. Implicit, of course, is the black community's ability to alleviate various life crises. Again, these laments typically engage in signifyin' communication, thereby speaking openly yet privately to black people. In this way, blues laments hold black people accountable for problem behaviors without publicly humiliating them. They become an arrestingly effective means through which the black community can "confront" and "transform" its own situation. When it comes to the black church, blues signifyin' laments are even more powerful, for they expose the disconcerting "ways of the black church" in a manner informed by what the black church holds sacred, the Bible. Bessie Smith's song, "Moan You Moaners," is an example of a signifyin' lament.

Smith recorded this song in 1930 during the Depression, when sales of blues were waning. Smith's record sales reflected this depression era slide. In an effort to boost her sales, Columbia had Smith record "On Revival Day" and "Moan You Moaners." Both songs were a departure for Smith, especially since they did not contain any of the bawdy lyrics and sexual innuendo for which she had become known. This departure has led some to label these songs "pseudo gospels," gospel-blues, or simply gospels. Whatever the case, even though they were not technically blues, they maintained the blues signifyin' aesthetic of humor and sarcasm as well as the blues spirit of speaking truth about the everyday experiences of black people, in this instance, black church people. Furthermore, Smith's performance of these songs reflected her spirit as a blues virtuoso; so, while not strictly blues songs, Smith delivered them as blues. In the end, notwithstanding the commercial motivation for recording "Moan You Moaners," and the sanitized lyrics, this song still reflected a blues play on the black church.

From the very outset of Smith's performance, the signifyin' intent of "Moan You Moaners" is obvious. When she speaks the opening lyrics of the song, she mimics the cadence and delivery associated with black preachers: Smith the blues singer—the one who is scorned in the black church—becomes a preacher of truth to the black church. The striking similarity between the blues performer and the black preacher has been remarked upon by many blues interpreters. Drawing upon the performance of Bobby Bland, Charles Kiel has observed that the way the blues singer brings the audience into the performance through cadence, enunciation, mannerisms, gestures, and other dramatic flourishes is reminiscent of what black preachers do in their pulpits. It is in this way that the stage becomes the pulpit from which the blues performer "closes the gap" between her or him and the audience, eliciting from the blues audience the same type of visceral responses that black preachers elicit from their congregations.[43] Friends of bluesman T-Bone Walker recognized in him the fine line between the blues performer and the black preacher, thinking that one day he would in fact become a preacher, because when he sang blues it reminded them of a sermon.[44] Certainly, no one embodied what it meant to be a blues performer/black preacher more than Bessie Smith. Her performances consistently reminded people of church revivals or "camp meetings."[45] Bluesman Danny Baker says of Smith:

> Bessie Smith was a fabulous deal to watch...she could sing the blues. She had a church deal mixed up in it...If you had any church background...you would recognize a similarity between what she was doing and what those preachers and evangelist from [the South] did, and how they moved people. The South had fabulous preachers and evangelists. Some would stand on corners and move the crowds from there. Bessie did the same on stage...Bessie was in a class with those people.[46]

That she as a blues singer would sing "Moan You Moaners" only reinforced her role as a blues performer/black preacher, especially given the songs signifyin' message from its beginning to end.

The opening spoken/preached lyrics immediately confront the sisters and brothers of the church with their hypocritical ways. In a signifyin' manner, this song questions who it is that is really "saved," blues people or church people, as it portrays the blues singer as confronting the sisters and the brothers of the church forthrightly, while the brothers and sisters of the church talk about the blues singer behind her back. The song goes on to label these "backbitin'" sisters and brothers as sinners. The very ones who consider themselves saved are called upon by the blues singer to get down on their knees and to repent so that they can save their souls. In the end, the song makes clear that the religion the black church professes to have made them so holy is the very religion that has turned them into "backbitin'" hypocrites. The closing line of the song brings this point home as it says, "Religion turns you inside out/Moan, you moaners." This closing refrain, "Moan You Moaners," draws our attention back to the title of the song, which itself serves a signifyin' function.

This title signifies upon the moaners bench in black churches. The moaners bench originated in the evangelical tradition as a place where those who were in need of repenting sat, especially during revivals. In "Moan You Moaners," however, those on the moaners bench are the very ones who consider themselves already saved. These saved ones are the focus of the altar call—which brings us to another signifyin' aspect of this particular "blues" song. The song itself serves as an altar call, as evidenced in the first sung lyrics, which literally call out to the sinners. In addition, throughout the song, various lyrics repeat stock fire-and-brimstone phrases used within the black church, such as "souls washed white," "blood of the lamb," and "see the light." The difference is that this blues fire-and-brimstone message is directed to those who are presumably "saved" by a presumably "unsaved" blues singer. Punctuating the signifyin' nature of the song are the amens and other spirited responses heard throughout. In the end, it is clear that the black church is being called to account for its duplicitous behavior toward blues singers and asked to change it—hence the lament.

Once again, a music form that suffers rejection within the black church community is the one that carries forth a biblical tradition that has been vital to oppressed people. This tradition provided an important self-correction for the Israelites so that they could remain faithful to what it meant to be a "chosen people" and hence continue on their road toward freedom. The blues as signifyin' lament has the potential to do the same for the black church community as long as the black church embraces them as faith testimonies. As signifyin' lament, blues helps the black church to remain honest to its own claims, true to its Exodus faith, and hence legitimate in the eyes of "blues people." As a cultural/historical/religious library, blues is the keeper of a radical black faith.

Blues as Radical Faith Testimony

> "Lord hear me prayin', My man treats me like a hound."[47]

Many have remarked upon the religious nature of blues, including blues artists. They have specifically noted the similarities between blues and the distinctly religious music of the enslaved, spirituals. Alberta Hunter described blues as being "like spirituals, almost sacred."[48] John Lee Hooker who began his career singing spirituals and thus, as he says, "reversed from spirituals to the blues," commented that "when spirituals were born it was born on the blues side." He went on to say, "I get just as deep a feelin' from the blues as I would from the spirituals."[49] What Hunter, Hooker, and others recognize is that both spirituals and blues emerge from the same existential black space, that is, from the experience of downtrodden black women and men making a way in a world oblivious to their very humanity. These two musical forms express the pathos and hope of these black people negotiating life in a hostile white environment. In so doing, both spirituals and blues provide a way for black people to release their innermost feelings and respond to their deepest desires so that they can "keep goin," especially through the hard and lonely times. W. C. Handy puts it best when he says, "Like the spirituals [blues] began with the Negro, it involves our history, where we came from, and what we experienced...The blues came from nothingness, from want, from desire. And when a man sang or played the blues, a small part of the want was satisfied from the music."[50] Notwithstanding the similarities between spirituals and blues, there are stark differences between the two that go beyond the fact of spirituals as songs that deal with antebellum black realities and blues as postbellum black songs. The most obvious difference is subject matter. Blues speaks about a side of black life that spirituals clearly ignore. Spirituals are concerned with the meaning of god for black people. They tell stories of god's presence in black history, thus they tell stories of god as liberator, confidant, friend, and healer, and they speak about god's promised future. Blues is concerned with the everyday happenings of black living. Blues songs tell uninhibited stories about black bodies. They most especially engage the sensual side of black existence: love, lust, sexuality, and life's pleasures. To some, the sexual dimension alone marks blues as secular music.[51] The intimate rawness of blues subject matter has led them to be called "secular spirituals."[52] To describe blues as secular spirituals certainly indicates the religious nature of this music. However, to refer to blues as "secular" insinuates a distinction that blues does not make. Blues does not distinguish between sacred and secular domains. It does not project a separation between sacred and secular concerns. Rather, it maintains a unified perspective on the universe and life. Levine tries to capture this unified perspective when he describes blues as "successfully blend [ing] the sacred and secular."[53] Jon Michael Spencer refers to it as a "synchronous duplicity" where apparent opposite aspects of the cosmos are held together.[54] Essentially, in blues there is no profane aspects of life; that is, there is no arena of life in which god is not present and about which god is not concerned. In blues stories, god embraces all of black life, the sensual as well as the nonsensual, thus all of life is sacred. In this same respect, blues does not recognize an aspect of life immune from evil. All of life is a mixture of good and evil. Again, within blues there is no sharp line of demarcation between what might appear to be divergent or even contesting dimensions of reality. It is in this way that blues carry forth a radical black faith.

To be radical is to reflect the basic, fundamental nature of something; it is to be true to one's roots. Blues songs are true to the African roots of the black faith tradition. Within black faith's African heritage "secularity has no existence." Furthermore, it is a heritage that presents evil as practically a looming presence in all of life—divine and human. In short, it is a heritage that maintains a view in which all dimensions of the universe are almost seamlessly intertwined; there are no abrupt breaks between differing aspects. There is, therefore, no protected "heavenly" space. Likewise, there is no protected good space. Heavenly and mundane realities engage one another, just as benevolent and malevolent possibilities coexist. All dimensions of existence are entangled and interact. Through their interaction a certain harmony is maintained. Indeed, as earlier mentioned, any such disruption or disharmony is a sign of evil—which again is a possibility within all of reality. Essentially, within the African religious tradition there is a "holistic tenacity."[55] Blues witnesses this "holistic tenacity" in several ways. It is readily seen in the way in which blues seeks god.

While there are instances when godlike references such as "Lawd, Lawd, Lawd" (Smith, "Dirty No-Gooders Blues") or "Mmmm, Lordy, Lordy, Lord" (Rainey, "Little Low Mama Blues") are little more than a figure of speech or rhetorical flourish, there are other times when the reference is intentional and god is purposively addressed. In these instances, blues lyrics virtually serve as a prayer or "little talk with God." In these little talks the African religious heritage comes through. These blues talks do not presume any aspect of black living to be an offense to god. They also assume that god will respond to whatever the issue is that is being expressed, including sensual issues. The sensual dimensions of life are not seen as profane, irreverent, or sinful. God is thought to be just as concerned with matters of the body as with matters of the soul. In blues the sensual is revered, even by god. Thus, in Ma Rainey's "Toad Frog Blues" when a woman tells god her troubles about a man who "treats [her] like a hound," she is confident that the lord will hear her "cryin'." Trixie Smith's "Praying Blues" goes even further when a betrayed woman asks for the lord to not simply listen to her man troubles, but to send her a man that will be faithful to only her. Again, she asks this because she trusts that even though "nobody knows" the depth of her "troubles," god knows.[56]

It is interesting to note that Smith's "Praying Blues" actually signifies on the slave spiritual, "Nobody knows the trouble I see," in the reference, "nobody knows." This kind of signifyin' is not unusual. Many blues songs—as mentioned earlier—signify on spirituals by adapting certain lyrics or even making specific references to a spiritual. "Ma Rainey's Mystery Record" does this when it refers to Nearer My God to Thee.[57] While borrowing between music forms is typical of black music, and borrowing of lyrics is particularly characteristic of blues, that blues so easily borrows from spirituals affirms the overlap between sacred and secular domains. It moreover affirms what others have observed, that blues and spirituals do emerge from the same historical experience and that this experience itself does not recognize sacred/secular splits. In appropriating spirituals, therefore, blues reinforces the notion that blues and spirituals compliment each other, as each musical form attempts in its own culturally nuanced way to shed light on the strivings and dreams of black women and men. Thus, both must be respected and held together if this experience is to be fully understood. Blues borrowings and blues prayers, therefore, echo an African religious heritage where all domains of reality, divine and human, are inextricably interactive.

Blues further witnesses this heritage in its unapologetic references to voodoo practices. Voodoo is considered one of the most successful of African religions to survive in the African Diaspora, particularly in Haiti. Voodoo reflects the African belief in the interactions between the worlds of the gods and humans. It affirms the insuperable power of the gods at the same time that it shows the human ability to access that power. Within African American culture, voodoo was translated into hoodoo, leading some to describe hoodoo as "the step-child of voodoo."[58] Notwithstanding the nuanced differences between the two, in African American cultures the two terms have become virtually synonymous, pointing to similar religious understandings and practices. To be sure, hoodoo is grounded in and deeply informed by voodoo. Like voodoo, hoodoo grants humans the capacity to influence the gods. In so doing, it realizes the intricate relationship between good and evil. In this respect, evil is considered a "shadow side" potential of both gods and humans.[59] Thus, through hoodoo, humans and gods can act in either good or bad ways. It is blues that boldly carry forth the "legacy of hoodoo." Hoodoo practices are mentioned in many blues as a way for black people to take control of their situations.[60] One such blues is Bessie Smith's "Red Mountain Blues."[61]

In this song a lovelorn woman is attempting to get a man to love her. After contemplating suicide, she sees a "fortune-teller." The fortune-teller advises her to get two powerful conjuring potions, "snakeroot" and "John the Conqueror," chew them, and put some in her pocket and some in her boot to bring the man she loves to her. There are numerous other songs in Smith's repertoire in which hoodoo practices are mentioned, such as going "to see the conjure man soon" in "Gin House Blues," or waking up to a "jinx around my bed" in "Mama Got The Blues," or "sprinkled salt" in "I'd Rather Be Dead and Buried in My Grave." There was perhaps no blues woman who sang more about the dark side of hoodoo than Victoria Spivey. In "Hoodoo Man Blues" Spivey tells how the hoodoo man is all the rave for women who may be having love troubles. Spivey's "Blood Hound Blues" goes as far as to talk about poisoning a man who abused her. In "Garter Snake Blues," "Spider Web Blues," and "Nightmare Blues" also, Spivey sings of hoodoo acts of revenge.

At the same time that these hoodoo references reinforce the belief that there is no unbridgeable gulf between human and divine worlds, since humans have the means to reach into the realm of the gods, they indicate something even more important about the meaning of authority. Blues consistently point to a power in the universe that surpasses human power. In blues, authority over human bodies ultimately belongs to this all-surpassing cosmic power; it belongs to the power of the gods. The regard for hoodoo shown in blues reveals black peoples awe for this overwhelming supernatural power. This was, for black people, authoritarian power. This was the power they feared and respected. It was for them at once a humbling and an empowering force. While appreciating that they were no match for the power of hoodoo, the black people realized that neither were white people. Thus, through its references to hoodoo, blues once again signifies upon the futility of white claims over black bodies. The only authority and power that blues people recognize and answer to is that suggested by the practice of hoodoo, which, no doubt, is the same power suggested by the jug, and perhaps is the power of the gods. Whatever the source of this power, what is clear is that blues affirms that there is an energy force in the cosmos, independent of human power, that enables the weak to resist the rule of the strong. It is to this intangible but potent force that blues people hold themselves accountable. Here again, blues reflects that dimension of the African religious heritage that allowed the enslaved to maintain an identity that tied their relationship to divine, not human, realities.

Blues songs are witness to a radical black faith in yet another way, which can also be seen in some of Ma Rainey's blues. These songs show how various African religious practices have traditionally coexisted with Christian beliefs within the black community. For instance, in "Lawd Send me A Man Blues," a woman "ask the good Lord" to send her a man.[62] This man can be a Zulu man, or a voodoo man, it does not matter as long as it is a man who can take away her loneliness. What is interesting is that there is no hesitancy in asking the apparently Christian god for a man who may hold African religious practices (i.e., Zulu man) or one who believes in voodoo. This shows the validity of each of these religious practices for the woman. It also shows the belief that the gods of these various religions harmoniously coexist in the same universe, since there is no hesitancy in the request. In this instance, the Christian god is not a jealous god. Therefore, in "Lawd Send me A Man Blues" the woman is assuring god that she will welcome a non-Christian man; presuming that god shows no partiality, she does not want god to think she is partial and so hesitate to send her whatever man is available. Blues songs such as these speak not only to the simultaneous existence of various religious belief systems within the black faith community but also to a belief in the harmonious world of the gods, bearing in mind that any disharmony is a sign of evil.

Without a doubt, blues songs have kept alive an African religious heritage that has too often been ignored and even at times forthrightly rejected within the black faith community. As we will see in later chapters, blues acceptance of a worldview that admits hoodoo practices and maintains a sacred sensuality, and thus reveres the body, contributes to the black church community's castigation of blues and blues people. It must be pointed out, however, that even as blues projected a radical faith tradition, many blues people, including blues performers, were profoundly influenced by a black church narrative that saw blues as devil's music. This created for them a certain ambivalence about their blues careers. This irony will be explored in later chapters. For now, it is important to recognize blues as a repository of radical black faith and, thus, meaningful for a black church that is to remain a vital force within the black community.

The Blues and Me

> "'Lord I'm down with the blues,' blues as I can be."[63]

When we were growing up, my dad would often exclaim to my sisters, brother, and me, "You got the world in a jug with the stopper in your hand." He most often said this when he noticed us indulging in some pleasurable event: be it watching our favorite television show or savoring every bite of our favorite food. We would laugh every time my dad said this. We did not know he was quoting a blues lyric, we thought this line was another example of our dad's creative wit—there was no one who could make us laugh more than dad could. While we did not know his wit came from blues, what we did know was that he was not just trying to get us to laugh. We knew that through this line, dad was trying to teach us a lesson. My father was signifyin' on our privileged existence as black kids. Ours was not a blues household. Not only did we not play blues in our home (at least not that I knew), we did not also lead a blues life. Dad was of the professional working class. Mom was a stay-at-home wife and mother. We lived in a neighborhood of other black professionals. We walked to a neighborhood school. Our stomachs were never hungry and our bodies were never cold. We had all the necessities for good living and indulged in many of life's luxuries. Ours was not the life that most black children in 1960s America enjoyed, let alone those in Dayton, Ohio. Ours was the life of what E. Franklin Frazier would call the "black bourgeoisie," replete with Jack and Jill membership, cotillions, boutillions, and European travel. We were not a blues people, yet my parents were determined to develop within us a blues bond. This began by making us aware of our privilege.

In making us aware of our privilege, dad and mom were not simply calling our attention to those less fortunate than ourselves, they were most importantly connecting us to blues realities. They often warned us not to forget from whence we came. They reminded us that our grandparents were blues people who migrated from the South to make a better life for their children. They cautioned us to never consider ourselves better than anybody else, regardless of how better-off our life circumstances may be at the time—because, they said, "by the grace of God go we." They reminded us that there was nothing inherently special about who we were that granted us a privileged life, and that there was nothing inherently wrong with those who did not enjoy such privilege. It had to do, they told us, with having certain opportunities. My parents held us accountable for the opportunities we had by diligently trying to instill within us a sense of responsibility to those less fortunate than ourselves. These messages about "privilege," responsibility, and humility were what was behind my dad's "jug" humor. Through my father's wit, this signifyin' line was signifyin' in yet another way: it was forging for four lucky black children a blues bond with blues people. It is because of this that I can claim, "I am blue."

I am not in the first instance a blues person. To suggest that I am would betray the integrity of blues. Yet, my understanding of who I am as a black person is defined by a blues bond. I know that to be black in America is to be blue, regardless of one's social status. I know that as long as there is a black body anywhere that is deprived, denigrated, or dehumanized because of its blackness, then my black body is being likewise treated. It is, no doubt, this blues bond that my parents fostered in my siblings and me that drew me to blues listening, and to this project. When I listen to blues, I am connected to my blackness in a way that is difficult for me to articulate. I feel in blues a deep connection and accountability to black women and men whose lives have been nothing less than a constant struggle just to exist. Blues songs evoke memories, emotions, and passions within me that quite simply no other music does. They make me laugh and they make me cry. It is through this laughter and tears that I can sing with Ma Rainey, "Lord I am down with the blues, I am blue as I can be." And, it is as I sing along with Ma Rainey and other blues women that I am also put in touch with another dimension of who I am, and that is who I am as a woman. It is to the story of blues women that we will now turn, on our way to appreciating the meaning of blues for the black church.

2

Somebody's Angel Child

She jes' catch hold of us somekindaway.[1]

You never get nothing by being an angel child
You'd better change your way and get real wild.[2]

"The blues?" T-Bone Walker says he was born with them. But, he recalls that his first memory of blues goes back to his mother. "I think that the first thing I can remember," he says, "was my mother singing the blues as she would sit alone in the evenings... I can't remember the words to those blues, but she could sing you blues right now like you never heard before... After I heard my mother play the blues and sing them, then I started in."[3] Walker's story is certainly not unique. There are, no doubt, countless other blues singers whose mothers introduced them to the music, just as they introduced them to other aspects of black life and culture. Given women's circumscribed role as the primary caretakers of the home, they have been the ones held primarily responsible for nurturing certain values, habits, customs, and practices in their children. It is presumably through women that a cultural legacy is inherited, if not maintained. It was certainly this way when it came to the blues legacy. Blues historian Giles Oakley rightly points out that women played "an important part in spreading rural musical culture, passing on songs and especially the feeling of the blues."[4] Just as black mothers introduced blues to their children, black women introduced them into "mainstream" society, white as well as black. It was fitting that Ma Rainey was called the Mother of Blues, and Bessie Smith, the Empress. These titles highlighted not just their specific roles but also the central role that black women in general played in fostering blues culture. Blues singing women ignited the blues spirit and imagination of the black community. Sterling Brown captures the blues woman's allure in his poetic tribute to Ma Rainey when he says, "she jes' catch hold of us somekindaway."[5] As blues women captivated their audiences, they gave birth to the "Classic Blues" era, the era in which blues reached its peak of popularity.

With the 1920s release of Mamie Smith's "Crazy Blues," the "race market" musical industry was born. Classic blues defined this market. These blues were not what some considered "pure" blues, that which the "wandering lone [guitar-playing] male" sang throughout the South.[6] Classic blues was a more commercialized rendition of blues. They typically involved sophisticated instrumental accompaniment and were entertainment- and performance-oriented. Nonetheless, it was the classic blues tradition that brought blues sounds from the rural South to the urban North. This classic tradition was dominated by women such as Ma Rainey, Bessie Smith, Ida Cox, Sippie Wallace, Victoria Spivey, Alberta Hunter, and more. For a time, to speak of blues was to speak of black women. When blues musician Buster Bailey remembered the blues singers he and pianist Fletcher Henderson accompanied, all the singers he named were women. "We did accompaniment for all the blues singers," he recalls. "All the Smith girls—Bessie, Mamie, Clara."[7] When recalling the glory days of the classic blues, Alberta Hunter further reveals the dominance of women when she remarks, "No, they don't have blues singers like they did then, except maybe Dinah Washington. There was Sara Martin, Ida Cox, Chippie Hill, Victoria Spivey, Trixie Smith and Clara Smith and Mamie Smith, who made it possible for all of us with her recording of 'Crazy Blues,' the *first* blues record."[8] During the 1920s blues heyday, black women were the primary caretakers of blues culture.

The implications of women being seen as the caretakers of any culture are immense. When they are not credited for preserving culture, they are likely blamed for cultural breakdowns. Likewise, when they are not affirmed for the positive aspects of culture, they are often castigated for the negative aspects. This occurred in regard to blues culture. At the same time that black women were celebrated as the Mothers or Empresses of blues, they were condemned for being blues women. They were considered poor role models for innocent black girls. They were seen as threats to black progress. Inasmuch as these women popularized blues, they were blamed for spreading a depraved and degenerate culture. The "disturbing" aspects of blues culture were virtually grafted upon the bodies of blues singing women. In this regard, these women represented the predicament of black female bodies in general. For, the black woman's body is a blues body. The highs and especially the lows of blues culture are associated with their bodies. It is the black woman's body that has been at the center of the contestations about blues in the black community. In order to appreciate the blues predicament that ensnares the black female body, we must first understand the black ethos that surrounded the classic blues era.

Moral Panic and Image Making

> "*there can be no issue more vital and momentous than this of the womanhood of the race.*"[9]

The classic blues emerged during the first wave of the Great Migrations when a major demographic shift was taking place in black America.[10] During the 1920s alone, almost 2 million southern black women and men moved northward. With this massive black movement, one thing became obvious within the black community—a cultural clash between the black southern arrivals and the black northern residents. As one black northerner puts it, "there is much difference in the culture of people who were tenant farmers down South than people who were raised up here."[11] In actuality, this perceived and exaggerated cultural difference was a reflection of a growing class divide within the black community. As mentioned earlier, the black middle- and professional classes considered themselves "respectable" and refined, while they considered the nonworking and working poor classes of blacks rough and unfinished. The new migrants from the South were regarded as the bottom of the poor black barrel. The northern black elites deemed these southern men and women as a "rough and ready" lot. They judged them to be uneducated, ill-bred, and lacking in morality. The self-proclaimed "refined and respectable" blacks of the North considered the "tenant farmers" of the South a threat to the strides they believed they had made into mainstream society. For, again, regardless of how different they judged themselves from the "tenant farmers" class, they were very aware that the white public lumped them all together into one black heap of people. The northern black elite were, therefore, extremely self-conscious of black peoples' public image and worked very diligently to make sure that the southern migrants did not tarnish it.

The influx of the southern black migrants into the North unleashed a "moral panic" within the staid northern black population.[12] The image conscious blacks of the North feared that the crude ways of the new southern arrivals would translate into an immoral image of blackness in the white mind. This moral panic contributed to an explosion of the narrative of civility within the black community. It is important to bear in mind that this was not a theoretical narrative. It was a productive narrative. It spawned clubs, training classes, and, most especially, literature—such as the manual "The Negro in Etiquette" mentioned earlier. As we will soon see, this narrative was contested by another public narrative that was produced through the bodies of blues women.

To reiterate, the narrative of civility was grounded in white/puritan standards of propriety. It promoted values of modesty, self-control, and cleanliness. Most importantly, it emphasized the virtue of hard work and sexual restraint. The black elite had two specific priorities in mind when advancing this narrative. First, they wanted to refute the stereotypes that labeled black people as tawdry, ill-kept, unreliable, lazy, lewd, and lascivious beings. Second, they wanted to demonstrate that black people were as civilized as white people, and thus could make a positive contribution to civil society. It was imperative that the values promoted in this narrative become the prevailing and public values of the black community, so that black people could be seen as worthy and moral persons. Black women were considered instrumental to this imperative being met.

Virginia Broughton, school teacher, Baptist missionary, and advocate of women's rights, wrote in 1902,

> The social status of a race is fixed by the character of its women: and all earnest promoters of Negro enlightenment should constantly apply the corrections that have proven most effective in the betterment of the social condition of our women. For by the virtue and integrity of our women, rather than by the courage and prowess of our men, will the race raise the standard of our social condition.[13]

Broughton's observation reflects the "uplift" ideology that was pervasive in the black community during the early decades of the twentieth century. The Negro Women's Club Movement, later to become the National Association of Colored Women (NACW), was most responsible for fostering this uplift ideology. This ideology presumed that women in general were vital to the survival and progress of any people, since they were the ones charged with child rearing and housekeeping duties. With its focus on the black community, uplift ideology regarded black women as the principle purveyors, if not the gatekeepers, of morality for the black race. Just as black women were expected to hand down cultural traditions, they were also expected to pass on proper moral values. For the club woman, these values meant Victorian white middle-class notions of "respectability," such as "cleanliness, thrift, domesticity, and sexual chastity."[14]

Uplift ideology was intrinsically gendered. Black women shouldered the moral burden for the entire black community. Their moral failings were read as the moral failings of the race. Wanton black women were considered indicative of a degenerate black people. As the moral barometers for the black community, black women were virtually required to be paragons of virtue. As club woman Ida B. Wells made clear, Black women were expected to refrain from bodily excesses like "drunkenness, gambling and fornication."[15] They were held accountable for the community's ability to progress. Who they were was to be the best case for the race. The uplift of the black woman was deemed crucial for the uplift of the black race. This is why club woman Anna Julia Cooper proclaimed, "When and where I enter, in the quiet undisputed dignity of my womanhood...then and there the whole *Negro race enters with me.*"[16]

The club women were right to suggest a relationship between the reality of black women and that of "the whole Negro race," even if they were misguided relative to constructing black women as the moral centers for the race. In actual fact, the various ways in which black bodies are put upon by structures and ideologies of oppression land upon the black female body. The dynamics of race, gender, class, and heteronormative oppression all play themselves out on the black female body in an interactive and intersecting way. Thus, that which imposes itself on the black community is grafted on the bodies of black women, and so they are the "gateway" toward black freedom. If they are free, then the black community is free. A gendered notion of freedom is not, however, what the club women or other civility minded black voices had in mind when making black women accountable for black advancement. Their focus was on moral uprightness.

Given the perceived relationship between black female morality and black progress, there was no issue more important for the self-proclaimed guardians of black civility to address than the state of black womanhood. Black women became the focus of the narrative of civility. They were "the primary targets for the moral panic" that penetrated the elite black classes.[17] Organizations such as the Urban League and National Association of Colored People (NAACP) adopted the gendered "uplift" ideology in their efforts to improve both black people's image and status in white society. These organizations paid special attention to the dress, demeanor, work, and social habits of black women. For instance, in 1917 the Detroit Urban League went so far as to found a "Dress Well Club." This club believed that improving the appearance of black women would help to improve the social and living conditions of black people. If black women appeared more acceptable, then perhaps the race would be more accepted by the white public. These stewards of civility already considered black women responsible for the black community's nonacceptance into the white mainstream. Forrester Washington, the president of the Detroit Urban League at the time, made this clear during his remarks at the opening of the Dress Well Club. After asking himself why segregation was increasing, he answered, "Chiefly on account of the loud, noisy, almost nude women in 'Mother Hubbards' [long housecoats] standing around in the public thoroughfares."[18] Fueled with gendered notions of uplift, Dress Well Club members, who were mostly men, met female migrants at the train stations upon their arrival into the city and provided them with pamphlets on how to dress. They further distributed brochures throughout the black community instructing black women on how to present themselves and their children when in public. One such brochure cautioned them not to "g'o about the streets in bungalow aprons and boudoir caps,' " and 'don't do your children's hair up into alleys, canals, and knots.' "[19] To say the least, black women were a closely watched group. Their private and public lives were scrutinized by the "respectable" black organizations. The narrative of civility was played out on their bodies. Their bodies were practically held hostage by this narrative. The black female body was nothing less than a policed body. It was into this climate of "moral panic" and image making that blues women entered.

Blues women were no angel women—at least for the civility minded blacks. These women violated the rules of civility. They constructed a competing image of the black female body. If the narrative of civility projected an image of the black female body as domesticated, demure, and chaste, blues women constructed it as a wild, wicked, and sensuous body. Ironically, while the body image that blues women modeled contributed to their being castigated and rejected within the black church community, it will be an appreciation for this contesting body image that becomes fundamental to preserving the integrity of the black church. To appreciate this we must first explore the contesting blues women body.

The "Wild" Female Body

"you better change your way and get real wild."[20]

In 1925, Bessie Smith recorded "Reckless Blues." In this song, Smith describes a woman whose lifetime love of men led her mother to call her "reckless" and her father to proclaim her "wild." These parental sentiments were no doubt similar to those of the image conscious and moral panicked "respectable" of the black community when it came to blues women. These guardians of black civility seemed to draw a straight line between the songs blues women sang and the lives they lived. They were, of course, concerned with the impact of both upon the community, especially upon the community's moral barometers—black women.

In actual fact, blues women did not write many of the songs they sang. Moreover, these songs were not meant to be biographies of their own lives. Nevertheless, it was because of their lives as black women that these female performers could sing blues with both integrity and passion, whether or not they authored the lyrics. In singing these songs, blues women made them their own, and most importantly, they sang them in such a way that other black women heard them as their own. The authenticity of the blues women's performances allowed their female listeners to hear their own life stories reflected in the music. As noted by blues historian Daphne Duval Harrison, blues women gave the songs they sung a "distinctly female interpretation" that had a "profound effect on their listeners."[21] "Through the blues," Harrison comments, "[blues singing women] became the principal spokespersons for black women in the North and the South."[22] There was an even more profound, if not intricate, relationship between blues and the lives of blues women. Whether or not the songs reflected precise aspects of their lives, their lifestyles as female performers began to reflect the songs. In this regard, blues singing women were doing more than putting on a show. They were providing musical testimony to their experiences as female blues entertainers. The world of blues created a lifestyle that was consonant with blues themselves. For many blues women it could rightly be said that "blues is life...the blues is art...is life," as their lives began to reflect a blues-like existence.[23] These were lives that did not comply with any scripts of the "respectable" elite, be they uplift ideologies or narratives of civility. These were lives of sometimes "reckless," but all the time "wild," bodies. These were bodies that undermined the narrative of civility's representation of the black female body as domesticated.

A major emphasis of the narrative of civility was to depict black women as models of domesticity. Reflecting the Victorian standards of womanhood that informed uplift ideology, the narrative of civility stressed the importance of the black woman's role as a homemaker. The Urban League and NAACP worked alongside the NCAW in training black women on the dos and don'ts required to maintain a "happy and respectable" household. These organizations offered classes and distributed literature that instructed black women on cooking, household cleanliness, good health habits, proper diet, pleasant attitudes, dress, and even personal hygiene—all in an effort to assure that black women were seen as worthy of being placed on the same domestic pedestal as white women. There was, however, a significant obstacle to black women sitting on this pedestal. Black women had to work.

Because of the adverse image in the white public consciousness of black males as shiftless, irrepressible, rapacious, and violent, it was hard for black men to find adequate work to support their families. There were many instances in which black men left their families behind in search of a better life. Given the uncertainty of black men's presence in black homes and financial support of their families, black women—along with being cultural purveyors and moral gatekeepers—were also expected to be economic providers. Black women were crucial to the economic well-being of black households. Bluesman Willie Thomas says of this situation, "You see, a woman could get a job at that time, but a man couldn't hardly get it. Want a little money, had to get it from her."[24] Even though they could secure work more easily than black men, black women still faced a very limited job market. Domestic service was the most reliably available job. Ironically, while they were maligned in the white public as unable to properly manage their own homes, they were called upon to manage the homes of white women. Capitalizing on this irony, the narrators of civility aimed to show black women's domestic fitness, even if it was in white households. They believed that if black women showed themselves to be skilled, fastidiousness, and wholesome in maintaining white houses, then they could altar the image of themselves as dissolute, as well as alter the image of the black household as disorderly. Moreover, by showing that they were hard workers, they could help to dispel the myth of black people as lazy and irresponsible. Essentially, the promoters of the narrative of civility were not deterred by the necessity for black women to work. Instead, they attempted to use this fact to their benefit. They did this by instructing black women on how to be good domestics. The NACW, for instance, worked to change the image of domestic work itself. They made every effort to professionalize it by opening schools to train future domestics in the professional art of domestic service. In 1909, club woman Nannie Helen Burroughs founded the National Training School for Women and Girls. This school trained the students in everything from how to work certain household appliances to proper dress and maintaining proper attitudes.[25] Essentially, the goal of the NACW and other civility minded groups was to elevate the job of domestic work. If black women were going to be relegated to domestic labor, then the tasks of the narrative of civility was to show domestic work as respectable, "clean work," befitting "respectable work." At the same time, civility minded organizations also trained black women for other "respectable" jobs, such as clerks, stenographers—though the likelihood of them being hired for such a job was rare. What was more important was that the jobs they performed be "beyond reproach ... 'clean' jobs disassociated from dirt and disorder" and, hence, from depravity and decadence.[26] Performing blues was not one of the acceptable clean jobs.

Often lost in the discussion of blues women is the fact that performing blues was their job. Like other black women, blues women took advantage of available job opportunities in light of their given skills and talents. Sippie Wallace probably spoke for many blues women when "she declared that singing the blues, 'is my job.'"[27] Blues women were wage earners. They worked to support themselves and their families. Harrison suggests that blues women's wages probably went further in this regard than the wages of most other black women, since the average blues women could earn up to 50 dollars a week while domestics earned only eight to ten.[28] Of course, the most prominent blues women earned much more. The Empress of blues, Bessie Smith, was perhaps the highest earning blues woman. At the peak of her touring success she brought in at least $2,000 a week. Her recording contracts with Columbia Records earned her as much as $200 dollars per side, with no royalty rights.[29] There are stories of Smith pulling thousands of dollars out from under her dress to pay for luxury items such as cars.[30] Yet, regardless of the money she pulled in, it never gave her a sense of celebrity entitlement that caused her to lose sight of her role as a family provider. She moved her several siblings and their families to Philadelphia from Tennessee, renting them an adjoining house to live near her. Much to the consternation of her husband, Jack Gee, she provided generously for them throughout most of her career. She doted even more upon her adopted son, known as Snooks (though there would be a time later in her career that Bessie would suffer much heartbreak when Snooks was placed in foster care).

Like Smith, Ma Rainey also maintained her role as family provider. While she may not have earned as much as Smith, the Mother of Blues was said to be wiser with her earnings than Smith. Her financial acumen allowed her to build a home for her family and to purchase two theatres after her retirement from the blues industry. Many other blues singing women capitalized on their talents and worked hard to support their families.[31]

It did not matter, however, to the narrators of civility that blues women were hardworking women creatively making a way for themselves and their families. All that mattered to these guardians of civility was that these women were doing what they considered unrespectable work. While their work may have removed them from the "dirt" associated with domestic service, it was still not regarded as "clean work." For the "dirt" of domestic service was associated with the nature of the job, and not associated with the character of the people doing the job. Put simply, the black "respectable" regarded it as dirtier than the grime of domestic duties, since it exposed the body in indecent ways and, thus, was an "immoral enticement" for young black girls.[32] Blues women were considered "immoral women," who, as Iowa club woman Gertrude E. Rush warned, could not be allowed to "spread evil influence and disseminate their immorality."[33]

Blues singing women essentially were viewed as reinforcing the racist stereotype of black women as promiscuous, incorrigible "Jezebels." In this respect, their work is perhaps best characterized as "body" work. This is the kind of work that embraces the body as a resource for employment. The body is highlighted as an asset. It is work that sees the body as an advantage to be maximized, not an obstacle to be overcome. Body work draws attention to the gifts of the body. The body is seen as a blessing to be appreciated, not a curse to be hidden. Of course, work that would put the body on display, such as blues, was an affront to the promoters of civility. A 1921 editorial in the *Detroit Contender* made this clear when it called blues singing "rot" that "poisons the soul and dwarfs the intellect."[34] Implied in this comment is the Protestant puritan view of the body and soul as antagonistic entities, with the body being seen as the seat of passion and the soul as the seat of reason. More will be said about this later in chapter 3. For now it is important to recognize the way in which blues women were maligned by the black respectable and their responses to it. In short, blues women were hardly fazed by the scathing attacks. Regardless of how much they were taken to task publicly and otherwise, they refused to be domesticated. They did not betray their bodies. They did not allow their bodies to be held hostage by class-driven notions of respectability. Integral to their personal integrity was to remain true to their body selves. They, therefore, exploited the gifts of their bodies and rebuffed any standards that did not allow them to use and celebrate those gifts. It is in this way that they projected an alternative image to the black female body as a domesticated body. They entered into the black female imagination a life beyond the domestic. They provided an option for black women to live in their bodies in the way they saw fit, not as others saw fit. Sippie Wallace's determination to become a blues performer is a case in point.

Not unlike other blues women, Wallace considered "singing and playing blues... her only tools for making a living."[35] With that being the case, she was not going to permit a prudish criterion of respectable work to stop her from doing a job that she was not only good at but one that also empowered her. For not only was blues her job, she said, "I sings the blues to comfort me on."[36] Essentially, Wallace was no different from her black female audiences, blues helped her to get through life, in this instance literally and figuratively. As Harrison points out, "blues [was] an integral part of [Wallace's] life," which meant that she was not going to give them up in order to conform to a model of domesticity.[37] She was going to remain true to herself and true to her body, regardless of the obstacles she had to overcome. One such obstacle was in fact the domestic niche into which black women were routinely slotted.

Recognizing that her best chance for breaking into the blues industry was through the various tent and vaudeville shows that traveled on the TOBA circuit, Wallace tried out to join the show of snake-dancer Madame Dante.[38] However, there was one problem—Wallace could not dance. Determined to be a part of the Dante troupe, Wallace accepted the job that was offered to her—the job as Dante's maid. That Wallace had to begin her show business career as a maid underscores the fact that domestic service was the job most available to black women—even when it came to the entertainment industry. Nevertheless, Wallace remained undaunted. She did not allow herself to become pigeonholed into this domestic space. Instead, she used the job as a stepping-stone toward becoming "The Texas Nightingale" of blues. She remained true to the call and gifts of her blues body.

By refusing to be confined to domestic service, blues women such as Wallace were not setting themselves above black domestics. They empathized with these women. They did not condemn them. What they condemned were the conditions that deprived black women from having control over their own working bodies. When Sippie Wallace refused to stay a maid, she was virtually claiming agency over her own body by determining the work that her body was going to do. Other blues singing women did the same. They decided what kind of work their bodies were best suited for. They acted as the "mistresses" over their own laboring bodies. This, of course, was no small accomplishment for a once enslaved people who did not have a say on the labors their bodies did. In the post-slavery era, blues women had their say. Their bodies would labor as performers, not as domestics. It bears repeating that having their say over their bodies did not mean that they were judging those black women who were domestics. It also did not mean that they were trying to lead innocent black girls astray. Rather, they were encouraging black women, young and old, to take charge—in whatever way they could—of their own bodies. Even if they were domestics, blues women showed them they did not have to become domesticated bodies. Bessie Smith's rendition of "Washwoman Blues" captures this sentiment.

While she did not write these lyrics, in interpreting them, Smith's identification with the plight of black domestics is clear. Her delivery is plaintive and heartfelt as she sings of a woman who bemoans the reality of having to "do washin' just to make my livelihood." Listening to Smith sing the first stanza, one can picture a black woman doing laundry, especially as Smith draws out the word "all" in the phrase "all day long" and the word "tired" when describing the state of the washwoman's hands. As she goes on to sing that the washwoman would rather be a cook, it is clear at this point that Smith is not truly ballyhooing the merits of being a cook for white people. She is instead signifyin' upon black women's limited employment options. In the final stanza, Smith's raised voice and agitated enunciation of the word "wringin'" suggest that she has more in mind than wringin' out laundry. It is a signifyin' message about wringin' out the "muddy" social conditions that have forced black women into washing white peoples dirty clothes. But perhaps most important of all, that Smith delivers this song as a plaintive complaint positions it as a protest song that asserts an independent identity. There is no tone of resignation when Smith sings this song. Smith's interpretation makes it clear that the washwoman is not happy with her circumstances. So, while the washwoman may be forced into domestic labor, she has not given herself over to being a domestic. She is a black woman doing what she has to do to make a "livelihood."[39] In this instance, her identity is not defined by her labor. The washwoman may be a domestic, but she is not a domesticated body. As Smith made clear in this song, blues women declared with their bodies: to be black and female did not have to become synonymous with being a domesticated body, even when forced into domestic service—and, of course, no one demonstrated this more than Sippie Wallace. For, again, though circumstances dictated that she work as a maid, Wallace did not give herself over to being a maid. She maintained her identity as a blues singer. She recognized that her body was more suited to singing than cleaning. Being a maid was a job, not an identity. Essentially, in song and in life, blues women represented what it meant to have a say over their laboring bodies and to maintain a sense of integrity. In so doing, they undermined the narrative of civility's notion of "respectable" jobs for black women by placing into the public consciousness an image of a responsible black female body that was not a domesticated body. These two competing images of the black female body come into stark relief on Ma Rainey's death certificate. In it, her profession is listed as domestic service. So entrenched was the image of the black female body as a domesticated body that what it could not domesticate in life, it tried to do in death. But, of course, the final word was still Ma Rainey's. For it is the case that her eternal image in the public mind is that of a nondomesticated female body.

Blues women contested the image of black women as domesticated bodies in another way. These women were not confined to the domestic realm. Blues singing women were traveling women. They embraced their lives as blues performers, which meant a life out on the road. Yet, as much as they liked being on the road, they still cherished their familes and their lives as mothers and wives. For some of them, like Bessie Smith, they sometimes longed to be home. Even though her relationship with her husband, Jack Gee, was volatile, she enjoyed being with her son Snooks and trying to make a home for him. But the reality of having to provide always took her back out on the road. Whether she wanted to or not, Bessie did not spend much time at home with Snooks or other family members. Other blues women such as Alberta Hunter tried the role as homemaker and wife, but quickly recognized that this was not who they were meant to be. For various reasons, not the least of which was to stop rumors about her sexual orientation, Hunter decided to marry Willard Townsend, a former soldier and waiter in one of the clubs in which she performed. Even though Hunter described him as a "fine young man and a perfect gentleman," it was not long before she realized her marriage was a mistake.[40] She confessed that she "wasn't the type to stay home and see that the man's underwear is clean or get him a good meal and all. I wasn't cut out to be a good wife."[41] Her husband told a judge that she left their marriage after only two months when he tried to convince her to become a housewife. Townsend said of his absent wife, "She insisted on going on entertaining at cabarets...She told me that she could make more money than I could give her and that she did not like domestic life. I kept after her and told her I would rather she would stay at home and not do that kind of work. After I told her the last time, she left."[42] When Hunter improvises on her song "I've Got a Mind to Ramble" in her performance at the Cookery, even though by this time she is well into her eighties, it is still clear that hers is not a domesticated body.

Like Hunter, many of the blues women sang about traveling. Whether they were singing about "Leaving in the Morning" to find a better man, or running away because they were not being "treated just right," or wandering "north to roam" for a better life, blues women sang of women like themselves—women who were not anchored to a home of domestic responsibilities. Through their lives as traveling women and in the traveling songs they sang, blues women disrupted gendered notions of the "stay at home" wife and mom tethered to domestic duties and relegated to the private sphere. They undermined the civility image of black women as happy homemakers. These women challenged the notion that leaving home behind for whatever reason was something that only a male had the right to do. Blues women made it known that women could hop on a train and leave just as easy as could a man. There was nothing gender-bound about being homebound. And thus, a man could "stay at home, wash and iron" just as easily as could a woman.[43] Essentially, blues women challenged notions of the gendered domestic space. They severed the link between the home and the female body. As traveling women singing about traveling women, blues women allowed black women to imagine themselves as a free body. Theirs could be bodies free from the "postslavery fetters of domestic responsibilities," making them even more free from relying on men for financial support.[44]

In representing the black female body as a traveling body, blues women gave new meanings not only to the black female body but also to the home. Home was no longer a closed domestic space. It was an open and free space. It was a space where blues women could live in the fullness of their bodies and be fully who they were. It was a space where blues women's bodies were fully embraced. Put simply, it was where their bodies found comfort and were free to be. It was no wonder then that Bessie Smith—as much as she loved being a mother—found more comfort on the road, given that her time at her house with her husband was always very volatile. This means that for blues women home was not a static place, and it was not necessarily the place where their families dwelled. Blues women projected an image of being at home that did not necessitate being a domesticated "homebody." Home was a space of affirmation and freedom. This understanding of home is enunciated in Smith's "Work House Blues."

In this song, Smith sings about the reality of those who have been confined to workhouses. Just as this song agitates for black bodies to be free from the social conditions that land black women, as well as men, into work houses, it also projects a new understanding of home. This song tells of a woman dreaming to hop on a train North to home. Home is not associated with a family and household that she will return to. Rather, it is associated with traveling, hopping on a train to a place that is supposed to be better on black bodies, a place that was often associated with "heaven" in the black religious imagination, "up North." Thus, the workhouse woman longs to have a "heaven of my own," and to give all of those poor girls trapped in work house predicaments "a long happy home." It is only in appreciating how blues women refigured the meaning of home in their own lives that the true message of this song can be appreciated. For the workhouse girl, home becomes a place of freedom as symbolized by going North. Notably missing in this song is any mention of returning to a family household. This song thus reiterates the idea of home as a place where black women can have control over their own free bodies. We will see later the implications that this notion of home has for the black church.

In the end, the narrators of civility perhaps were right to be concerned about the influence that blues women would have on other black women. For blues women did undermine the image of black women that the black "respectable" were trying to cast into the public consciousness. Theirs was an image of a domesticated female body. In song and in life, blues women contested this image. They used the lyrics of the songs they sung to project an image of the black female body as a "wild" body. To be wild was to be free from the chains of domesticity—be they gendered notions of work and household duties or domesticated notions of home. To be a wild body was for black women to be independent from any claims that prevented them from expressing the "disposition" and "way" of their own bodies.[45] So, while they may not have been enticing black women into an immoral lifestyle—as the narrators of civility believed—they were calling these women to be "wild bodies." It was only as they were "wild bodies" that they could escape the "blues" that came with being who they were not. This is the message that Ida Cox was trying to get across when she proclaimed that there was no benefit in trying to be an "angel child," and so black women are better-off changing their ways and getting "real wild."[46]

Even as these blues women called black women to be "wild," there was a seeming contradiction to the message they were projecting. These women sang songs about black women who endured, if not accepted, physical abuse from their male lovers. How is it that blues women can affirm at once being wild and abused? If we are to answer this question, we must appreciate who these blues women were as "wicked" bodies.

The "Wicked" Female Body

> "Shoot everybody done me any wrong
> Now, I am all confused, 'cause I got the wicked blues."[47]

When dealing with intimate abuse, once again, blues women defied the civility minded blacks. The narrative of civility attempted to project black women as modest, humble, and demure. This narrative tried to counteract images of black women as uncontrollable, aggressive, and vulgar. It attempted to prove wrong those who thought it impossible for black women to be virtuous or genteel bodies. The civility guardians wanted to project an image of them as "Victorian ladies," which meant, among other things, meek and mild. Blues women were many things, but one of those things was not meek and mild "Victorian ladies." These women were known to assert themselves and to fight back when they believed that somebody had "done [them] wrong."[48] Stories of their outrageous outbursts were not uncommon. There was perhaps no blues woman more volatile and given to defending rage than Bessie Smith.

Stories of Smith's violent rages whenever she believed someone had offended her are almost legendary. Ruby Walker, Bessie's niece by marriage and best friend, tells the story of Bessie beating up one of her chorus girls and shooting at her husband Jack Gee when she was told of their affair.[49] Walker also recalled the time when Bessie took off in a rage after her young lover Eggie when she caught him with another woman—beating the woman during the chase.[50] There is perhaps no incident that best captures the fiery side of Smith than the one that took place at the home of the white patron of black artists Carl Van Vechten. Perceiving herself insulted by Van Vechten's wife when she asked Smith for a kiss as Smith was leaving, a drunk Smith flew into a rage. She cursed and flung Fania Maninoff Van Vechten to the floor before she could be led out the door.[51] That Bessie Smith apparently "took no tea for the fever," and was poised to fight and even to shoot anybody that done her wrong—as she tried to do to her husband—gave a certain credibility to her singing "Send Me To the 'Lectric Chair." In this song Smith sings of a woman who "went insane" and knifed her lover to death after catching him with another woman. The murderous woman then pleads for the judge to send her straight to "the 'lectric chair," because she knows she has to reap what she sowed. The Smith who dares to shoot and fight those who offend her and who sings "Send Me to the 'Lectric Chair" is not meek and mild. Knowing the feisty, fiery side of Smith makes it almost incomprehensible that she would be involved in an abusive relationship, as she was with Gee. In fact, Walker recalls that there were times when Gee hit Smith so hard that Walker thought he was going to kill her.[52] Just as hard to reconcile is the fact that she and other blues women, who were also women who fought back, would sing about women who remained in violent relationships. Even as they sang songs about leaving their lovers because of infidelity and abuse, as Sara Martin sings in "Mistreating Man Blues," or poisoning them because "he beat me and blacked my eye," as Victoria Spivey sang in "Blood Hound Blues," they continued to sing songs that appeared accepting of male abuse.[53]

Notwithstanding the fact that it was men who wrote many of these songs about intimate violence, blues women willingly and passionately performed them. The question becomes why? Why would wild women perform such self-effacing songs? The answer to this question will perhaps always be little more than speculative; however, the nature of blues and the demeanor of blues women may help us to understand it.

One of the first things that must be remembered about the songs these women sung is that they typically reflected the "raw facts" of black women's lives. Whether they wrote the songs or not, blues women sang songs that spoke of black women's everyday struggles. The songs about intimate violence are no different. Intimate violence blues revealed at least two truths at once, that intimate violence did exist within the black community and that "a good man is hard to find."[54] Thus, blues women sang songs that accepted intimate violence as a fact of life for women who wanted to have a good lover. The choice of having a good lover who was not in some way abusive did not seem to be much of an option for black women—at least judging by women's blues. One blues song that made this painfully clear was "Sweet Rough Man." In this song, Ma Rainey gives voice to a woman who says that it is alright for her lover to beat her, split her lip, and give her a black eye, because he is a phenomenal lover.[55] His sweet love makes up for his rough treatment.

Admittedly, "Sweet Rough Man" is one of the most violent songs that Ma Rainey sang; and as her biographer Sandra Lieb points out, given the profound acquiescence to abuse in the song, it is out of character in terms of Rainey's blues repertoire.[56] And, of course, one cannot forget that it was authored by a man. Caveats notwithstanding, as difficult as the song may be to hear in terms of a woman accepting such raw and brutal violence, we cannot dismiss the fact that it likely pointed to a truth about black male/female relationships. These were relationships burdened by the hardships of living in a racist world—as pointed out in the previous chapter. The reality of various social stresses made intimate relationships, let alone good ones, hard to come by—as blues women also testified to in song. Thus, it is not beyond the realm of possibility that far too many black women put up with violence just to have a relationship. Unfortunately, it is as if they believed they could not fulfill one of their bodies' needs, the need for intimacy, without their bodies also being abused. As "Sweet Rough Man" depicted, there was, no doubt, many a black woman who believed that "brutality and eros [were] inseparably wed."[57] With this being the case, it is no wonder that blues women sang these "hit me I love you" type blues.[58] In so doing, they were speaking to a harsh truth.[59] It is also telling that men authored these songs—for even if these songs reflected a pathological sense of male entitlement and power, that men wrote them suggests something about the black male sense of self and prerogative when it came to the black female body. Essentially, if one of the defining characteristics of blues is that they speak truths about black realities, then we must accept the fact that intimate violence blues speak to a hard truth about black male/female love. At the same time, there is another aspect of blues that must not be forgotten—their signifyin' nature.

As previously explained, many blues signify, that is, they speak publicly about private matters in a way that only the black community understands. Clearly, if blues women are signifyin' on intimate violence, they are not doing it in a covert way—there is no mistaking what they are talking about. There is no coded language involved. Nevertheless, there still may be signifyin' intent. While, on one hand, these women were singing of compliant females, on the other, they were exposing violent males. By doing so, they were serving notice to black men that black women were not as passive as these men might believe. First, blues women were at least talking about the violence and thus entering it into public record. Second, even as the songs showed women who accepted this violence, they were exposing the social situation that placed black women in this no win predicament. I agree with black cultural analyst Angela Davis when she suggests that there is more than meets the eye when it comes to these intimate violence blues, and that in fact they may be offering a "scathing critique of male violence"—and, I might add, the social conditions that produce such violence.[60] I further agree with Davis when she asserts that Smith is offering such a critique in her performance of "Yes Indeed He Do."

In this song, Smith sings of a woman who declares that her "sweet daddy" loves her despite the violent ways he treats her. Yet, it is hard to miss the sarcasm in Smith's delivery when she sings about the so-called luxury of being trapped into domesticity, because she only has to wash clothes, mend clothes, and scrub floors as opposed to work. This sarcasm seems to set the stage for how one is to hear the last pronouncement of the song "sweet daddy loves me." Smith's emphatic delivery of this final lyric seems to drive the sarcasm home. In this instance, the truth is found in the signifyin' sarcasm of Smith's performance—she portrays the woman as really knowing that the relationship is not about love, even though she continually says that her "sweet daddy" loves her.[61] It is as if she protests too loudly that black men would be wise to hear this signifyin' message—for hidden behind the literal words is the voice of a woman who is not passive.

The possibility of signifyin' notwithstanding, there is no getting around the fact that these intimate violence blues reveal black women who put up with abuse from their male lovers and seemingly accepted such abuse as a way of life. That blues women sang these songs certainly interrupts the image of them as wild bodies who are free, independent, and strong. There is no song that shows this stark contrast more than Smith's rendition of "Tain't Nobody's Bizness if I Do." With the sassy tone that listeners come to expect from Smith, she sings that since there was nothing she could do to stop criticism from coming her way, she was going to do just what she wanted to anyway, and that it was nobody's "bizness" what she does.[62] But, then, almost in contradiction to this defiant attitude, the last stanza approves of a man that beats her up, with the final pronouncement that such approval is nobody's "bizness." What is one to make of such startling contrasts in the lives of wild women? For, again, not only did blues women sing about abuse, some also endured it. How are we to explain these blues?

The seemingly contradictory messages revealed in intimate violence blues actually speak to a deeper truth concerning the nature of people and the world. They point to the inherent contrasting aspects of all reality. In so doing, they are honest concerning the full complexity of the black community and they celebrate the fullness of the black female body. They reveal what it means for black women to be proud "wicked" bodies even as they affirm the wicked side that lurks in all existence. They do this in at least two ways.

First, in singing these songs, blues women were singing about what everybody knew existed in black households and in black relationships, but refused to openly admit. They were, as earlier mentioned, making public that which was only spoken of in private. They dared to do this despite the narrative of civility that attempted to hide, if not deny, any issue that might portray the black community in a negative light. The civility narrative with all of its productions allowed the black community to remain in denial when it came to male abuse of women. Perhaps most troubling of all, under the guise of protecting the black image, the narrative of civility served to protect abusive males. In the process, it rendered black women silent. It stripped them of the power to name their abuse. To do so, according to this narrative, was to betray the black community and thus to impede its advancement into mainstream society.

By singing songs about intimate violence, blues women seized the opportunity to break the silence. They took the songs that men wrote and, as they did with all their songs, gave them a "distinctly female interpretation."[63] In the very least, through their performances of the songs, blues women presented intimate violence as a cruel fact of life, not as a male prerogative. They, however, had the last word on the issue, not men—not even the men who wrote the songs. They essentially put the issue of intimate violence into the public space from a black female perspective. By doing so, they once again allowed other black women to hear their stories and thus discover that they were not alone. Inasmuch as these blues songs provided black women a space to vent their pain and emotions when it came to abuse, and perhaps to talk about it, or even free themselves from it, then these blues were empowering not humiliating. Indeed, Smith perhaps provides the ultimate last word on this issue in her song "I've Been Mistreated And I Don't Like It." In this song she tells of a woman who has for a long time put up with an abusive relationship. However, something has changed within this woman because she is finally had enough. The first sign of change is in the fact that the woman introduces him as a "no good man." In this song the man is given no credit for being a good lover, he is simply presented as a no-good mistreating man. By contrast, the woman recognizes herself as a "good woman" who is undeserving of such treatment. And, so, she says that though she has "stood" for his mistreatment a long time, that has ended. She is no longer going to stand for it; she doesn't like it and there is "no use to say I do." Perhaps this song says it all. It recognizes the presence of the abuse and even the fact that women have put up with it, but it also lets black women know they indeed have the ability to say they don't like it and to accept it no more.[64]

Daring to break the silence is one of the ways in which blues women reveal what it means to be a wicked body. These women were willing to expose the wicked side of the black community, even if the narrators of civility were not. By doing so, they were not vengefully exposing the flaws of black men. Rather, they were being honest about the wicked realities of living and witnessing a truth about humanity. Ironically, they were attesting to that which the narrative of civility was intent on demonstrating—that black people were as human as white people. For what these blues affirmed was that all human beings have a potentially wicked side. Blackness does not exempt one from the sometimes disturbing paradoxes of human existence.

In this respect, blues women's refusal to conform to the narrative of civility's efforts to romanticize the black community is reminiscent of the African worldview discussed earlier, which assumes two natural givens: the inherent paradoxes that are a part of all existence and the fluid line between paradoxical realities, such as good and evil. Thus, wherever there is good there is also evil. The two realities interact with each other in the sense that all beings—human and divine—have the potential for expressing both. African worldviews, in general, appreciate that there is a "wicked" side to all existence. Blues women recognize this by naming intimate violence, thus making known that not even the black community, regardless of how pristine the narrative of civility would want it, is without a wicked side. In naming intimate violence, Davis says that blues women are carrying forth another African tradition—that of naming. She rightly points to the West African process of "nommo," which maintains that by naming things one can gain some control or power over them (much more will be said about nommo in chapter 5).[65] Placing the intimate violence blues into this interpretative framework certainly resonates with the earlier assertion that blues women were indeed claiming a certain power over male abuse by the mere fact that they named it from their vantage point as women. To be sure, it is not until a reality is named that it can be dealt with. In naming intimate violence, at least blues women were dealing with it.

With all of this said, however, it still may be the case that we are reading too much into these intimate violence blues. Perhaps blues women were simply giving voice to the contradiction in which they and other women lived. Despite how strong and independent they may have been in other areas of their lives, they might just have accepted abuse as a fact of life. These songs may just be testimonies to the fact that they were not one-dimensional or perfect women. In this sense, the intimate violence blues witnessed their deep integrity. For through them, blues women state the obvious: they are not in any way paragons of virtue, and they don't pretend to be. In so stating, they freed themselves and, no doubt, many of their black female listeners from being tethered to unrealistic models of womanhood. They showed that black womanhood was not about pedestals or damnation. They made clear that being a black female body was not a matter of being either all good or all bad, it was just a matter of being who they were, good and bad all mixed up together. Essentially, by singing about black women putting up with abuse, blues women were liberating black women from feeling guilty or ashamed about the contradictory sides of themselves. It is again in this way that blues women reveal what it meant for them to be wicked bodies. To be a wicked body was to own unapologetically the rich, sometimes puzzling, complexity of who they were, claiming their power while also recognizing their vulnerabilities, and valuing their strengths while also not denying their flaws. These were strong women who were also vulnerable to love. These were good women who were sometimes bad.

The proclamation "I have the wicked blues" should be heard as not just a statement about a woman who shoots her man, but also as a bold affirmation of what it means to be a richly complicated body. Such an affirmation is in keeping with who blues women were as sensuous bodies. For when all is said and done, blues women were in touch with their body selves.

The "Sensuous" Female Body

I need a little sugar I my bowl
I need a little hot dog on my roll[66]

As it is now clear, the narrative of civility was deeply concerned with the black female body. This narrative was sensitive to the white stereotype of this body as a lewd, seductive, and promiscuous body. It was also hyperreactive to the white male gaze when it came to the black female body. This was a vile and rapacious gaze. It was a gaze that viewed black female bodies as a means for white men to fulfill their most lustful desires. In the white male consciousness, the black female body was one that could never be sexually satisfied, and therefore constantly longed for sexual fulfillment. As for the white female gaze—the black female body was seen as a dangerous body inasmuch as it was a temptation to their husbands. The narrative of civility's response to the white disrespect and disdain of black women's bodies was with a hyper-focus on the way in which the black female body was presented. This meant instructing black women not to draw undue attention to their bodies by dressing in a flashy or suggestive manner. This narrative denounced any type of gaudy or loud dress. It called for black women to dress in a plain and simple fashion that covered as much of the body as possible, as demonstrated by The Dress Well Club's concerns. Essentially, instead of attacking the stereotype of the black female body, the narrative of civility actually fed the stereotype by treating the black female body as something that had to be controlled or hidden away, given its lascivious allure. Needless to say, blues women did not surrender their bodies to the stereotypes. They did not allow either white sexualized caricatures or black hyperreactive prudishness to dictate how they related to their own bodies. Even if others were disdainful, afraid, or ashamed of the black female body, blues women were not. These women were comfortable with their embodied selves. They affirmed who they were as feeling bodies. Most significantly, they were proud of the uniqueness of their bodies and they were proud to embellish their bodies in a manner that was pleasing to them. The controlling gaze was theirs, not of white males, white females, or even that of the black "respectables." There was perhaps no blues woman who better demonstrates the pride and agency that blues women had for their own bodies than Ma Rainey.

Most people who encountered Ma Rainey did not view her as attractive, at least according to white cultural standards of beauty. Bluesman Little Brother Montgomery said, "she was the horrible-lookingest thing I ever see!" Her one time pianist and Father of Gospel music, Thomas Dorsey, said that she was nice but he "couldn't say she was a good-looking woman."[67] Rainey has been described as "an extraordinary-looking woman, ugly-attractive" at the same time.[68] Pictures of Ma Rainey reveal her as a full-bodied, dark-complexioned woman with short coarse hair, round eyes, a broad nose, thick lips, and gold teeth. Although she did not conform to the white norms of beauty that called for slender bodies, long silky hair, light complexions, and narrow features, she did not deserve to be called "the ugliest face in show business."[69] Beauty in this instance is definitely in the eye of the culturally biased beholder. Culturally biased or not, people did not hold back in their responses to Rainey's appearance. Even her audiences were sometimes cruel. Ruby Walker recalled a time when they screamed "Phantom, Phantom" as they awaited Ma Rainey's appearance. Walker initially thought that they were merely restless and acknowledging the popularity of the recently released silent movie *Phantom of the Opera*. She soon discovered, however, that they were referring to Rainey because they thought she was so ugly.[70] Rainey remained undaunted by reactions such as these. She did not let others' responses to her body dictate her responses. She continued to boldly display her body and accentuate all of its features with flamboyant dress and flashy jewelry. Her entrance onto the stage illustrates her comfort in her own body. Thomas Dorsey provides a detailed description that is worth repeating in full. He said,

> Ma Rainey's act came on as a last number or at the end of the show. I shall never forget the excited feeling when the orchestra in the pit struck up her opening theme, music which I had written especially for the show. The curtain rose slowly and those soft lights on the band as we picked up the introduction to Ma's first song. We looked and felt like a million. Ma was hidden in a big box-like affair built like an old

> Victrola of long ago. This stood on the other side of the stage. A girl would come out and put a big record on it. Then the band picked up the "Moonshine Blues." Ma would sing a few bars inside the Victrola. Then she would open the door and step out into the spotlight with her glittering gown that weighed twenty pounds and wearing a necklace of five, ten and twenty dollar gold pieces. The house went wild. It was as if the show had started all over again. Ma had the audience in the palm of her hand. Her diamonds flashed like sparks of fire falling from her fingers. The goldpiece necklace lay like a golden armor covering her chest. They called her the lady with the golden throat.[71]

Dorsey's description shows two things. First, Rainey's talent quickly took the audiences attention away from her appearance. Second, it shows Rainey's utter disregard for people's opinions about her body. Only a woman comfortable in her own body could make such an audacious entrance onto the stage. This pride of body-self was also evidenced by the way in which she embellished her body on the stage and off it. She was indeed known for being bedecked in extravagant if not garish jewelry. The point of the matter is that she fed the needs and desires of her body. She responded to the calls of her body, not to the catcalls of others. It is fitting then that Rainey would sing songs that reflected her own attitude toward her body. As it was the case for Rainey, it was so for other blues women too.

Blues women sang, seemingly without shame or restraint, about their bodies' sexual needs, desires, and preferences. It is clear what Smith is clamoring for when she sings that her man is gone and she needs "a little sugar in [her] bowl" and "hotdog on [her] roll." There is no doubt what Alberta Hunter is referring to when she sings, "My man is such a handy man," because of the way he keeps her damper down and feeds the horses in her stable.[72] It is also clear what Ida Cox means when she says she is a "One hour mama," so she does not need a one minute papa.[73] It was lyrics like these that raised the ire of the stewards of black civility. While sexual, these songs are about more than sex, and subsequently living into a sexualized stereotype surrounding black people. As titillating as songs such as these can be, to become preoccupied with their suggestive lyrics is to miss the underlying meaning of this admittedly "sexualized" music and the subtlety of what blues women were doing. For, instead of reinforcing the stereotype, they were subverting it. That they sang so fervently and so often about sexual matters should be considered a form of signifyin' protest against the sexualized stereotype of black bodies. Unlike the civility narratives, blues women did not attempt to hide from or avoid the white cultural stereotypes. They confronted them head-on by repeating them, but with a difference—true to signifyin' tradition. In so doing, they provided a different approach to dealing with them, turning the stereotypes on their head by not granting them any power over their bodies. They did not validate them. They transcended them and crafted a new identity for the black female body. Through their lives and songs, blues women projected an image of the black female body, not as an over-sexualized body but as a sensuous body.

Crucial to being a sensuous body is to be in touch with one's feelings. Blues in general is in touch with the feelings of blues bodies. It is sensuous music. As earlier mentioned, blues does not begin with ideas in the head. This is music that begins with the experiences of the body and passionately expresses those experiences. As this is true of blues in general, it is even more true of blues that women sang.

Through their songs, blues singing women gave voice to the calls of the black female body. They made visible that which was oftentimes invisible. Through their performances, they boldly uttered that the female body was alive and full of feelings and desires. Blues women witnessed the feelings of pain, sorrow, and loneliness, as well as the desires for joy, happiness, solitude, pleasure, and satisfaction. If their blues was provocative, as the narrators of civility believed, it was because they provoked their female listeners to recognize and answer the feelings and desires of their own bodies. Blues women provoked black women to celebrate their body selves by validating all that their bodies go through and by providing a vehicle for them to vent all that they feel, as suggested in the discussion about intimate violence. Their songs serve as a virtual "looking glass" into black women's bodies, revealing unarticulated sensations and emotions. Blues women literally gave back to their black female listeners the experiences of their own bodies. They allowed these women to get in touch with their bodies. Once in touch with their bodies, they could then claim who they were as sensuous bodies.

A sensuous body is a body that is not ashamed of itself. It is a body that is not embarrassed by what it feels and desires. A sensuous body celebrates its individuality in terms of color, size, shape, and other physical attributes. A sensuous body claims it is hurt or disappointed. It also asks for what it needs to be fulfilled, be it physical, emotional, or sexual fulfillment. A sensuous body does not surrender to the sensitivities of others; rather, it is sensitive to itself. Again, beneath all of the sexual innuendo and bawdiness, blues women projected an image of black women who do not cave in to cultural phobias or stereotypes about the black female body. These were women with sexual agency.

In talking about sexuality, it is always important to keep in mind that one of the ways in which a dominating power attempts to seize control over a people is through their sexuality. As evidenced by the way in which black reproductivity and romance were regulated, as well as the prevailing white stereotypes, this has been the case for black people since slavery. The lack of freedom has meant the lack of sexual agency, or the inability to determine how to express one's sexuality and to choose one's sexual partners. In many respects, the narrative of civility was a further intrusion upon black women's sexual agency. Even if it was a counter to white infringements on black sexuality, it attempted to regulate how black women related to their bodies and hence to their sexual selves. By taking back their sexuality without shame or fear, blues women were stripping the oppressing power—whether it was in the form of white caricatures or black narratives—of its central controlling tool. In the end, as blues women created a space for black women to embrace the dynamism of what it means to be sensuous bodies, they further established a space for them to be free bodies.

Ruby Walker recalled that her aunt Bessie was well aware of the attitudes that the black respectables, whom she referred to as "dicty," had toward her and other blues women. Bessie knew that dicty blacks regarded them as "being too much the image from which they had escaped." Walker said her aunt "would pay these uppity Negroes no mind."[74] However, Walker also recognized that though she acted otherwise, Bessie was sometimes hurt by the way these black people rejected her. Nevertheless, despite her hurt and disappointment, Walker said Bessie Smith still refused to compromise just to be accepted. Bessie, Walker recalled, "never put on airs…She wasn't going to change for anyone, she just wanted people to like her for what she was—a real person."[75] Being a real person, a real woman, was what blues women were all about. Without a doubt, they defied "respectable" models of womanhood and undermined the narrative of civility's image-making agenda. But, if not for them at least for those black women who came after them, the gains outweighed the losses. As Daphne Duval Harrison rightly points out, they "introduced a new, different model of black women—more assertive, sexy, sexually aware, independent, realistic, complex, alive."[76] While blues singing women may have been castigated and rejected, they were "a [bold] highway through de[civility] wilderness" for other black women to be wild, wicked, and sensuous.[77] And, as we will soon see, they were an embodied testimony in the face of body-phobic narratives to the meaning of a faith tradition.

In "Reckless Blues," the reckless and wild woman proclaims that she is for somebody an angel child. This lyric serves as virtually a signifyin' response not only to the black respectable who viewed blues women as "no angel child," but most particularly to the black church who would call the songs they sing devil's music and come to reject them as virtually the devil's own. It also reveals an ambivalence that blues women have in regard to the church. Nevertheless, through this lyric, blues women are claiming an identity that is not dependent upon, and overcomes, oppressive social narratives. They are claiming a divine identity and more. Inasmuch as angels are messengers from god, these wild, wicked, sensuous blues women were angels to the black church. They were living messages concerning the meaning of an incarnate god.

Blues Women and Me

> "But I'm going to do just what I want to anyway."[78]

Growing up, I preferred balls over Barbies, jeans over dresses, playing sports over playing house. I was not a "fly" girl with light skin, long hair, and straight teeth. I was not prim and prissy. My weekends were not filled with dates and I was left out of debutante balls. I was called a tomboy, asked if I was "funny or something," and told that if I did not change my ways "boys would never like me." I was routinely teased and ridiculed, all because I did not fit the black elite standards of what it meant to be a "young lady." My family was a part of the black elite, so it bothered me that I did not fit in. From time to time, I tried to conform and play with dolls, wear more dresses, and join the drill team. But these excursions into conformity never worked. They just were not me. I returned to my comfortable ways. However, self-acceptance remained a struggle for far too long. I didn't know about Bessie, Ma, Alberta, Sippie, Ida, or other blues women when I was searching for myself and struggling to find a way to be comfortable in my own body. If I did, perhaps the journey toward self-affirmation would not have been full of so many tortuous twists and turns. But I know them now, and I am glad I do.

Today, I still prefer running over ballet, slacks over skirts, watching sports over keeping house—and most days I know that it is okay that I do. In the times of self-doubt, when I hear the whispers of those who call me "funny or something," I hear Bessie calling me to do what I want to do anyway. And so I do. It doesn't matter anymore that I don't fit comfortably into models of what a female should act like. The more I listen to the blues singing women, the more I am at home with myself. They have become a part of my life. Listening to them and learning about their lives empower me to keep growing into my embodied self, regardless. These women who were rejected by many help me to not reject myself. This is their everyday legacy to me. And theirs is an even greater legacy to a black church community, of which I am a part. They are legacies of an incarnate faith. It is to the black church that we now turn.

3

The Devil's Gonna Get You

"Ah, the Devil's gonna get you, the way you carryin' on"[1]

Blues woman Ida Goodson remembered her parents making clear to her that "The Devil's got his work and God's got his work." In the Goodson household, blues was definitely the devil's work. Consequently, when growing up, Goodson had to hide from her parents the fact that she played blues on her piano.[2] Mary Johnson tells of how she was torn between going to church and earning money, so from time to time she "would go back to the church [and] quit singin' the blues."[3] Sippie Wallace recalls how she wavered between the church and blues. When, as a little girl, she determined she wanted to become a blues singer, she says she did not think she could do so because she "was in the church."[4] This tension between the church and blues followed Wallace throughout her career even after she left blues to become a church musician. Wallace was not unlike other blues women—or men, for that matter. Although many of the blues singers recognized the intrinsic relationship between spirituals and blues, and developed their singing talents in the church (especially black women), they also recognized that singing blues meant that they were condemned by the church. They were aware that the good church folk considered them sinners, and indeed some of the blues singers believed themselves to be sinners—as long as they sang blues. They were afraid that if they kept "carryin'on" with blues the devil was going to get them. Emily Williams made this clear to her blues singing daughter, Mary Johnson, when she warned her that if she continued her blues career "she was pavin' her way to hell."[5]

Of course, hanging over the blues performers was the lore that suggested a pact has been made between accomplished blues guitarists and the devil. The most known of the stories is about Robert Johnson. As the story goes, Johnson presumably met the devil at a Mississippi crossroads where he traded his soul for the gift of superior play on the devils own instrument, the guitar (this crossroads legend will be more fully explored later). This legend seemed to have had at least an unconscious impact upon many blues singers. They acted as if their own blues skills were, at the least, the devil's playground, if not gifts from the devil, and so they felt compelled to abandon blues and leave the devil behind.

Regardless of the private comfort blues may have provided them, blues performers accepted that the church most of them grew up in and still loved condemned the music they loved as the handiwork of the devil and judged them to be the devil's own. They reconciled themselves to the harsh truth that there was little mercy to be found for them in the black church. They understood that, as long as they sang blues, they would not be fully embraced by this church. What blues people perhaps did not understand fully was why the black church so easily rejected them and their music.

Blues singing women and men clearly saw themselves as violating the black church's norm of piety by living a blues lifestyle—performing in juke joints, buffet flats, indulging in drink and dance. They were also aware that many black church people believed blues performers endangered the salvation of souls other than their own—not only because they sung about the devil and excesses of the body, but also because they tempted others into a blues life. Bluesman Lil Son Johnson made this clear when comparing church songs with blues when he said, "A man who's singin' the blues—I think it's sin because it cause other people to sin. But church music, is from the Lord and I never knowed anybody to sin over that."[6] The belief that blues was sinister and sinful led many blues singers to return to the church after retirement—as if to atone for their blues singing sins. Ma Rainey was one who did just that. After her blues career, she joined the choir of Friendship Baptist Church in Columbus, Georgia, where her brother was a deacon. Devoted to her faith, she reportedly refused to sing blues during the latter years of her life.[7] When Ethel Waters's singing career came to an end, she became a born-again Christian and joined Billy Graham on his Evangelical Crusades. The uneasiness with blues forced others into early retirement to begin ministries as church musicians, like Sippie Wallace, or as preachers, like Blind Willie McTell and various other bluesmen. Lizzie Miles would abandon her career for a life as a Catholic nun. For the most part, the very gifts and talents that set them apart as performers were used by these "redeemed" blues singers in what they considered a more religiously acceptable manner. Many who took this route simply decided they had been on the "wrong side" of the road long enough.[8] Jon Michael Spencer describes them as "prodigal sons and daughters," following the pattern of the biblical "prodigal son," who, after a life out in the world, repented of his worldly ways and returned home.[9]

Essentially, these blues singers saw themselves as having a problem that required their repentance. What they did not realize was that the problem was not with them or with their music. The problem was with the black church. This was a problem that went far beyond the blues singers' moral disposition and the music's devilish nature. The uninhibited lyrics and stories of demonic pacts were not the source of the problem for blues when it came to the black church. There were narratives already present within the church that predisposed the black church to denouncing blues. The "controversial" aspects of blues only served to validate a preexisting prejudice toward certain expressions of black bodies, perhaps serving to also justify the biased narratives as well as the black church's treatment of blues singers. It is through the black church's response to blues and the people who sang them that we can begin to penetrate this problem and understand the nature of these narratives, and thus learn what it is that compels the black church to deem blues as devil's music and to reject certain black bodies.

What is it about the black church that led it to demonize blues? The answer to this is connected to two identifying characteristics of the black church: its blackness and its faith.

Blues and the Blackness of the Church

"I'm a good hearted woman just am a slave to the blues."[10]

As mentioned earlier, the black church is not a singular monolithic institution. It is a vast grouping of churches that reflects the complex richness of the black community itself. Black churches are often as different from one another as the black community is diverse. These churches vary in terms of size, denominational identities, worshipping ethos, and numerous other factors. While black churches are typically identifiable by their membership, the blackness of these churches actually goes beyond the racial makeup of its members. It is a matter of history and sociopolitical commitment that determines the collective identity of these churches as black.

The black church emerged as a fundamental part of black people's resistance to white racist oppression. From slavery, through the 1960's civil rights movement, to the present day, the black church has been prominent, if not in the forefront, of black people's movement toward freedom. At the same time, the black church has been one of the most significant influences upon black values. As evidenced by the way in which many blues people regarded their very profession, the black church plays an inordinate role in shaping black people's notions of what is morally acceptable or unacceptable. The black church's importance to black life is undeniable, if not insurmountable. It is this church's distinct involvement in the struggle for black life and freedom that determines its blackness. Essentially, the blackness of the black church is inextricably linked to its commitment for the overall welfare of black people's body and soul. Simply put, it is the black church's active commitment to the social, political, emotional, and spiritual needs of black men and women that makes it black.[11] The role of the black church in the black community, therefore, has been immense. W. E. B. DuBois captured this, and hence the essence of what it means for the black church to be black, when he wrote:

> [the black church] has accomplished much. It has instilled and conserved morals, it has helped family life, it has taught and developed ability and given the colored man his best business training. It has planted in every city and town of the Union with few exceptions, meeting places for colored folk which vary from shelter to luxurious and beautiful edifices.[12]

Ironically, it is its very commitment to the black community that has caused the black church to reject certain black bodies. This can be readily seen when considering the black church's embrace of the narrative of civility, a narrative that is inherently condemning and exclusive. Northern black churches' response to the "sudden and simultaneous departure" of black people from the South during the great migrations—again a halcyon time for classic blues—helps clarify the black church's relationship to the narrative of civility and consequent demonizing of blues and blues people.[13] Just as this time of southern migration had a far-reaching impact on black demographics, it had an equally telling impact upon the way in which the black church relates to black bodies.

As the black church is not a singular institution, the response of established northern black churches to the massive influx of black southern migrants was also not singular. Their responses varied and were complicated by numerous factors. For instance, not all black church leaders believed that black migration to the North was expedient. They reasoned that with access to education and jobs, the potential black migrants would be better-off staying down south. African Methodist Episcopal [AME] Bishop Benjamin F. Lee asserted this position during a South Alabama conference of the AME church when he said, "We beg to advise you who are still in the South to remain on the farms, and buy small or large tracts of land while you can, and practice honesty, industry and frugality. Practice the habit of saving; purchase lots and build houses; cultivate a friendly relationship with all races."[14]

Lee and others of like mind held a naïve, if not self-interested, hope that southern whites would eventually see the light leading them to improve social and educational opportunities for blacks. Such improvements, they hoped, would entice black men and women to stay in the South. Perhaps Lee and others worried more about the impact these migrants would have on their lives in the North than they did about the life black people had to endure in the South. There were other black church leaders who actually favored black migration out of the South, but they feared that they did not have ample resources for helping the migrants when they arrived North. Many of the established black denominations such as the AME, Colored Methodist Episcopal [CME}, and African Methodist Episcopal Zion [AMEZ] had funneled most of their financial and institutional resources into the South, where the majority of the black population resided and, thus, where most of their members belonged. Consequently, a major reallocation of funds and personnel was required if they were to adequately meet the needs of the shifting black population. Given regional and denominational power struggles, such a reallocation was easier said than done. Furthermore, while black churches were characteristically involved in meeting the social needs of their congregants, they typically partnered with other black social and civic institutions to do so. They also counted on black people pooling their resources to help one another. Black church leaders encouraged a version of self-help, making clear to their members that "God helped those who helped themselves." When it came to addressing the myriad concerns and needs of the black community, the black church gladly did so, but it rarely had to rely on just itself. When those needs swelled to unprecedented proportions with the southern migration, even with assistance, the black church was overwhelmed. It was simply not equipped to respond at the level that was necessary to meet the urgent demands of the new arrivals. They became taxed beyond capacity not only in terms of their congregational growth but also in terms of their urban mission programs.[15]

It is interesting to note that in many instances black women stepped into the breach to address these demands. Organizations such as the aforementioned Women's Convention Auxiliary to the National Baptist Convention founded by Nannie Helen Burroughs established a variety of programs to help the southern blacks assimilate into northern urban life. Even though the women's work sometimes antagonized black male leadership and caused them to be accused of compromising the feminine image of black women with their assertive presence in the public arena, that black women's organizations acted as "caretakers" and "guardians" of the new black arrivals was in keeping with the "uplift" ethos of the time. Perhaps adding to the antagonism was the fact that the leadership of these organizations did not miss the opportunity to chastise the black male clergy class for their inability to adequately support the migrants. Burroughs, for instance, blamed uneducated and unscrupulous clergy for the black churches' failure to respond. She warned that "No [black] church should be allowed to stay in the black community that does not positively improve community life."[16] In calling the black church to task, one thing was very clear in Burrough's stinging remarks: her high expectations for the black church. She expected the black church to provide for the needs of black bodies and thus to be an instrument for black progress. With all of the obstacles for doing so notwithstanding, northern black clergy expected this as well. Black church leadership did not take their role in the black community lightly. They accepted the fact that black churches bore primary responsibility for the care of the southern newcomers. They knew how much black people relied on the church for their well-being. And they knew that the white community considered the black church a window into the character and state of black people. One 1919 newspaper editorial put it best when it said of the black church,

> [it] is the greatest institution that exists among the colored people today. The Negro Church represents a larger number of the members of

> the race than any other organization. It has the masses of our people in its membership. It has their confidence and they give it a support that is remarkable when we consider their small means. The churches have for a long time been the community centers for our people...It is also true the church has molded the public sentiment of our race in a very large measure.[17]

These lofty opinions further illustrate the very meaning of the black church. Its very existence in the black community depends upon how it responds to the needs of black bodies at any given time. The black church is judged by its care of black bodies.

During the time of migration upheaval in the black population, all eyes were on the black church. Black church leadership was well aware of this. They viewed this unparalleled time in the life of the black community as a crisis time. They accepted the migration as the "social challenge of [their] generation" and as a monumental opportunity for black churches to affirm their pivotal role in the life of the black community.[18] It was a time for black churches to live into their very black identity by advancing the cause of black people. This required the black church to not only address the practical needs of the new arrivals, but to also refine these arrivals' social and cultural habits (with, of course, a special focus on women). One thing was clear, many in the black clergy class shared the view of other black leaders when it came to the cultural and social sophistication of the southern migrants. They believed that these new arrivals were a rough hewn people and subsequently might jeopardize any gains that northern blacks had already made. With this concern in mind, black clergy, again like black leadership in general, had differing views on the best way to deal with the southern migrants. The differences in views generally reflected differing philosophies regarding the meaning of black freedom.

There were those who measured black freedom by black people's ability to integrate into the social and political mainstream. There were others who believed that the only way black people would enjoy freedom was by establishing a separate community, if not emigrating to an African nation. In appreciating these differences it is far too simple to assume that the separatist-minded were members of independent black denominations while the integrationist-minded were members of churches within white denominational systems. There were integrationist-minded clergy who were part of independent black churches and separatist-minded clergy who were not. For instance, two Episcopal priests, Alexander Crummell and James T. Holly, were two of the strongest advocates of emigration. One of the strongest agitators against emigration was the bishop and founder of the AME church, Richard Allen. The point being made is that the black church has always been a very complex and complicated church that defies simple categorization. This complexity again points to the fact that the blackness of this church is unrelated to denominational identity or even political philosophies—it is a matter of commitment. Even as widely different as black church leaders were in their views regarding the black migrants, these disagreements typically reflected their allegiance to the cause of black advancement. In this regard, passionate disagreements within the black church leadership reveal the passionate commitment to the black community. So was the case during the migration crisis. It was out of a commitment to black advancement that the narrative of civility became a prevailing narrative within the black church.

Typically, those black churches that readily embraced the narrative of civility were integrationist-minded. The leaders of these churches were concerned with black people's public image, which meant for them a concern for the image of the black church. Inasmuch as the black church was the face of the black community, these black church leaders were vigilant in their efforts to make sure the black church was viewed as "respectable" by the white public. They thus implemented a narrative of civility within their churches. This had strong implications for the black migrants when it came to how they were received by many of the established northern black churches, first and foremost was because it was a class-driven narrative.

The class divisions that developed in the wider black community during the period of migrations manifested themselves in the black church. The growing black professional and middle classes (which many black clergy considered themselves a part of) tended to flock to the more established and mainline black churches of the North, like the AME church. Black church historian Gayraud Wilmore says, "most of the Northern-based bishops of the three major [black] Methodist bodies were members of this relatively [black] privileged class."[19] Reflecting the values and concerns of these elite classes, these churches tended to mimic the religious life and worshipping culture of their white counterparts. They emphasized a rational engagement of faith and sedate worship. They discouraged worship practices that elicited loud or emotional responses from the congregation. This bias brought attention to the black migrating class.

One of the major concerns that civility-minded churches had about the southern migrants was their behavior during worship. This concern was expressed even prior to their migration North. In his observations on life in the South after emancipation, African American slave narrator and novelist William Wells Brown proclaimed the religion of southern blacks as one of the primary reasons for their "moral and social degradation."[20] He further warned, "It will be difficult to erase from the mind of the negro of the South, the prevailing idea that outward demonstrations, such as, shouting, the loud 'amen,' and the most boisterous noise in prayer, are not necessary adjuncts to piety."[21] Civility-minded black church leaders considered such loud and demonstrative worship a sign of an uncivilized and ignorant people. There was no voice stronger than that of prominent AME Bishop Daniel Payne when it came to condemning boisterous and animated worship. He was clear that this type of worship signaled ignorance and was "heathen." He became convinced of this after several occasions witnessing black people participating in what he called "Praying and Singing Bands (no doubt a carryover of the African ring shout)."[22] In one instance, after watching black worshippers respond to a sermon by forming a ring, clapping their hands, and stamping their feet in what he called, "a most ridiculous and heathenish way," Payne asked the pastor to put an end to it.[23] The pastor refused to do so and explained to Payne the importance of the dramatic and emotional responses to the religious life of the people. Dismissing the pastor's explanation, Payne retorted that such behavior was "a heathenish way to worship and disgraceful to themselves, the race, and the Christian name."[24] Fueled with this belief, Payne attempted to ban such practices from AME worship. He said that "The time is at hand when the ministry of the A.M.E. Church must drive out this heathenish mode of worship or drive out all the intelligence, refinement, and practical Christians who may be in her bosom."[25] Reminiscent of the civility-minded blacks who believed that blues people would spread their immoral practices, Payne believed the same might occur if these boorish black worshippers were allowed to continue their practices. He said that it would be better to "let such people go out of the Church than remain in it to perpetuate their evil practice and thus do two things: disgrace the Christian name and corrupt others."[26] Payne was clear that people who worshipped in this way and the preachers who permitted it were "grossly immoral."[27] Payne was not alone in his beliefs.

Though less strident, W. E. B. DuBois was similarly inclined when it came to uninhibited worship practices. This was made clear in the resolutions from a conference that saw the end of an extensive study DuBois conducted under the auspices of the University of Atlanta on the "religion of the Negro and his moral habits." Though this study was careful to name "notable preachers," those considered "leading the best elements of the Negroes," the resolutions that emerged from the study focused on what was needed to "elevate" the church and its members. One such resolution called for "a religious evolution when the low moral and intellectual standard of the past and the curious custom of emotional fervor are no longer attracting the youth and ought in justice to repel the intelligent and the good."[28]

Negro club women also joined the voices of those who had no patience for the "emotional fervor" of black worship. Anna Julia Cooper considered this type of worship "ludicrous." Others called it "monkey" kind of behavior. Mary Church Terrell wrote that it was "discouraging and shocking to see how some of the women shout, holler and dance during their services."[29]

DuBois, Payne, and other civility-minded leaders and black churches were determined to counter the stereotype of black people as nonrational and given to emotional excesses. They wanted to show that black people were not driven by the emotions of the body, but the rationality of the mind. Given the prominence of the black church, this meant developing a black religious culture that was quiet and reflective—one that resembled the culture of mainstream white churches. This was of urgent concern to these self-conscious black clergy. Again, they believed cultivating the ways of black worshippers according to white practices was necessary if black people were going to continue to make gains into the white mainstream—and, of course, if they themselves were to maintain the status they enjoyed in mainstream society. They wanted to make sure that the status they and other "respectable" blacks had achieved would not be "permanently drowned by [the]torrent of migration."[30]

For the most part, the black migrant class was the target of black churches' efforts to purge their worship of emotional and unrestrained behavior. They felt the brunt of black churches' promotion of a narrative of civility. Similar to white people stereotyping all blacks as incorrigible, lewd, and irrepressible, the civility-minded clergy caricatured southern migrants as backward, ignorant, and unsophisticated, even though many of them were in fact educated and wise to the ways of urban living. Nevertheless, while the social and civic organizations of the black respectable may have targeted the public demeanor of these migrants, the black church focused on their worship behavior.

Inasmuch as the southern migrants insisted on exuberant worship, they were not welcome in the civility-oriented black churches. Interestingly enough, many of these migrants did not care to be welcomed, for they found the sedate ways of these black churches as unappealing to them as they were to the churches. Moreover, they found the people of these churches less than warm. Expressing her dislike for one Chicago black Baptist church, a female migrant commented, "nobody said nothing aloud but there were whispers all over the place."[31] The woman no doubt knew that the people of this church were whispering about her. She recognized the "back bitin' goin' on" that Smith signified to in her blues, "Moan You Moaners."[32] Even though many of the mainline northern black churches treated them with disdain, the southern migrants, for the most part, did not give up their worship practices. Instead, they stayed away from black churches that were unwelcoming or that they perceived to be "high-and-mighty." What they looked for were churches where they felt appreciated and at ease. This sometimes meant founding their own churches. In the words of novelist Richard Wright, "To retain the ardent religious emotionalism of which they are so fond, many of them...group[ed] themselves about a lonely black preacher and help[ed] him to establish what is called a 'store front' church, in which they are still able to perform their religious rituals on the fervid levels of the plantation revival."[33] As suggested by Wright's remarks, the northern black church landscape became even more diverse with the new arrivals. Storefront churches emerged, Holiness and Pentecostal churches flourished, and a whole new generation of charismatic religious figures appeared.[34]

Nevertheless, as inhospitable as the civility-conscious churches may have been to the worshipping ways of the migrants, black churches generally adopted this narrative out of a genuine, albeit ill-advised, concern for black advancement. Their detached reserve toward the southern migrants did not indicate a conscious betrayal of black identity. What it pointed to was a problem endemic to the narrative of civility itself, which in fact did undermine the blackness of the black church. This problem again begins with this narrative's elitist, class defined nature.

The narrative of civility is predicated on a "talented-tenth" logic. This logic projects the "elite" black classes "as guardians" of the race. They are considered the "gateway" for black social advancement, as they are the practical black link to the white mainstream. They are the class of black men and women privileged to enjoy a place within the white mainstream, usually by dent of education. It is they, therefore, who are presumed to protect the interests of the black race and advocate for their rights as they rub shoulders with the white "guardians" of society—always, of course, bearing in mind the special burden of the women in this class. It is for this reason that the narrative of civility is seen as important. For, it is only as the talented tenth are able to maintain their privileged place in white society that the black community will be able to advance. Refining the ways of the black masses is seen to be in the best interest of the masses themselves. So goes the "talented-tenth" logic of the narrative of civility.

This logic shows this narrative as inherently patronizing and excluding. It naturally creates a superior in-group and an inferior out-group within the black community itself. As it applied to the civility-minded black churches during the migration crisis, those black people who did not conform to "white" styles of worship became a part of the inferior out-group. These were considered people who seemingly allowed the passion of their bodies to overwhelm the reason of their minds as evidenced in the way they worshipped. The way they engaged their bodies in worship determined what kind of people they were, those of the mind or those of the body. Of course, when it came to the southern migrants, they were considered those governed by their body. And these were the people who were a threat to black advancement, and thus a people in need of cultivation or rejection. Through the way in which black churches regarded southern migrants, we can come to understand the dynamics of the narrative of civility that demand the rejection of blues and the blues body. That it in fact lends itself to such rejection is an inevitable if not purposeful outcome of this narrative. There are several factors that support this claim.

The first thing that is clear is that the narrative of civility is defined in relationship to mainstream norms and standards—that is, standards of whiteness. That which is considered civil in this narrative is what is considered acceptable to white society. The intent of the narrative is to craft an acceptably white image of black people. By its very nature, the narrative is shaped by white self-interest, not black self-interest. Adding to the white bias of this narrative is the fact that it is an outward-looking narrative. It turns black people away from their own cultural/historical resources. It does not mine the ways of black folks to determine how they have survived and made it in a hostile white world, instead it mines the ways of white folks to see how they have maintained their privileged status. It essentially ignores, if not belittles, the culture that put-upon black bodies have crafted to sustain their well-being. It ignores the "taken-for-granted" wisdom of black bodies that gave them the know-how, the drive, and the hope to keep going in face of almost insuperable odds. As white culture subjugates black culture and wisdom, so too does the narrative of civility. This brings us to another disturbing implication of this narrative.

The narrative of civility, by nature, functions to maintain white supremacy. It basically functions as a discourse of power. To repeat, the standards of civility that this narrative has traditionally adopted are those that are acceptable to white society. This means they are values and ways of being that serve to maintain the cultural and social status quo. They are standards that reinforce white privilege. To adopt such standards is to certainly affirm not to contest the privileged place of whiteness, at least culturally. What is white is considered what is right. Essentially, the narrative of civility is a narrative that accepts a white status quo; it does not seek to change it. This is therefore not a narrative that actually supports freedom from white oppression. It is rather one that finds a way to accommodate it, which means finding a way for black people to advance within systems and structures that privilege whiteness—not to be freed from such systems and structures. In this regard, perhaps it remains true to the civility-minded black leaders' concern for black "advancement," a term often used in their rhetoric, as opposed to freedom. In a bizarre way, the narrative of civility fosters a minstrelsy of whiteness, that is, black people performing whiteness. Needless to say, the implications for the black church when implementing such a narrative are grave.

This is a narrative that is inherently at cross-purpose with the black church—regardless of the reasons for the black church adopting it. To reiterate, the black church has been one of the central resources for black well-being. Its integrity is bound to the fact that it reflects the very cries of black bodies. What black bodies have needed to survive and be whole, they have poured out into their world to give birth to the black church. That which is the black church, in worship and in mission, is that which black bodies themselves have cried out for. The measure of the black church, therefore, is taken in relationship to black bodies. It is by listening to black bodies that this church exists. Furthermore, the black church is by nature organic. To repeat, it did not emerge as an institution apart from the life of black bodies. It was not imposed upon them. Instead, it evolved organically from within them. As it first emerged out of the cauldron of slavery, in "hush harbors" and slave quarters, it was a place where black bodies could be "wholly themselves," a place where tired black bodies could "dip . . . in cool springs of hope . . . and retain . . . wholeness and humanity" and know their god in the midst of a world that would deny them of themselves and deprive them of their gods.[35] To be such a place was the black church's defining identity. The integrity of its existence depends upon it continuing to be that oasis of comfort, empowerment, and hope where black people can know their god. This means that the black church must continue to be organic, that is, transforming itself in terms of the needs of black bodies at any given time. It is its organic nature that allows it to maintain its relevance within the black community. To impose contrived and static narratives upon black bodies, especially ones for which black bodies have not been considered, is antithetical to the dynamics of the black church and threatens its very vitality. This brings us to another aspect of the narrative of civility that threatens the blackness of the black church.

Inasmuch as the blackness of the black church is predicated upon responding to the needs of black bodies, the black church is a body-centered church. The black church at its best is an institutionalized response to the calls of black bodies. For the black church to adopt a narrative that denigrates or diminishes the primacy of the body in any way is to adopt a narrative that is by nature anti-black. Such is the case with the narrative of civility.

Again, the southern migrants are illustrative of this. The migrant class was defined by the way in which their bodies were engaged in labor and in worship. Because their bodies were the central resource for their labor, as opposed to their minds, they were considered body people. These black men and women whose bodies were exploited in labor were regarded as people who gave in to the indulgences of their bodies in unacceptable, indecent, ways. The first thing to be noted is that just as white narratives have defined black people by the work they do—seeing them as laboring beasts instead of as human beings—so too did the civility-oriented black churches of the migration era. The nature of one's labor virtually defined the nature of one's character. It became a mark of one's identity. In this instance the laboring men and women were deemed as virtually out of control, mindless bodies. As such, they were presumed to be people who were ruled by their bodies and, thus, given to unrestrained behaviors—in leisure and in worship. These were people assumed to be unduly attracted to unseemly body pleasures, such as blues. So it is unsurprising that the black church would not look to blues as a resource to navigate a white world. More will be said about this later. For now, it is interesting to point out that these civility-minded churches were right in one regard—these were the bodies of the most put-upon people, those that are exploited in labor and seek the most release in both leisure and worship.

The body that has been so restrained and exploited five days a week begs to be free and relaxed when the workweek comes to an end. These bodies cry out for relief from the pain and hardships of being exploited. Such relief is found in play and in worship. It is through play and worship that these bodies *re-create* themselves. In re-creation, bodies are transformed from being disrespected bodies into bodies that are valued and treated like humans not animals. It is through play and worship that these denigrated bodies can actually experience what it means to be a sacred body. It is through play and worship that these bodies are empowered to keep living, even in a world where their lives are little valued. In this regard, both the juke joints and church become spaces of re-creation, that is, spaces where put-upon bodies experience release, comfort, and hope, the zest necessary to go forward. In speaking of the importance of his church when growing up, Benjamin Mays says, "This was the one place where the Negroes in my community could be free and relax from the toil and oppression of the week."[36] Richard Wright expresses the importance of re-creation from the perspective of the weary migrant bodies when he writes,

> When off duty after a hard day of fighting, we are like spent troops, ready to plunge into pleasure to obliterate the memory of this slow death on the city pavements. Just as in the South...we managed to keep alive deep down in us a hope of what life could be, so now, with death ever hard at our heels, we pour forth in song and dance, without a stint or shame, a sense of what our bodies want, a hint of our hope of a full life lived without fear, a whisper of the natural dignity we feel life can have, a cry of hunger for something new to fill our souls, to reconcile the ecstasy of living with the terror of dying.[37]

The civility-minded churches of the migration era did not seem to appreciate the "hunger" of these browbeaten and weary bodies of the black laboring classes. The narrative of civility prevented them from doing so. Consequently, these churches were unable to meet the needs of these bodies, and worse yet, they did not feel obligated to do so. Instead, they felt obliged to browbeat them even more for being such hungering needy bodies. They castigated them for their frenzies of relief and their gyrations of hope. And, if they did not conform to the decorum of civility, then they were rejected. The meaning of the blues body as refracted through a narrative of civility is now clear. To be a blues body in the black church is to be a rejected body.

The narrative of civility produces an image of the blues body that is in stark contrast to blues' own narrative regarding the blues body. Within the blues narrative the body is something to be celebrated, not abhorred. This narrative, as seen in the previous chapter, does not define black people by the labor they do, especially given the fact that it is typically not labor of black people's own free choosing. By separating the labor from the person, the blues narrative is able to affirm both the body and the humanity of black laboring bodies. It is the work that exploits the body that is seen as immoral, not the bodies that are exploited by the work. According to blues, therefore, it is the body-negating work that is to be rejected, not the body itself. The body at all times is to be appreciated. To be a blues body is therefore a good thing within blues, for this is a body that cherishes and values its very black embodied self. The way in which the narrative of blues and the narrative of civility differs in regard to blues bodies obviously results in differing responses to these bodies. Blues affirms them while the narrative of civility rejects them. Herein lies the fundamental problem for the black church when it comes to the narrative of civility.

As long as this narrative provokes the rejection of any black bodies, it defies a commitment to the well-being of the black community—the very mark of what it means for the black church to be black. Inasmuch as a body cannot be both black and blue in the black church, then the church cannot be black. When the black church rejects blues bodies, it all but rejects its very unique self.

It is no accident that a narrative that is defined by white standards of acceptability is at once body-negating and antiblack. As mentioned earlier, this is an inevitable outgrowth of such a narrative. The signature mark of white oppression has been the profound and lethal disrespect of black bodies. It has negated the value of black bodies. Moreover, it has caricatured black people by the way in which they have engaged their bodies, particularly as they have engaged them in re-creative activities. For instance, as black bodies have sang and danced, black people have been labeled shiftless and given to frolic, not work. And, of course, as black people have loved, they have been labeled hypersexual. Through its various discourses concerning the black body, white power has rendered certain bodies dangerous bodies, and thus been able to justify the destruction of those bodies. The narrative of civility is a continuation of the white gaze and predisposition toward black bodies. By adopting a narrative of civility, the black church essentially looks upon the black body through the lens of whiteness. While it may no longer judge black people according to the way in which their bodies are engaged in labor or engage worship, it does judge them by the way they engage their bodies in their spaces of re-creation. The way these bodies play and love, as we will see later, has become grounds for their rejection. Again, the minute the church becomes a place that rejects black bodies, it has bartered away its blackness.

Paradoxically, the more bodies the black church rejects, the more blues bodies it actually creates, in the sense of people who seek to celebrate and find release for their bodies. Essentially, as blues bodies are rejected bodies, they are people of blues themselves. They are bodies who sing blues, figuratively and/or literally. For they are bodies that seek re-creation. Blues is music of re-creation. It is the music of the most excluded black class, excluded by wider society and within the black community. It is the music of the most put-upon black bodies. The more excluded they are, the more put-upon their bodies, the more their bodies sing a music of re-creation, like blues. Ma Rainey gives voice to this as she sings *Ya Da Do*. In this song she sings of people who, every evening after work, come home and play blues. She says it is the "ya da da do" blues that they sing. While this is blues without a name, it still takes away the pain after a long day of work. The "ya da da do" refrain in this song is the call of re-creation for these blues bodies as they seek and experience relief.[38] This understanding of blues as a refrain of re-creation gives new meaning to Ma Rainey's song "Slave to the Blues." For when she sings about a woman whose very life existence renders her slave to blues, implied is not only the blues quality of her life but also the significance of singing blues to such a life, to such a put-upon body. As blues people have readily attested, blues is a music that returns them to themselves in a world that does everything to strip them of themselves. Bluesman Little Eddie Kirkland makes this clear when he says, "you can get to yourself and sing the blues."[39] Blues is a music that re-creates black bodies.

Unfortunately, the prevailing civility narrative within the black church has rendered this church virtually incapable of exploring blues narratives. It has only been able to see it as a destructive music as opposed to a re-creating music. If a narrative of civility has prevented the black church from appreciating the positive value of blues for the black body, it is another narrative within the church that has made it impossible to appreciate it as having any value for the black soul, and leading even some blues people to doubt their own soul-stirring experiences when it comes to blues. This is a narrative of faith that renders blues not just body music but the devil's music, and renders blues bodies not simply rejected bodies but demonized bodies. It is thus a narrative that colludes with the narrative of civility in a way that has been lethal for blues and bewildering for the people who sing them.

Blues and the Faith of the Church

"Everybody cryin' mercy, tell me what mercy means."[40]

During the eighteenth-century religious revivals across the United States, especially across the South, a significant population of black women and men were converted to Christianity. It was during these revivals that Christianity made its greatest inroads into the antebellum black population. Consequently, most black people's introduction to Christianity during this period was through an evangelical Protestant puritan tradition. This tradition is therefore deeply rooted in the black church. It is a prevailing part of the black church's identity.

A defining aspect of this tradition is a body-denying ethic. This ethic is based on a Western philosophical worldview that places the body and the soul in an antagonistic relationship. The soul is seen as the seat of salvation while the body is seen as the site of sin. When it comes to human qualities, it is reason that enhances the soul and thus connects one to god, while it is pleasure that feeds the body and thus alienates one from god. The source of the bodily sin is pleasure, namely, sexual pleasure. Desires of the body are to be overcome at all cost, especially sexual desires. Sexual desire is considered the ultimate temptations of the devil, since in states of sexual ecstasy all reason is presumed suspended.

The ethic of evangelical Protestant thought is nothing less than a body negating/sex phobic ethic. It is an ethic that is expounded in the New Testament teachings of the Apostle Paul. Hence, the writings of Paul are typically normative ethical resources within evangelical Protestant traditions. Black churches most influenced by this tradition have tended to emphasize Paul's assertion that "one should make no provision for the flesh, but if one must engage in sexual activities it is better to marry than to burn." In accordance with this Pauline pronouncement, gratuitous sex is prohibited—which means sex that is engaged in for other than procreative purposes.

The relationship between this evangelical body-negating ethic and the narrative of civility is clear. Both view the body, particularly the black body, as a problem. For the narrative of civility it is a social problem. For the evangelical faith narrative it is a religious problem. According to the narrative of civility the body is an impediment to black progress. According to the faith narrative it is an impediment to black salvation. Either way, the body is a danger to black people. Its excesses are something that has to be overcome. As for its sexual longings—these are even more dangerous. According to the civility narrative, they play into the worst of the white stereotypes about black people. According to the evangelical faith narrative, they play into the hands of the devil. These two narratives come together in the black church to make indulging in bodily pleasures not only a betrayal of blackness but also a violation of faith. Sexual gratification is seen not just as a social breach, but as a sin. The evangelical faith narrative is in many respects a sanctified version of the narrative of civility. This consigns blues bodies to an almost inescapable outsider space in relation to the black church. This is clearly exhibited through the relationship of blues people to the black church especially during the classic blues era.

Those black churches that were not influenced by a civility narrative and welcomed the blues bodies, at that time most notably southern migrants, were oftentimes influenced by an evangelical faith narrative. Consequently, these churches did not necessarily accept blues performers or appreciate blues. While these churches may not have supported a narrative of civility in terms of its attitudes toward the poorer classes of blacks and their worship, they did support the evangelical narrative and its attitude toward the body. Ironically, many of the churches that the southern migrants found or joined when they came north were churches where this body-negating faith narrative prevailed. Again, this was a narrative that many of them brought with them from the South. It was a part of their religious heritage and upbringing. Thus, it was not contrary to their own religious beliefs to affirm a faith tradition that attempted to save black souls from the passions of the body. They were already steeped in a tradition that viewed bodily excesses as jeopardizing their soul salvation. They did not believe, however, that their body-involved worship was one of these excesses. If they danced, clapped their hands, and shouted in church, this was compelled by the spirit and was meant for the Lord. That which was considered sinful had to do with indulging in lustful pleasures, meant to feed the body not the soul—like drink, dance, and nonreproductive sex. Also sinful was anything that tempted the body to engage in such activities—this meant blues and, of course, the people who spread them. These southern migrants and others like them, therefore, supported the black churches' demonizing of blues and the people of blues. While these rejects of the civility-minded church may not have cared whether or not they were acceptable to the "dicty" blacks, they did care whether or not they were acceptable to the Lord. This meant that they had to distance themselves from the people who carried on with blues in the same way that civility-minded blacks felt they had to distance themselves from them. Ironically, the people who were rejected by the churches that considered themselves vanguards of black civility saw themselves as vanguards of salvation and thus rejected blues singing bodies.

Blues singers found themselves with few places to go when it came to the black church. They, particularly the ones most responsible for the moral disposition of the race—the women,—were viewed as virtual Eves. They were temptresses, luring good black people away from god with their lewd music and lurid ways. Blues women were very aware of the churches' characterization of them as modern day Eves. This is evidenced in the songs they sang that alluded to the Adam and Eve story. Sippie Wallace went so far as to write "Adam and Eve Blues," which was made popular by her niece Horciel Thomas. In this song, Eve is portrayed, true to biblical mythology, as tempting her husband into acting against god. In so doing, Eve becomes the source of black peoples life of blues; as Wallace says, "Eve is the cause of all of us having the blues."[41] For Wallace, the personal blues experience that motivated her to write the song was the break up of her marriage. Even with that being the case, it still reveals Wallace's affirmation of a belief that a woman is the source of all blues troubles, reinforcing the churches very view of blues women. These women are seen as having made the legendary "pact with the devil." Angela Davis explains it this way,

> Blues singers were (and to a certain extent still are) associated with the Devil because they celebrated those dimensions of human existence considered evil and immoral according to the tenets of Christianity...from the vantage point of devout [black] Christians, blues singers are unmitigated sinners and the creativity they demonstrate and the worldview they advocate are in flagrant defiance of the [black] community's prevailing religious beliefs.[42]

Blues performers found themselves in an intolerable outsider space as rejected bodies. They were rejected by the "respectable" black classes, demonized "by the most authoritative institution in [their] own community, the church," and tormented by their own religious conscious. They were left without a home, that is, a place to be comfortably and freely who they were—blues people of faith. This was the outsider predicament that caused many blues singers to waver between their profession and their church. It was a matter of being true to their bodies, or saving their souls. As Elizabeth Cotton, a former blues singer, said, "I couldn't play those worldly songs and serve God. I had to serve God or the devil one."[43] Annie Pavgeau, a former blues performer, offers, "you know you can't serve two people. Jesus said that. You can't serve God and mammon, too. Everything that is not right is wrong. Everything that does not pertain to God is sinful."[44] Being Christian and blues singers was for many blues women and men an almost unbearable predicament, even if they did not readily admit to it—as was perhaps the case with Bessie Smith.

By most accounts, Smith was a very religious person. There were differing accounts, however, regarding the way in which Smith reconciled being a blues singer with her religion. Her sister-in-law Maud remembers that Bessie would go to church on Sunday mornings even when they were on the road. But she said Smith was not troubled with a conflict between her blues life on Saturdays and her church life on Sundays. Though Maud did offer that she believed that "Bessie was getting ready to turn," meaning leave blues for the church, Bessie's friend Ruby did not agree that Smith was ready to give up blues life for church life.[45] Whether or not Bessie experienced a crisis of faith, she perhaps gave voice to it in song. In *Blue Spirit Blues* she sings of being haunted by a dream in which the devil has carried her off to hell. The reason for this trip with the devil is clearly connected to blues, as Smith sings, "Mean blues spirit stuck they fork in me." The song goes on to describe the creatures of hell as "spittin' out blue flames."[46] The ominous piano accompaniment and Smith's slow, tense delivery makes this haunting dream come alive. In this song, it is as if Smith is giving voice to the haunting dreams of blues singers, if not to her own dreams of hell. There is perhaps double signifyin' meaning in these lyrics. At the same time they may be giving voice to the blues, as they represent life's troubles, they may also suggests the tortured reality of the blues performer. It's perhaps because of such haunting dreams that Ma Rainey can sing with passion, "Everybody cryin' mercy, tell me what mercy means," because it is a fact that those of the black church who boast of the mercy of god offer not even the faithful blues singers any mercy, all but consigning them to hell.[47]

The paradoxes and ironies are numerous when it comes to the relationship between blues and the black church, and hence between blues singing women and the church. It is a complex relationship, which sometimes placed blues women in a conundrum with their own blues singing bodies. For while it was easy for them to affirm who they were when it came to black social narratives of civility, and even easy to criticize what they viewed as hypocritical ways of the church, it was not so easy for them to affirm themselves in relationship to sanctified narratives of faith. They were no less concerned about the state of their souls as were other black people. That they were blues women did not mean that they were not religious women. What they struggled with was reconciling these two particular aspects of themselves. When they looked to the church for guidance, the only answer it provided was for them to choose to be either blues bodies or church bodies. This for them was nothing less than a Sophie's choice. This choice forced them to choose between two genuine aspects of themselves that made them who they were and that they loved. They would not be the only black bodies to face this existential catch-22 situation. We will soon see that there will be other black people who rebuff social narratives that claim them unacceptable, but who find it virtually impossible to do the same with regard to faith narratives that deem them hell-bound simply because of who they are.

Given the choice that the black church's evangelical faith narrative provides, this narrative lends itself to a kind of existential disharmony—compelling people to live over and against their very selves, thus creating personal confusion and anguish—the kind that cries for "mercy." It is this kind of disharmony that African religious traditions deemed evil. It is this kind of disharmony that the black church fosters as long as it maintains an evangelical faith narrative with an unyielding body-negating ethic. This brings us perhaps to the irony of all ironies when it comes to the relationship between blues and the black church.

While it is the evangelical faith narrative of the black church that compels it to deem blues the devil's music, it is actually this narrative that places the black church on the side of evil—as it is a narrative that fosters division and disharmony within the black church community as well as within black bodies themselves. The same can be said of the narrative of civility. In contrast, it is blues, with its narrative that witnesses a unified universe and affirms the coexistence of opposites, that nurtures harmony, thereby making it a force that contests the reality of evil in the universe. It is to their own blues narratives, therefore, that blues women should look for mercy, as it is to blues narratives that other demonized blues bodies should look. And so perhaps there is even more meaning to be found in Rainey's blues song that cries for mercy. For, in this song, after pondering what mercy means, she says, "If it means feeling good, Lord have mercy on me." This final proclamation affirms that it is the good feeling that comes from blues that is nothing less than the mercy of god.

Blues that blues people sung were the antidote not simply for their put-upon bodies but also for their troubled souls. Unfortunately, the prevailing narratives of the churches in which they grew up overshadowed their ability to hear their own testimonies of faith. For, while they were tormented by the faith of their churches, they were the actual carriers of a black church faith. The church that cast them out as betraying their blackness and their faith was the actual betrayer of both. It was blues people who were the keepers of a radical black faith tradition. This is seen through the narratives of the songs the blues women sang, as well as through the narratives of the lives they lived. As blues call blues bodies back to themselves, it is blues that call the black church back to itself. This call becomes clear as we hear the signifyin' laments of blues.

The Black Church and Me

"Make [me] feel so peculiar... on revival day."[48]

I grew up in St. Margaret's Episcopal Church in Dayton, Ohio. It was an all-black congregation. The rector was Father M. Bartlett Cochran. I was baptized and confirmed at St. Margaret's. It was there that my faith was nurtured. I liked going to church on Sundays. I would go even on the Sundays when my parents did not. On those Sundays, I would wake them and ask them to drive me to church. If they did not stay I would ride home with a neighbor. I would go to Sunday school and stay for the service. Sometimes I would attend the service before and after Sunday school. There was no loud music in my church. There was mainly sedate hymns from the Episcopal hymn book, with an occasional spiritual sung during black history month or on some other special occasion. The sermons were typically reflective messages about what it meant to follow Jesus. There was no foot stomping, hand clapping, or shouts of amen in my church. The worship was quiet and sedate. It was just the way I liked it. It resonated with my spiritual personality. I liked my church because it was where my quiet spirit came alive.

My church also left me wanting and feeling left out. I wanted to be an acolyte. I wanted to work at the altar like my male peers. I could not, because I was a girl. There was nothing I could do, nor that I wanted to do, about my gender. Nevertheless, I felt trapped—I felt called to serve at the altar but was told, as a girl, I could not. I simply could not reconcile the fact that the church I loved so much would not let me serve in it. I felt rejected by my church.

As time went on, I decided to live out what I believed to be my call to the ministry of the church by becoming a theologian. Even though the Episcopal church was now ordaining women to the priesthood, I suppressed my call because I feared once again being rejected by my black church. The first step toward ordination is through one's home church. I knew that there were still many men, especially black men, who believed that ordination was a violation of faith. The same Pauline narratives that rendered blues people as body people did the same to women. We were seen as being driven by the passions of our bodies and thus not suitable vessels for giving witness to god. I did not want to risk that the church in which I grew up and the priest who baptized me would reject me. After all, this was the church that would not permit me to be an acolyte. The existential dilemma soon became too much. My call was weighing me down, so I took the chance and called Father Cochran. I told him about my call. Before I could barely finish speaking, he was telling me what we needed to do to get the process started. My eyes filled with tears of joy and peace. In that moment, I felt whole again. I felt I had a church once again, a place where I could be fully black, fully female, fully Christian—fully ME. This for me was what a black church was all about. Four years later, Father Cochran presented me to be ordained in the Episcopal Church.

It would not be long before I was told that I was not a member of the black church. My seminary colleagues told me a church that did not shout, clap hands, and say "Amen" out loud could not possibly be black. Besides, my church was a part of a white denomination, this in itself made it white. Once again I found myself in an almost untenable situation. It was in black Episcopal congregations that I felt most alive, most myself. Now I was being told that I could not be black and Episcopal at the same time. I was made to feel peculiar because my church was not a revival-spirited church. This was a dilemma I lived with for a long time, until I listened to myself. I was black and I was Episcopalian—problem solved. The issue was not with me, it was with the churches that rejected me because of who I was in all of my black womanhood.

I have now served as an assisting priest at Holy Comforter Episcopal Church for over 21 years. It is a church with a rich and diverse membership from across the African diaspora. It is a church where all bodies are wanted and affirmed. Occasionally the congregation may applaud at the end of a sermon or after a choir offering, but ours is quiet worship. There is no dancing, spontaneous clapping, or loud Amens. On the rare occasions that someone may shout aloud Amen, it is alright. Nobody complains. We are a caring church. We address the needs of our communities as best we can, often stretching ourselves to the limits to do so. But this we see as our mission.

I teach Adult Sunday School at Holy Comforter. We study the bible, we read books on issues of faith, and we read black novels and talk about blues. It is a church where I can share with the congregation my very journey through blues, and be affirmed by them as I do so. When I leave church each Sunday, I feel as I have been re-created. I am ready to engage the week. It is a church, by the way, that people don't like to leave. The congregation sticks around way past the time of mass, eating, talking, sharing, affirming one another, re-creating. This is a church where you can be black and blue. This is the black church to me. It is for a black church that blues bodies cry in their signifyin' laments, to which we will now turn.

II

Blues Truth

4

"Hear Me Talkin' to Ya"

"Ah, you hear me talkin' to you, I don't bite my tongue."[1]

It happened in the darkness of Sunday morning on September 26, 1937. It took place on a two lane stretch of Route 61. Bessie Smith and her devoted lover Richard Morgan had just left Memphis, Tennessee, where Bessie had performed that Saturday night. They were headed to Darling, Mississippi, where she was to perform that Sunday afternoon. Bessie sat in the front passenger seat while Richard was driving. They rode in silence, apparently both still smarting from a heated argument about leaving Memphis. Richard wanted to stay overnight (apparently to play cards with friends), Bessie wanted to leave. After an intense exchange, Bessie got her way. They got in the car and headed south. About 75 miles into the trip, seemingly out of nowhere, to a tired Richard, a huge truck appeared. Even as he tried to avoid it, he was not able to do so. Richard's car and the truck met on the passenger side where Bessie was sitting. It was a violent collision. Richard made it through practically unscathed, at least physically. All who knew him said he never recovered from that night. He died in 1943, by most reports suffering from heartbreak. Bessie died that September morning as a result of injuries sustained during that accident. The Associated Press ran a brief report of her death that day under the headline, "Blues Singers' Queen Dead."[2]

These are perhaps the only uncontested details of Smith's death. The finer details of her death became quickly clouded by the racist climate of the 1930s South. Exploiting the racial tensions of the times, John Hammond wrote a rather dubious article that appeared in the November 1937 issue of *Down Beat* magazine. In this article

Hammond reported that Bessie Smith ultimately died as a result of delayed treatment because a white hospital refused to take her, forcing her to be transported to a black one. As sketchy as the facts are of what actually happened in the aftermath of the accident and the circumstances surrounding Smith's treatment, Hammond's version of events was not substantiated by any of the persons involved, including the doctor who offered initial treatment at the scene of the accident, the black ambulance driver who took Smith to the hospital, or the doctor who attended to her at the black hospital. By the time Hammond timidly retreated from his version of events, it was too late. His article had done perhaps what he intended for it to do. It stirred the pot of racial tensions. It raised questions and created controversy. It became a part of blues legend, much like Robert Johnson's crossroad's pact with the devil on that same Route 61 highway. It made Smith's death a symbol of protest against the viciousness of southern racism—that which forced many blacks to migrate North.

That a blues singer's death would provide the "perfect cause celebre" to protest southern racism was a bit of an irony. To some, particularly the younger generation of black men and women of Bessie's time, blues was the music of "Yassuh an' nosuh," black people who had accepted their Jim Crow place in the white world.[3] Smith's biographer rightly points out that "for many years the stigma of Uncle Tomism was attached to the music of Bessie and her contemporaries."[4] In the minds of many, blues was not a music of protest, it was a music of accommodation.

Various blues interpreters have agreed with this assessment. Sam Charters says that "there is little protest in the blues." He explains that while blues often contain "a note of anger and frustration ... there is little open protest at the social conditions under which a Negro in the United States is forced to live." Given that the "oppressive weight of prejudice is so constricting," Charters goes on to say, "it is not surprising to find little protest in the blues. It is surprising to find even an indirect protest"[5] Paul Oliver develops an elaborate culturally narrow perspective to support his contention that "protest themes" in blues "are exceedingly small." He asserts that not only were recording companies reluctant to release blues that spoke to volatile issues like racism, but so too were blues singers. He argues that blues singers were not unlike other southern blacks in their "acceptance of the stereotypes." He explains,

> They were primarily concerned with the business of living from day to day, of conforming and making the best of their circumstances. As

> surely as the southern Whites intended them to "keep their place" the majority of Blacks were prepared to accept it. They knew that they could not change the world but that they had to live in it.[6]

Perhaps the only accurate observation that Oliver provided in his "content darky" caricature of southern blacks was that it was "scarcely conceivable that the [blues] singers... would deliberately ignore or reject [the facets of black life] that were a result of racial prejudice and intolerance."[7] He is right, they would not fail to comment on the virulent racism of the South. And neither would they fail to protest it. If the response to Bessie Smith's accident did not suggest as much, her legendary encounter with the Klan did.

As the story goes, Bessie chased about a dozen hooded Klansman away with a "hands on hip" barrage of obscenities when she discovered them trying to collapse her show tent.[8] This was not a woman afraid to speak out against racism, and neither were other blues women. Blues did protest the impact of racism and other oppressive impositions on black bodies, especially bodies of black women. For, again, blues realities of racism, sexism, and poverty intersect on the black female body in a rather paradoxical way. Black women are denigrated for doing the work of men, yet they are forced into the work place. Their femininity is questioned, on the one hand, yet they are projected as paragons of virtue, on the other. As we have seen, blues women were not reluctant to challenge those opposing oppressive realities. They protested the various assaults against their bodies and contested the caricatures that circumscribed their identities. In standing up for themselves, they were standing up for the black community as a whole, including for men, since, again, the various narratives that oppressed black bodies converged on the black female body. To protests for themselves was to protest for the black community. The blues that black women sang did, in fact, protest. But, it was a blues protest. This means it rarely came in the form of a frontal attack and it was seldom directed outward. Blues protests were signifyin' laments. True to their signifyin' nature, they were, as Davis observes, "secretly expressed and understood only by those who held the key to the code."[9] Reflective of being laments, they were directed to the black community, again, the intended audience of blues in the first place.

As described in chapter 1, blues signifyin' laments was meant to provide an opportunity for the black community to confront its own ways and transform them so as to change what they had the power to change when it came to their oppressing situation. To the extent that black men and women perpetuated offenses against black bodies, they were called out for it. Given the lamenting aspect of blues, it did not typically challenge various racial injustices and social inequalities head-on. It did not engage the stereotyping narratives and structures of power in direct conversation. Rather, blues engaged black men and women in conversation about their absorption of these narratives into their public conscious and re-enactment of subjugating power relations in their private and social relationships. When blues protest did confront the source of black suffering directly, it was still a signifyin' protest. Such is the case in "Washwoman Blues," which, as earlier mentioned, challenged the conditions that forced black women into domestic service. Ma Rainey also offers a signifyin' protest against the social conditions that encumbered black lives in "Chain Gang Blues."[10] In this song, Rainey sings of a woman who is sentenced to the chain gang for what was apparently a minor offense involving a conflict with another woman over a man. Lieb, Rainey's biographer, says that a stanza left out of the final version of the song makes clear the minor nature of the offense, as it admits that no "hanging crime" was committed.[11] Yet, even though a minor offense, the woman knows that she will not be able to escape the harsh realities of the chain gang, as she says, "Just a poor gal in trouble, I know I'm country road bound." This song goes on to speak about the tortuous conditions of chain gang life in its references to bear "a ball and chain" and a padlock. "Chain Gang" blues serves as a veiled protest against the injustice of the criminal justice system as well as the inhumanity of chain gangs, to which black people—even boys and girls—were disproportionately assigned. There are also blues that confront the economic inequalities of the day that left white people rich and kept black people poor. One such blues is Bessie Smith's "Poor Man's Blues," which Smith authored, providing further evidence that she was not an apolitical "get along to go along woman." In this song Smith delivers an insightful critique of black poverty. In one stanza she comments on the irony of the working man's wife "starvin'" while the wife of the rich man lives "like a queen." This lyric is prescient as it foreshadows the caricature of the black woman as the "welfare queen." Heard in the context of a welfare system, one would wonder precisely who the welfare queen is, for it is the rich woman whose welfare of wealth depends upon the starvation of the poor woman. Nevertheless, this lyric is just as penetrating when heard in the Depression era context in which it was sung. For it makes clear that the wealth of the rich man depends upon the poverty of the poor man. Smith sings, "If it wasn't for the poor man, mister rich man what would you do?" Smith's song also protests the irony of poor men going to fight for a country that will not fight for them. Clearly, this song offers a poignant and timeless (perhaps not so veiled) critique of capitalism. The power of this critique is punctuated in Smith's draggy delivery with a signifyin' horn response.

"Chain Gang Blues" and "Poor Man's Blues" are not the only blues to offer signifyin' commentary on the social-economic conditions that weigh down black bodies. Various other blues, such as Rainey's "Ma and Pa Poorhouse Blues," Ida Cox's "Pink Slip Blues," and even Victoria Spivey's "Dope Head Blues," signify on the difficult and uncertain conditions that seem to come with the territory of living black in America. In fact, it is virtually impossible to listen to any of the blues as they speak about the "raw facts" of black life without hearing an underlying protest—unless, of course, one is blinded by their own cultural parameters. Davis is right to say that those who criticize blues for lacking protest have defined "what constitutes protest and what constitutes acquiescence" in a way that "prevents them from [hearing]more deeply" the way in which blues is talkin' to them, and hence to the wider society.[12]

Nevertheless, most protest talkin' of blues is not directed to wider/white society. Through signifyin' lament, such blues talkin' is directed to the black community. This does not mean that the black community is blamed for its own oppression. Rather, by calling the black community to account for the ways in which it has fostered oppressive social narratives and social arrangements, blues is exposing the menacing and subtle nature of subjugating power. Even so, it holds the black community responsible for that which they should be held responsible—their cooperation with the ways of power that divide the community and set black men and women against their own black bodies. In the end, blues is talkin' to black people about their pact with forces of evil. This comes through loud and clear in signifyin' laments on colorism, sexuality, and saved bodies.

High Yella Blues

I'm as good as any woman in your town
I ain't no high yella, I'm a deep killer brown[13]

Bessie entered show business like many blues women, in the chorus line of traveling shows. She was once in the chorus of a show produced by Irvin C. Miller, who had at least two shows traveling through the South at the turn of the century. Her place in the chorus line was, however, short-lived. She was fired not for her lack of talent but for her abundance of color. Miller considered her too black to be in one of his shows, especially since he billed them as "Glorifying the Brownskin Girl."[14] This would not be the last time that Bessie was confronted by the matter of color on the chorus line. Apparently, a rift between Bessie and Frank Schiffman, who owned Harlem's Apollo Theatre, involved the color of the chorus line. Prior to Bessie performing there, Schiffman reportedly became disturbed by the number of dark-complexioned girls Bessie had in her line. Ruby Walker says that Schiffman approached Bessie after a rehearsal and said, "you got a dancing bunch of girls with you this time, but they are so black that with the makeup on they'll look gray—especially that little one at the end of the front line, she's *exceptionally* dark, and I wouldn't want to bring this bunch into the Apollo." Needless to say, this infuriated Bessie, who told Schiffman in no uncertain terms that if she was going to perform in the Apollo, so too were all of her girls. With Bessie's help the story of the incident spread throughout the black community, resulting in long lines to see the show since, as Ruby reported, "all those Ma Rainey's [were] gonna be there."[15]

Blues women were very aware of the codes of color perpetuated by white racist stereotypes. While most people considered Bessie an acceptable shade of brown, most considered Ma Rainey unacceptably black. As confident as she was in her own body, Rainey was sometimes not as comfortable in her skin, or at least she recognized it to be a problem. Responding to the dark skin prejudice, she reportedly applied heavy makeup and rouge when performing so that she could look more "gold-colored" under the stage lights.[16]

To grow up black in America, regardless of the era, is to be well-schooled on the color-coded standard of beauty and acceptability. The closer one's skin tone, physical features, and hair texture are to those of white people, then the more accepted one is in white society. This code has its roots in slavery where the lighter-complexioned blacks, who invariably had white features, were typically allowed the so-called privilege of working in the master's house, while the darker-complexioned blacks with more African features were relegated to the fields. Of course, this color variation within the black community during slavery was evidence of the master's crime of rape against black women, an unspoken white male prerogative of the slavocracy. Such favoring of light-complexioned black people continued after slavery. During the migration era, for instance, it was the light-complexioned black women who were most likely to get the few available nondomestic jobs. It was rare to see dark-skinned women working as elevator operators or in industrial and clerical positions. While blackness was the mark of a slave during the antebellum period, thereafter it became a mark of an immoral, lewd, ignorant, irresponsible, and volatile person. E. Franklin Frazier, author of the classic study *The Black Bourgeoisie*, bluntly states,

> Since the Negro's black skin was a sign of the curse of God and of his inferiority to the white man, therefore, a light complexion resulting from racial mixture raised a mulatto above the level of the unmixed Negro. Although mulattoes were not always treated better than the blacks, as a rule they were taken into the household or were apprenticed to a skilled artisan.[17]

Unfortunately, this color-coded narrative penetrated the collective consciousness of the black community in the form of internalized racism, perhaps best described as "colorism."

There is no denying colorism's pervasive impact on black life. As class divisions emerged within the black community, the elite classes were generally made up of lighter-complexioned blacks. Deborah Gray White aptly describes the budding issue of color in the black community when she explains, "In turn-of-the-century black America color mattered, too. While a light-skinned complexion was not a prerequisite for upper- or middle-class status, in the period before World War I, the black middle and upper classes were lighter than the black working and lower classes."[18] Of course, this was not unrelated to the aforementioned fact that a wider variety of job opportunities were available to these black men and women precisely because of their skin tone. Although they were not immune from countless other forms of racial discrimination, they were afforded the privilege of relatively stable employment. Furthermore, those who were, as Frazier calls, "descendants of the mulatto class" considered themselves the black "talented-tenth." As such, they assumed leadership positions within the black community. They subsequently enjoyed a racialized privileged status in mainstream society. They were not considered equal to whites, but neither were they considered as low as the uncouth black masses. It was as if their light skin signaled that they had just enough white blood to perhaps mitigate the worst instincts of blackness. Even as white civil society considered one drop of African blood a sufficient qualification to be a black person, it considered a physical manifestation of white blood a "tonic" for the worst maladies of blackness. Whatever the case, light-skinned black people were presumed to be the "genteel" blacks, well cultured in the morals and manners of white society. And on their part, to show that they were as different from the black masses as white people thought, these light-skinned "ladies" and "gentlemen" rarely interacted socially with the darker "vulgar" blacks.

From black social clubs to civic organizations, skin color was an issue. As early as the Reconstruction era, social clubs emerged whose membership was restricted to "mulatto" or light-skinned men and women. There was, for instance, the "Blue Vein Society" of Nashville, Tennessee, and the "Bon Ton Society" of Washington, DC. Not only were black Greek societies associated with "molding" the values of the black middle and elite classes, but they also developed within their ranks a distinctive color code. Certain sororities, for instance, became known by whether they admitted lighter-complexioned or dark-complexioned women. Various black fraternities instituted the ritual of a "color tax" in the 1920s, which continued for four decades. This ritual required that the fraternity brothers pay a tax at the door of a party for their dates. The darker the date, the higher the tax a brother had to pay. The paper bag test was also a part of black Greek life. This test required a black person be lighter than the color of a paper bag for acceptance.[19] Skin color was presumably a factor in the National Association of Colored Women [NACW] as well. Gray White explains that while there are no precise records that might suggest the complexions of NACW membership, prior to 1920 most of the leadership of the organization was light-skinned. At times, some of the leadership may have passed for white, as Mary Church Terrell is believed to have done. Gray White goes on to suggest that skin color probably played a part in these women calling themselves the National Association of "Colored" Women as opposed to Negro. There were those, she says, who preferred this term because it acknowledged their "white or Indian ancestry."[20] Perhaps most unfortunate of all, the institution that was held most responsible for shaping black peoples values also reflected a color line—that institution being the black church. Frazier says, "Even in their religious affiliations, the descendents of the free mulattoes held aloof from the Negro masses."[21] For the most part, light-skinned black people were members of black churches within white denominational systems, such as the Episcopal, Presbyterian, and Catholic denominations. Black denominational systems embraced the color code as well. Traditionally, there have been various independent black Baptist and Methodist congregations that became known for their light-skinned membership. In general, at the turn of the century the black church community had its own versions of paper bag qualifications. Some churches employed this test precisely. Other churches painted their doors the darkest shade a person could be to enter. Still other black congregations hung a fine-tooth comb at the entrance to be used. If the comb could not pass through the potential black worshipper's hair, then he or she would be denied entrance.[22] The point of the matter is that most segments of black private and institutional life, especially at the turn of the twentieth century, were deeply influenced by the politics of color. This palpable aspect of the narrative of civility trickled down into the black poor and working classes as well. Just as the elite blacks used color as a mark of respectability, so too did the black masses. Within the wider black community, the color bias was most evident in terms of the black perception of beauty. A white gaze shaped the black aesthetic. This white-informed aesthetic became the basis for sexualized moral assessments, especially as it related to the female body. The "attractive" light-skinned body was considered chaste and demure while the "unattractive" dark body was seen as promiscuous and volatile. Essentially, the black community took over the sexualized white narrative of black people and used it against themselves to sustain various social distinctions.

In singing about the truths of everyday black living, blues women did not ignore the color complex. They provided signifyin' laments on its confounding impact on black bodies. In so doing, they revealed its evil consequences within the black community.[23] They drew particular attention to the multidimensional way in which the issue of color played itself out on the black female body.

In her own composition "Young Woman's Blues," Smith signifies on the way in which civility narratives of gender and color intersect in black women's lives. In so doing, she reverses the stereotypic assumptions of both. Her song begins with a woman waking to find a note on the pillow saying her male lover has left. Initially this sounds like nothing new—a woman singing about being abandoned by a man. As the song continues, however, we discover the twist: he left because the woman did not want to settle down, and it was she who was running around with other men. With this gender twist, Smith signifies on the gender privilege that men have enjoyed in these relationships—they have been entitled to treat black women the way they want, according to their male needs. She also reverses the gendered presumption that women want to be tied down in a monogamous relationship. In this instance, what is good for the goose is good for the gander. The man is left wanting. Smith goes further by signifyin' on gendered valuing. If a man runs around there is no presumption concerning his character. This is considered a badge of masculinist identity. If a woman runs around, however, she is considered a loose, evil woman. It is here that Smith's song engages the gendered morality of the color code. According to the color code, it is the darker-skinned women who are more prone to such promiscuous behavior. The light-skinned women are considered the marrying type, as their skin color suggests a purity associated with the desexualized Victorian white female. In this regard, dark-skinned women become legitimate objects for carnal pleasure, not light-skinned women. Smith attacks this sexualized color-coded morality head-on. She lets it be known that even though the running-around woman is a "deep killer brown," she is just as good as any "high yella" woman. The only difference between the two is that the high killer brown woman is not ready to settle down into marriage. Interesting to note is that, in challenging the sexualized interpretation of dark skin (again reflective of the white stereotype of black bodies), Smith does not reverse the stereotype or in any way denigrate the light-skinned woman. She presents both women on equal terms, both as victims of the objectification that comes with the gendered/sexualized narrative of color. In this regard, Smith frees both bodies from such moralizing objectification while still attacking the stereotype itself. This is in keeping with blues women's absolute refusal to be constrained or defined by cultural narratives, such as the sexualized notion of blackness produced by white society and internalized by the black community. Even in this matter of color, blues women claim agency over their bodies. In one signifyin' lyric, therefore, Smith contests the insidious interaction of two narratives that have infiltrated black lives: that of gender and that of skin privilege, as informed by sexualized white racism.[24]

In her song "Brown Skin Blues," Lillian Glinn also signifies on the color code. In this song, a woman is advising "high yeller" women of the best kind of man to have. She advises against the extremes, the yellow or black man. She favors the brownskin man. She says a "brownskin man's all right with me." In this song, Glinn, like Smith, makes a mockery of the color codes by simply calling out the various color conscious categories as she, a brownskin woman, gives advice to a "high yeller" woman. In giving this advice, there is the unspoken assumption that light-skinned women need this advice since men of all colors will be going after her because she is so light skinned.[25]

Sara Martin's "Mean Tight Mama" signifies on the color code by affirming the connection between the dark body that does not conform to the white model of respectability and sexual prowess. Martin proclaims that her hair is nappy, and that she does not conform to standards of "respectable" dress. Yet, she says, "the cow that 's black and ugly has often got the sweetest milk."[26] Instead of hearing this as a validation of the moral implications of color, in the blues tradition on signifyin', this should be heard as a mocking repetition.

Alice Moore's signifyin' lament "Blue Black and Evil Blues" clearly struck a chord with black people, since she found a need to record four versions of it. In this song she also signifies on the association of blackness with evil. She says that she wishes she had made herself, presumably a different color, so that she could make sure that her man did not stray. Of course, the implication is that she would have made herself "high yeller," thus assuring that her man would have absolutely no reason to stray. But she resigns herself to being black, which means she resigns herself to being evil, which ultimately spells trouble for the woman that was with her man. Embedded in this song of being "blue, black and evil" is a caveat about living in the white informed civility narrative of color. The evil black woman essentially projected back onto the man the evil he had projected onto her and which white society had projected upon him. This song shows the way in which white racist discourse infiltrates the black psyche and wreaks destructive havoc on black relationships. In this regard, Moore's song points to the reality of a self-fulfilling prophecy—tell people enough times that they are of a certain way, and they themselves will begin to believe it and act it (we will return to this later). "Blue, Black and Evil Blues" clearly sounds a warning about the color complex—this complex creates disharmony; it is evil manifest in the psyche and on the bodies of black women and men.

While, as mentioned above, colorism found its way into the black church as a part of its narrative of civility, resulting in light-skinned and darker-skinned blacks worshipping separately, it also penetrated the black church in an even more incisive and unsettling way—through its Protestant puritan evangelical faith narrative. Color symbolism within Christianity is a complex matter that deserves the kind of examination that goes far beyond the scope of this book. Nevertheless, what is obvious is that Christian symbolism has provided a sacred canopy for white racism and the demonizing of black bodies. Within Christianity, whiteness has long been associated with that which is innocent, spiritual, and angelic, while blackness has been associated with that which is corrupt, carnal, and demonic. Historically, the more European Christians came into contact with darker races of people who were not Christian, especially Africans, the more the culturally biased white/black Christian symbolism took root. This symbolism began to develop practical consequences as it shaped the way various peoples were viewed and as it impacted Christian iconography and art. Essentially, Christianity went through a process of whitenization as evinced in artistic representations. The central figures in Christianity were depicted with white features, including Jesus. In Christian art and iconography, Jesus came to be portrayed as a member of an Aryan race rather than the Palestinian Jew that he was. That Jesus was made to be white was consistent with the notion of dark skin signaling evil. With such an understanding, it would be virtually sacrilegious to portray the sinless Savior as anything but white. Protestant Puritanism not only inherited this white/black oppositional color symbolism, but expanded upon it.

As Protestant Puritans came to North America and encountered Indians who were not Christian, and resisted becoming Christian, these puritans became even more convinced that dark skin was a mark of an evil, incorrigible nature. The new Protestant arrivals to North America grew even more confident in this belief through their brutal interactions with African peoples. In the religious mind of the puritans, the color of one's skin indicated the state of one's soul. Sociologist Roger Bastide explains, "The association of the darker color of skin with a parallel blackness of the soul became for the Puritans arriving in the New World a fact of experience. The symbol of color was confirmed as an obvious truth."[27]

Protestant puritan evangelical traditions have had a special concern for the salvation of the soul. These traditions, as already said, view the body as an impediment to salvation. Thus, they maintain that one must do all that is necessary to protect the soul from bodily corruptions. This has typically meant leading a chaste life. For those with dark bodies the corruptions of the body are even more sinister. A chaste life is not enough to insure their salvation. They must do something about their black bodies. Given the association of blackness with evil, the black body becomes virtually an evil cauldron in which the soul is trapped. In this regard, it is not a matter of controlling the passions of the body, it is a matter of the body itself. A perfectly chaste black body is still a black body. No matter how chaste, a black body still endangers the purity of one's soul. The problem is the stain of blackness. It is that which must be overcome so that it does not taint the soul. The question is one of how to overcome it. A popular evangelical hymn provides the answer as it carries forth Christianity's dubious color symbolism. This hymn voices the plea to be washed in the blood of Jesus so that one's soul can be "made as white as snow." A white soul becomes the saving grace of a black body. Even if your body cannot become free of blackness, at least your soul can. Conversion equals a spiritual whiteness. This song is testimony to a racialized spirituality. It is the sanctified legacy of white cultural arrogance and supremacist notions that have associated blackness with the devil and black bodies with heathen bodies. And, unfortunately, this song found its way into the black church.

For black people this song, "made as white as snow," has dire implications, especially as it continues to be sung in contexts that are not yet free from white racism. Simply put, this song is not innocent. It carries with it a history of cultural bias. Therefore, its imagery is problematic. It affirms whiteness as a blessing from god and blackness as a curse from the devil. On white lips these words become a statement of sanctified white supremacy. On black lips they become a sanctified self-loathing. Moreover, within the context of the black church, this song serves to reinforce the color code, making this code holy as it renders blackness a badge of sin and whiteness a sign of righteousness. It carries forth the logic of the early puritans, the darker/black body is an inherently defiled body. In asking to be "made white as snow," masked by a plea for salvation is a black plea to be white. In the black church, this hymn virtually provides sacred cover for the minstrelsy of whiteness that defines the narrative of civility. Recognizing the intense self-loathing and white envy implied in this song, prominent nineteenth century AME Bishop and bold nationalist voice during the Reconstruction era, Henry McNeal Turner, interrupted the playing of it while attending a church conference. Upon hearing the hymn announced, Turner reportedly jumped to his feet and ordered the organist not to play, as he shouted, "That's the trouble with you colored folks now... You just want to be white. Quit singing that song and quit trying to be white. The time has come when we must be proud that we are black and proud of our race."[28]

Turner was not exaggerating the implications of blacks singing such a song, and the color-biased evangelical narrative from which it emerged. Such a narrative inevitably leads to a Jobian soul-searching moment where one questions why indeed one was ever born to be black, given the suffering that one must undergo in life and the uncertainty of salvation after death.[29] Such a moment is found in the autobiographical satire of Harriet E. Wilson, *Our Nig*, in which the young black female protagonist wonders why she was ever created if she had to be made black and suffer as she was made to suffer. She then goes on to wonder, "*is* there a heaven for blacks."[30] Novelist James Baldwin recognized a similar sanctified self-loathing in his father. His father's holiness, Baldwin believed, was an attempt to wash away the stain of his blackness. Baldwin said of his father, "He was defeated long before he died because at the bottom of his heart, he really believed what white people said about him. This is one of the reasons he became so holy."[31] This problem of sanctified whiteness was not lost on blues singers. Bessie Smith signified on this in her aforementioned song, "Moan, You Moaners." As she signifies on the "backbitin" hypocrisies of the sisters and brothers of the church, she goes on to signify on various other aspects of the church, most notably the faith that is imparted through the fire-and-brimstone preaching. In calling this out, she mocks the preacher who calls on sinners to get their "souls washed white."

In his letter to his 14-year-old nephew, the same letter in which he commented on his father's self-loathing, Baldwin cautions his nephew that he "can only be destroyed by believing that you really are what the white world calls a nigger."[32] In this instance, and throughout the letter, Baldwin speaks to power's most imposing weapon, its ability to get those it subjugates to believe in their own inferiority. Power does this through discourse. One of the greatest tools of power is the discourse it produces or commandeers to sustain itself, discourses, for instance, that make white supremacy appear divinely determined. Ironically, the narrative of civility as earlier mentioned serves as a discourse of power, and so too does the evangelical narrative, particularly in regard to purity of souls. The evangelical narrative testifies to a divinely established color code. It projects a god that is partial to color, it essentially establishes the whiteness of god—a black god is inherently impossible, given the evil nature of blackness. This discussion concerning the color of god will be taken up in a later chapter. For now, it is important to look at the implications of this color-biased faith narrative for the black church. Indeed, these implications are far-reaching, as they actually go beyond the matter of color itself.

Before looking specifically at the implications for the black church, it is important to recognize the unfortunate fact that colorism continues to be a vexing part of black life. Dark-skinned and light-skinned biases remain a source of division within the black community. This will probably remain the case as long as white society continues to discriminate between black persons on the basis of color, which it does.[33] The songs of blues women are as timely today as they were at the turn of the century. They continue to sound a signifyin' lament as they confront black people with the ways in which they have rejected their very embodied selves by taking over white racist narratives. As for the black church, as long as colorism exists in the black community, it will be reflected in the church. Nevertheless, while color codes, no matter how subtle, are certainly a part of black church life, the notion of blackness as a marker of sin and black bodies as intrinsically sinful bodies is no longer a prevailing narrative. Yet, it must be said that black congregations can still be heard singing lustily on Sunday mornings that they want to be "made white as snow." Remnants of a sanctified self-loathing clearly still linger in the black psyche. However, this self-loathing is not the only pernicious consequence of the color-biased evangelical faith narrative. The most far-reaching consequence of this narrative is that it introduced a paradigm of faith that asserts the creation of sinful bodies, that is, bodies that are by their very nature antagonistic to god.

The evangelical faith narrative, with its remonstrations about the corrupt nature of black bodies, opened the door of possibility for corrupt creations.[34] Hence, this narrative provided the framework for giving divine justification to the alienation and rejection of bodies that offend certain predominating cultural sensibilities. Such rejection is an inevitable extension of a narrative against the body. For, as shown earlier, when certain people become defined by their very bodies, they become the rejected class. They are blues bodies. When those characteristics that make them body people are innate characteristics, they then have no way of becoming a "saved people" except to somehow step outside of their own bodied selves. Invariably, as we have seen, bodied people are subjugated people. One of the tools of power is to make sure that the people it oppresses are defined by their bodies in the most offensive way—that is, as sexualized bodies. It is in this way that an evangelical faith narrative provides the foundation for human biases to be projected into the divine realm, for this narrative derides both the body and sexuality. To repeat, the body is that which must be overcome if one is to enjoy soul salvation, and sexuality is viewed as the primary sign of the body's sinful nature. Thus, people who are depicted as innately sexualized bodies are called to virtually overcome themselves if they want to be "saved."

Evangelical narratives essentially allow for the sanctification of cultural biases and social ostracizing, making both appear consistent with divine realities. In short, social constructions of race become cosmic constructions. Thus, the white rejection of black bodies seems the righteous thing to do, given the sinful nature of these bodies. The evangelical narrative becomes self-authenticating for those who seek to take comfort in their prejudices. Essentially, the evangelical faith narrative with its juxtaposition of pure white souls with evil black bodies allowed for the possibility that there are certain creations that are by nature sinful, like the black body. Ironically, the black church has exploited this possibility of sinful creations.

The black church has used the evangelical faith narrative as a self-authenticating narrative as did early white Protestants. In rejecting the innate sinfulness of black bodies, the black church has not rejected the notion of sinful creations. It has in various instances simply replaced the black body with other bodies, and the matter of skin color with other intrinsic givens. The issue of colorism has essentially transformed itself within the black church community. From time to time it has both literal and symbolic significance. For, to reiterate, vestiges of a self-hating color-consciousness exist in the black community, along with color-based class stratifications, hence the continued literal manifestation of color-coded narratives. More pervasive and blatant, however, are the symbolic realizations of this narrative. This is seen in the "righteous" proclamations that certain bodies are sinful and need to be converted from their state of sin: we will look at this in relation to specific bodies in the next section. Important to grasp for now is the fact that in taking over the evangelical narrative of corrupt black bodies, the black church has constructed symbolical black bodies. Again, bodies they consider corrupt by nature and thus in need of being saved from their very selves. These bodies are to be washed in the blood of Jesus so as to essentially become some version of whiteness, that is, a body more befitting certain mainstream norms. These norms are, of course, invariably sexist and heterosexist. Thus, women and non-hetero-defined persons have taken the brunt of this narrative. They have been called upon to overcome their very being through the redeeming blood of Jesus. The penalty of not being so "washed," and thus converted to salvific whiteness, is to suffer in death as they are made to suffer in life. They will be as marginalized or rejected in "heaven" just as they are in the black church. The ways of the earth get projected into eternity. As it is on earth, so it will be in heaven.

The theological inconsistencies and implications of this evangelical paradigm will be taken up later, particularly as it runs counter to radical black faith understandings. Essential for the current discussion is recognizing the insidious way in which the color-coded faith paradigm continues to play itself out in the black church. This is an excluding paradigm. It is one that offers sacred cover for oppressive and alienating ideologies. It sanctions the rejection and condemnation of bodies rendered black. Ironically, therefore, the black church has taken over a paradigm of faith that has demonized black bodies, and it has employed it well. One of the clearest manifestations of this paradigm is seen in the way various black churches have responded to particular sexual identities—an issue upon which blues women also readily signified.

Prove It on Me Blues

Went out last night with a crowd of friends
They must've been women,' cause I don't like no men.[35]

Ruby Walker recalled a time when Ma Rainey and Bessie Smith were together gossiping and laughing about old times. One of those old times involved an incident in Chicago that proved to be embarrassing for Ma Rainey:

> [Rainey] and a group of young women had been drinking, and they made so much noise that a neighbor summoned the police. The impromptu party was getting intimate, and as bad luck would have it, the law showed up just as everyone began to let their hair down. Pandemonium broke loose as girls madly scrambled for their clothes and ran out the back door, leaving Ma, clutching someone else's dress, to exit last. Ma did not get away, however, for she had a nasty fall down a staircase and practically into the arms of the law. Accused of running an indecent party, she was thrown in jail, where she stayed until Bessie bailed her out the following morning.[36]

Both Ma Rainey and Bessie Smith were intimately involved with women as well as men. Ruby says that Bessie became particularly enamored by Lillian Simpson, a former schoolmate of Ruby's who she introduced to Bessie. It did not take much convincing from Ruby for Bessie to make Lillian a part of the chorus line. Shortly thereafter, Bessie let Ruby know that she "like [d] that gal" and began a sexual relationship with her.[37] While Ma and Bessie were apparently sexually attracted to both men and women, Alberta Hunter's preference was presumably more female-oriented. Though she was very careful not to reveal much about her intimate life, it is fairly certain that she maintained at least two long-term female relationships, one with Lottie Taylor and another with Carrie Mae Ward. As mentioned earlier, her marriage to Willard Townsend may have been an attempt to divert attention away from her sexuality. The details and peculiarities of these three and other blues women's intimate relationships are not important. What is significant is the fact that they rebuffed the prescribed parameters of sexual identity just as they transgressed the expectations of gender roles. These women contested not only the hetero-normative standard for expressing one's sexuality, but they also challenged the either/or paradigms of sexual identity and expression. Blues women, through their lives and songs, complicated the issue of sexual identity. No song does this more forthrightly than Ma Rainey's "Prove It on Me Blues."

Ma Rainey authored this particular song. In terms of its actual structure, "Prove It on Me Blues" is not considered an actual blues. Nevertheless, Rainey's delivery is certainly consistent with her blues style. Moreover, as this song is a part of her blues repertoire, it is hard to hear it as anything other than a blues signifyin' lament, especially with its kazoo and washerboard accompaniment reminiscent of Rainey's country blues' roots. In this song, Rainey sings about a woman who has a fight with her female lover. The lover leaves as a result. This causes the abandoned woman to reveal her possessive nature as she suggests that she does not know where the woman "took it," it referring to sexual prowess, but she will follow this woman wherever she might go. This story has a strange ring of familiarity, as it is the same old story—a lover leaving another. The difference is, of course, that the two people involved are both women. True, therefore, to signifyin' tradition, Rainey repeats, in this instance, a lover's tale, but with a difference. It is a tale not of male/female love, but of female/female love. This difference is the point. It serves to normalize same-gender intimacy. It shows that same-gender relationships are vulnerable to the same volatile dynamics as different-gender relationships. The song goes on to establish the difficult predicament of same-gender loving in a hetero-normative society.

The abandoned lover acknowledges the whispers regarding her sexuality. She speaks boldly of going out with women and not liking men. She also speaks of defying gendered roles of dress, as she admits to wearing shirts and ties. These proclamations suggest a woman who is brazen and self-confident in her sexual identity, and will do what she wants in this regard. But then there is the refrain, "prove it on me." This refrain points to one who is very aware of the possible repercussions of same-gender attractions, so, as bold as she may be, she is not going to do anything to provide evidence of her not liking men. It is in this way that "Prove It on Me Blues" signifies on cultural and social standards that force persons who do not comply with hetero-restrictive codes of sexuality to live bifurcated lives. On the one hand, they are not ashamed of who they are, yet, on the other hand, they must hide who they are as if they are ashamed. It is worth noting that missing from this song is any condemnation of the female-defined intimate relationship. The signifyin' condemnation is directed to the society that has virtually criminalized same-gender love. This interpretation is reinforced by the advertisement announcing the release of this song. It shows a woman dressed in a man's hat and a skirt, with a shirt and tie, who is obviously flirting with two other women, while a police officer looks on in the background.[38] This interpretation is also consistent with Hazel Carby's analysis, as she explains,

> "Prove It On Me Blues" vacillates between the subversive hidden activity of women loving women and a public declaration of lesbianism. The words express a contempt for a society that rejected lesbianism...But at the same time the song is a reclamation of lesbianism as long as the woman publicly names her sexual preference for herself.[39]

In another song, "Sissy Blues," Ma Rainey gives voice to male-gendered intimacy. In this song, Rainey sings of a woman who has lost her male lover to another man, who is called "Miss Kate." The woman wakes up one morning only to find her lover in Miss Kate's arms. Miss Kate is labeled a "sissy." The man eventually chooses Miss Kate, whose sexual prowess apparently far outweighs that of his female lover. This is made clear as Rainey sings, "my man's sissies got good jelly roll."[40] This particular blues signifies on sexual and gender norms in several ways. By labeling the other man in the relationship as a sissy and by calling him Miss Kate, this song brings into focus the interaction between homophobic and sexist narratives. Essentially, the discourse that surrounds same-gender loving men is *heterosexist*, because it is a combination of homophobic and sexist ideologies. Same-gender loving men are equated as being like the inferior gender, women; they are therefore femininized, as "Miss Kate" was in the song. At the same time that this heterosexist stereotype is repeated, it is also challenged. For, there is no indication that the male lover is effeminate. He is not called a "sissy." The male lover as seen through the woman's eyes is masculine, given her lack of recognition that he also enjoyed male bodies. The hidden message is a warning about these facile stereotypes and gender constructions. Specifically, social constructions of masculine identity are contested. In addition, this song also calls into question the either/or notion of sexual identity. Clearly the male lover is attracted to both the female and male bodies. His sexuality defies the easy hetero/homo categories. This song testifies, therefore, to the fluid nature of sexual identity, a fluidity that blues women showed in their own intimate relationships.

Overall, as blues women sing about same-gendered love, they continue to exhibit their freedom from restrictive narratives of civility and evangelical narratives of faith. As mentioned earlier, they refused to be restrained by white stereotypes that hypersexualized black bodies, and by hyperreactive black narratives that virtually denied black sexuality. If nothing else, blues women broke the silence regarding matters of black sexuality. As they did so, they undermined sexual and gender binaries. They confounded definitions of masculinity and femininity that were linked to one's intimate sexual expression. They suggested that the way in which one expresses his or her sexuality is not an indicator of masculine or feminine identity. In blues, masculinity does not assume heterosexuality. At the same time, femininity does not assume hetero-intimacy and does not require chaste living. Women's blues essentially projected sexual identity as a human characteristic that transgresses rigid boundaries. And perhaps most significantly, blues such as "Prove It on Me Blues" and "Sissy Blues" portray same-gendered intimacy without any hint of moral rebuke. They simply name the issue and tell the story. That songs such as the aforementioned ones serve as signifyin' laments is clear. Indeed, the message to the black community and especially the black church remains striking given the attitudes toward sexuality that have continued to prevail within the black church community.

Within the black church community the LGBTQ body has become the new black body. In various black churches LGBTQ people's salvation requires a double conversion—a saved soul and a converted sexuality. While this double conversion is not unique to black churches, it is more troubling when it is promoted by them. As seen above, it makes use of the evangelical narrative in the very same way it was used to condemn black bodies. The black church has taken over the "master's sanctified tools," and used them against itself, namely, against its LGBTQ brothers and sisters. In so doing, it has gone a step further than anti-black uses of this narrative. Instead of requiring a "straight" soul, various black churches literally require that LGBTQ persons become heterosexual, in a way in which the evangelical narrative did not require black bodies to become white. Of course, black churches who promote conversions of sexual identity argue that blackness is a created/biological given, while LGBTQ sexual identity is not. While engaging this debate is beyond the parameters of this discussion, it is important to recognize that such an argument is clearly hetero-biased. It blatantly ignores the stories and discounts the experiences of LGBTQ persons. These persons often state that their sexual identity is as innate to who they are as physical blackness is to black people. Becoming heterosexual would be as unnatural to them as it would be for black people to become physically white. With this said, the more common black church response to the LGBTQ body is the infamous declaration of "loving the sinner, but hating the sin." However, even this response is an indictment of the LGBTQ body. For the sin, same-gendered intimacy, is as natural an expression of LGBTQ's bodies, for those who chose to engage in intimate expressions of their sexuality, as differently gendered intimacy is for non-LGBTQ bodies. Once again, LGBTQ persons are being asked not only to live against their very selves, but also to view that which is natural to them as sinful. In effect, this logic of conversion as well as the sinner/sin distinction is the same as that which rendered blackness an affront to god. It is virtually a continuation of black minstrelsy of whiteness, in this instance cloaked in narratives of faith. For, to be "made white as snow" is in this instance to follow the norms of white morality, as they are rife with racist, heterosexist actualities. Heterosexuality is symbolically white, while any other sexual identity is symbolically black—the latter is sinful and the former is not. But again, black women's blues offer a contesting narrative. As blues women sing about sexuality, they refuse to validate any narrative, civil or religious, that categorically condemns or excludes human bodies. This is further seen in their signifyin' laments on the "saved" bodies.

Preachin' the Blues

Lord, one old sister by the name of Sister Green
Jumped up and done a shimmy you ain't never seen[41]

"When I sing [blues]," Alberta Hunter says, " 'I walk the floor, wring my hands and cry. Yes, I walk the floor, wring my hands and cry...' what I'm doing is letting my soul out."[42] Bluesman St. Louis Jimmy called blues a "soul feeling."[43] While many blues women and men were torn between their blues identity and their Christian faith, others were not. Both Hunter and Jimmy testified to the fact that blues spoke to their very souls. Such testimony is in keeping with blues as a music that does not reinforce separate sacred/secular realities. Rather, as mentioned in previous chapters, blues maintains a unified perspective on all dimensions of existence. Blues does not recognize the sacred and secular as different dimensions of living. The reality of life itself is a reflection of both. What we have seen thus far is that blues witnesses what might be considered "the sacralarity of reality," that is, the interpenetration of what are often considered distinct domains. They do this not just in respect to the universe but also in relationship to the human person. Within a blues framework, there is no divine/profane distinction within human beings. All persons are both body and soul, flesh and spiritual. To be human is to be at once both. As a music that speaks to the truth of human existence, it is no wonder that it stirs at once the bodies and souls of people. In this regard, blues undermines religious narratives that assume discreet sacred and profane dimensions of human beings, and which force people to choose between the two and thus to live divided realities. It does so not only as it elicits passionate responses from those who might consider themselves saved, but also through signifyin' lament. Bessie Smith's "Preachin' Blues" is one such lament.

Using lyrics ripe with sexual innuendo, Bessie Smith sings about Sister Green. To know black church culture is to know that the "sisters" of black churches are routinely considered the most holy, sanctified, saved ones. In many instances, they are held in high esteem as models of virtue and salvation. They are also known to cast a scornful and harsh eye on the "unsaved." For Bessie Smith to suggest that Sister Green is shimmying to the blues (a dance often done in the juke joints at that time) is to signify upon this self-righteous high-and-mighty black church culture that relishes in the distinctions between saved and unsaved persons. Smith does this specifically by mocking the point in many black church services when the choir's soul-stirring rendition of a particular hymn or spiritual leads a sister in the church to "get happy" and jump up and shout, that is, to engage in a holy dance. This dance supposedly demonstrates the sister's salvation and how touched she is with the Holy Spirit. The is the very emotional behavior abhorred in the civility-minded black churches, similar to what Bishop Payne was said to have witnessed, as mentioned earlier.

Playing upon this dramatic display of salvation, Smith portrays Sister Green as jumping up to the blues. In this instance, Smith employs a signifyin' tool of humor. For it is as if Sister Green herself has confused the devil's music with the church's music. Her shimmy is her shout. Resonating with the message of the blues, she cannot help but jump up and shout/shimmy. It is as if blues touches her in a place that perhaps the church does not. Through the blues she is put back in touch with the whole of who she is, body and soul.

While "Preachin' the Blues" certainly contains other signifyin' messages, one message is especially clear: Smith is signifyin' upon a church culture that draws a judgmental line between the saved body and the unsaved body. In singing about Sister Green, Smith suggests that no matter how holy Sister Green may be, she still has a blues body that calls out to be satisfied and re-created. Thus, try as the black church might to keep the blues out of its holy space, blues resides in the bodies of those in the pews, even in the holiest of people. Smith therefore reveals the black church's misguided view of the saved and the hypocrisy of its scorn for blues and blues-singing/blues-loving people. This particular blues serves to reinforce the flawed nature of an evangelical faith narrative that makes body/soul distinctions and then foists those distinctions upon human beings. Through a blues lament, Bessie Smith draws attention to the black church's ill-advised compliance with this narrative. Again, it sets the black church in an antagonistic relationship to black bodies and, as we will further show, to its own radical faith. This brings us, perhaps, to the ultimate signifyin' irony of "Preachin' the Blues."

That Smith sings about Sister Green shows her profound wisdom concerning the ways of the black church. The implication of such a song is that Smith, who is a blues-singing woman, undoubtedly knows the black church better than it knows itself—and, to be sure, she knows the Sister Greens of the church better than they know themselves, and the Bessie Smiths of the blues. This signifyin' knowledge suggests the wisdom gained from blues' standpoints. The blues standpoint in this instance is what sociologist Patricia Hill Collins has identified as an "outsider/within" perspective. The outsider/within perspective is that of the domestic worker in the white household, or the janitor in the white law firm. It is the perspective of one who is in a place of power but remains on the outside of that power. Such positioning, Collins says, allows for " distinct views of the contradictions between the dominant group's actions and ideologies."[44] This is certainly the perspective that blues women had of the black church. Even though they were members of the black church community, they were marginalized within that community, if not rejected by it. They were virtually outsiders on the inside. Theirs was a "faithful blues space," for they were at once "blues people of faith." This space allowed them so see the contradictions within the black church and in other people of faith. Simply put, they could see that the good church people were no different from themselves, even as they were no different from the good church people; they were all faithful blues people—people with bodies that needed to shimmy and souls that needed to shout. The blues allowed for both.

There are many other blues, particularly those of blues singing men, that serve as signifyin' laments on black church hypocrisy and self-righteousness, especially that of black preachers. For instance, "He Calls That Religion," sung by the Mississippi Sheiks, tells of a preacher who likes "jelly roll" and a deacon who likes to shake his thing.[45] Hambone Willie Newbern sings of a deacon who indulges in the pleasures of the body when the lights are down in "Nobody Knows What the Deacon Does." This song compares the deacon to the shimmying Sister Green.[46] In the main, as they identify particular behaviors of the black church leaders and congregants, these blues are likewise drawing attention to the false dichotomy between profane and sacred dimensions of living, and thus between the saved and unsaved people. What they once again reveal is the impossibility of people living such compartmental lives, because people are simply not compartmentalized beings. To demand that people deny the needs of their bodies to be saved is to place them in the same untenable space as blues people—having to make a Sophie's choice between two real aspects of their very beings, their bodies and their souls. To demand such a body-denying "saved" commitment inevitably results in hypocrisy, as the whole person cries out to be satisfied. The saved/unsaved dynamic is one more way in which the evangelical faith narrative forces people to live against their true selves.

In the concluding lyrics of "Preachin' the Blues," Smith sings that she is not trying to save a person's soul but rather to save a persons jelly roll. This is a song about making people whole again. It serves as the culminating criticism of the black church's allegiance to an evangelical faith narrative that places the body and soul in opposition. This narrative creates disharmony not only within the black church community but also within black individuals. It causes black church people to reject other black bodies, and it causes them to reject their own bodies. And as it does these things, it alienates the black church from its own faith tradition.

Black church historian Gayraud Wilmore described the black church as becoming deradicalized at the turn of the twentieth century. He said that it had begun to mimic the ways and beliefs of white churches. With the death of Bishop Henry McNeal Turner, Wilmore said that it lost one of its most prophetic voices, and thus a voice to hold it accountable to its radical black faith tradition.[47] Indeed, Bishop Turner was a witness to a radical black faith, but so too are the blues. With signifyin' laments on colorism, sexuality, and saved bodies, that which was perhaps implicit becomes explicit—the ways in which blues carries forth a radical black faith. It is the music of the black faith tradition. It carries forth a black faith that is at once African and Christian. In the concluding lyric of "Preachin' the Blues," Smith calls for people to sing the blues so that their souls will be saved. This is a call to the black church. The blues witnesses the very soul, as in the heart, of the black church. We will discuss this in Part III as we explore what it would mean for the black church to hear the blues talkin' to it.

Blues Talk and Me

"Tryin' to count these blues."[48]

I don't remember why I was home from school that day. But I will never forget what took place on that day. It was during the time of a rising black consciousness. African Americans were just declaring that they were "Black and Proud." I was in the fifth or sixth grade. It was a weekday afternoon and I was flipping through the three television channels that were available to see what was on. As I flipped through the channels, a black face appeared on the screen. As I often did anytime there was a black person, I stopped to see who it was. At that time, to see black people on television was still a very rare sight. The show was Phil Donahue. He was still broadcasting from my city, Dayton, Ohio. His guest that day was James Baldwin. I was instantly mesmerized by Baldwin. He was a very dark-complexioned man with definite black features. I found his blackness strikingly attractive. That day, Donahue asked him why African Americans, he probably said Negroes, wanted to be called black. I remember Donahue pointing out how blackness had evil and sinister connotations. He asked

Baldwin what message black people were trying to get across. I don't remember most of Baldwin's response. What I do remember was the confident way in which he answered the question. I remember that he did not stammer or stutter or back down. I remember that he said something about black people naming themselves. And I remember that something changed in me that day. I, for the first time, boldly proclaimed to myself that I was black and proud.

The color-complex was a part of my growing up. My grandmother, who was light-complexioned, often warned my siblings and me not to play in the sun, or else we would get dark. I often heard the adults whispering about someone being too dark to be a part of some event or organizations. I remember that all the boys we thought cute were the ones with "good hair" and light skin. I also remember that those boys were not attracted to me, because I was not a light-skinned, longhair girl. That day, James Baldwin connected me to my blackness. He changed my aesthetic. I no longer tried to get the "good hair" boys to like me. I suddenly discovered how cute the dark-skinned boys actually were. Baldwin, on that day, made a preadolescent black girl feel good about herself. From that day onward, I looked in the mirror and liked what was looking back at me in a way I never had liked before. I was glad that I was black. I was black and I was proud. I felt whole again. He also did something else that was very important to my blackness. He changed by aesthetic of beauty. The black body with its dark skin, broad nose, and thick hair became for me attractive in a way I had not noticed before. Baldwin was, and still is, for me a blues muse. He inspired me to claim the fullness of who I was in my black bodied self. He inspired me to see the richness of black bodies. Perhaps it is no accident that I would be led to the blues, as this was the music that consistently spoke to James Baldwin and inspired his own writing. And so it is in many respects that I have come full circle, the one who discovered her black self through Baldwin remains true to herself through the music Baldwin loved, the blues.

Blues is a music about being whole. It is a music that reminds me that it is all right to be who I am with all my complexities and imperfections. It reminds me to measure who I am in relation to my inside self, not in relation to the outside world. It is also a music that holds me accountable to the ways in which I participate in the sense of inadequacy of others. And so it is that I count the blues. I count the blues that signify on color. I count the blues that signify on sexuality. I count the blues that signify on self-righteousness. I count the blues that signify on the ways people are forced to live against themselves.

I count the blues because they remind me of the ways in which I still need to grow into my whole self. I count the blues because tapes still play in my psyche that consider white ways as the right ways. I count the blues because they keep before me the ways in which I participate, even unknowingly, in sustaining narratives that harm others. I count the blues because of the most important job I now have—raising an African American male. The blues reminds me of the insidious ways in which social and religious narratives can poison the psyche and the soul of who we are. So they keep me ever so vigilant in trying to raise my son so that he is whole and at home with himself, and that allows others to be whole and at home with themselves. I count the blues because they are about being whole. This is what makes blues a radical music—for those who can hear it talkin' to them, it puts people back on the road to claiming their whole selves, their truth. And so it is for the black church. Blues talk sets the black church on the crossroads of discovering its truth. It is to a crossroads theology that we will now turn.

III

Blues Crossroad

5

Down at the Crossroads

I went to the crossroad
fell down on my knees[1]

It was in the dark of night at the Mississippi crossroad of Route 61 and Highway 49. He was sitting alone with his guitar. When time struck midnight, a mysterious black man appeared. Robert handed him his guitar. The black man took it and tuned it. He offered the guitar back to Robert. Robert took it. With that exchange a pact was made. Robert received the gift of playing the guitar, the devil gained Robert's soul. This was a story that many believed. It was one that Robert no doubt encouraged. There was no other explanation for it. When Robert left Robinsville, Mississippi, sometime around 1936, he was just an average guitar player, trying to pick up anything he could from Charley Patton, Willie Brown, and Son House. He followed them around everywhere. When he returned several months later, his playing had "supernatural electricity."[2] He could now outplay Patton, Brown, and House. There was no doubt in the minds of many that the devil had given Robert his talent. It would not be the first time that a bluesman had entered into such an ominous pact.

When Tommy Johnson (perhaps a distant relative of Robert) left his home in Crystal Spring, Mississippi, as a teenager, he was still very much a novice musician. When he returned several years later, he was a polished and innovative blues guitarist, surpassing Charley Patton and Willie Brown, the same greats that Robert would follow and from whom Tommy had received tutelage. When his brother Ledell asked him how he got so good, he gave this explanation,

> If you want to learn to play anything you want to play and learn how to make songs yourself, you take your guitar and you go to where a road crosses that way, where a crossroad is. Get there, be sure to be there just a little 'fore twelve o'clock that night so you'll know you'll be there. You have your guitar and be playing a piece sitting there by yourself. You have to go by yourself and be sitting there playing a piece. A big black man will walk up there and take your guitar, and he'll tune it. And then he'll play a piece and hand it back to you. That's the way I learned how to play anything I want.[3]

This story that Tommy and Robert told had been around long before them. It circulated decades earlier on the slave plantations, which were now the farms on which they grew up. Anthropologist Newbell Niles Puckett reported an almost identical story in his 1925 collection, *Folk Beliefs of the Southern Negro.* He said a New Orleans conjurer told him,

> If you want to make a contract with the devil...go to a lonely fork in the roads at midnight. Sit down there and play your best piece, thinking of and wishing for the devil all the while...After a time you will feel something tugging at your instrument. Do not try to hold it. Let the devil take it and keep thumping along with your fingers as if you still had a guitar in your hands. Then the devil will hand you his instrument to play and will accompany you on yours...When all is quiet you may go home. You will be able to play any piece you desire in this world, but you have sold your eternal soul to the devil and are his in the world to come.[4]

That this story became a part of blues lore, especially through its association with Robert who would go on to sing many blues about his own tussles with the devil and die in a mysterious way, no doubt cemented in the minds of many that which they already believed—blues was the devil's music. After all, it was long understood that the guitar was the devil's instrument and that crossroads was the devil's hangout. But behind this story is another story, which makes blues not the devil's music at all, but music, perhaps, of the gods. That this story is a part of blues lore substantiates blues as a carrier of a radical black faith tradition.

The crossroad experience that was told by Robert, Tommy, and in the enslaved community has its roots in West African religious beliefs. The one who hung-out at the crossroads was called Eshu-Elegbara, by the Yoruba and Legba by the Fon. African Americans have referred to this crossroads guardian as Esu.[5] In West African belief systems, the crossroads is where two worlds meet, the world of the gods and the world of humans. Esu is the guardian of the crossroads. As guardian Esu is a divine communicator. Esu relays messages from one god to and another god, and between the gods and humans. But Esu does not always relay the messages in a straightforward manner. Rather, Esu takes liberties and plays tricks, forcing the recipients to figure it out and to read between the lines, in many respects crossing the boundaries between a truth and a lie to get the message across. One story tells of Shango, the god of thunder, asking Esu why it was necessary to speak in riddles. Esu replied, "I like to make people think."[6] Another story tells of Esu tricking two friends into a violent quarrel. This is indeed a story that was a part of my own cultural upbringing. As the story was told to me, there were two best friends who did everything together and had farms right next to each other. They bragged that nothing would ever tear them apart. One day Esu (who was simply identified to me as a man who liked to play tricks) walked down the boundary line of the friends' two farms making sure that each friend saw him. As he walked down, he wore a two-colored hat, one side was white and the other side was black. At the end of the day, when the friends talked about the mysterious man walking through their fields, they argued over the color of the hat. They argued so violently that neighbors had to break them apart.[7] Of course, Esu appeared on the scene to resolve the situation. When hearing this story in my youth, I heard it as a lesson on how easy it is for things to really come between a friendship, and that everything was not always so black and white. As my cultural education grew and as I learned more about Esu, it remained for me a story about the vulnerability of human relationships while also providing lessons on the limits of human knowledge. This story suggests the importance of taking various perspectives into account. If the friends had come together, rather than fight over who was right, they would have gotten the whole picture and realized Esu's trick. In the end, this story reveals Esu as an ultimate trickster, but one with a purpose. Esu exists along the boundaries, or crossroads of life, showing the necessity of entering into these crossroads. The crossroads are the spaces where disparate realities intersect, thus revealing their intrinsic connections. Essentially, as a trickster at the crossroads, Esu makes a farce of lines that divide one space from another space, one realm of being from another realm of being, revealing such division as a false construction of human and divine realities that prevents people from perceiving the whole truth.

Not only was Esu known for being a trickster, but also for having an insatiable sexual appetite. There are many tales of Esu manipulating a situation with sexual cunning and prowess. Esu's insatiable sexual drive became so well known that icons portray Esu with big lips (pointing to this god's role as a messenger) and an erect penis. The prominence of sexuality in Esu tales and iconography suggests the centrality of sexuality to divine and human realities. It is also interesting to note that there are statues that portray Esu with both male and female characteristics. Esu thus becomes the embodiment of both genders. Once again, mockery is made of lines of demarcation. In this regard, Esu undermines the social constructions of gender difference and points to the fluidity of sexual identity.

Overall, as guardian of the crossroads, Esu affirms the West African belief in the unity of all being. Even those things that appear to be in opposition to one another are actually different parts of a whole. Esu undermines binary constructions of reality, be they gender, sexual, or even spiritual binaries. Esu's trickery is an attempt to achieve harmony between what appears to be oppositional, so as to fend off ultimate chaos—which is nothing less than evil. Again, through Esu, opposites are exposed as being a part of a unified whole. The trick is in achieving harmony between that which has been presented as disharmonious. As a trickster, Esu acts as a disruptive force, interrupting human ways of knowing and relating that compartmentalize aspects of existence. Esu oftentimes creates the chaos to expose the false fabrications of oppositional ordering and to reveal the underlying harmony. As anthropologist Robert Pelton explains, occasionally for Esu "the resolution of order begins with a dissolution of false order."[8]

Essentially, Esu helps people to reclaim the paradoxes inherent in all existence. In so doing, one recognizes that, if navigated properly, these paradoxes are places of union and not discord, they are sources of strength, not weakness. It is in the crossroads that unity can be achieved, and thus where the meanings of one's life begin to emerge and where one's power can be claimed. It is fitting, therefore, that it would be a story about a crossroad pact through which the musical genius of Robert and Tommy is explained. The pact that these bluesmen made was not as it would first appear, with the devil, but perhaps with the spirit of Esu. This is a spirit of a god who called them to cross whatever boundaries they needed to cross, to claim the paradoxes of their own living in order to realize their power as blues people. Both men were able to claim their own blues realities with the help of the guardian at the crossroads. Theirs was not a Faustian pact, as blues legend would have it. They did not trade their soul for their gifts. Rather, they found the soul of who they were so that they could know the power of their gifts. And again, it is not inconsequential that such a crossroads story would become so much a part of blues culture.

Blues is virtually a musical embodiment of Esu. Blues' signifyin' nature, transgression of boundaries, and sexual themes reflect the spirit of this African guardian at the crossroads. As Esu tramples over boundaries in order to reveal the power of crossroad realities, so too does blues. To appreciate the blues body, to know the lives of blues women, and to hear the talk of blues signifyin' laments is to recognize that for blues everything comes together in the crossroads. Blues is a crossroads music. As such, it keeps alive the African foundation of black faith and hence testifies to the god that has brought black people a mighty long way. It is in this way that blues suggests a crossroads theology. Such a theology is vital to the black church if it is to remain true to its identity and thus relevant to black bodies. It is to a crossroads theology that we will now turn.

Crossroads Locations

"When we sing blues," Alberta Hunter said, "We're singin' out our hearts, we're singin out our feelings. Maybe we're hurt and just can't answer back, then we sing or maybe even hum the blues."[9] Lillie Mae Glover echoed Hunter's sentiments when she said, "You got to sing the blues with your soul. It looks like you hurt in the deep-down part of your heart. You really hurt when you sing the blues."[10] As Hunter's and Glover's testimony suggests, blues women sang from out of their own experiences of pain and hurt. Whether or not they wrote the lyrics they sang becomes an insignificant issue after hearing them sing the lyrics. For one thing is certain, their own experiences bring the lyrics to life and give the lyrics transforming power. Because of their intersecting realities of being black female blues performers, these women could sing blues with passion. Moreover, as their experiences brought the blues lyrics to life and gave the lyrics their power, singing blues empowered them and also other black women who heard them sing. When they sang about the "loves and troubles" of being black and female, they were able to recognize the contradictions in their living, denounce some perhaps, affirm others, and in doing so claim the strength and power that came from these intersecting realities. They recognized the power in their own embodied multiple identities. That which was often turned against them and viewed as a weakness, they reclaimed and saw as a strength. This very transformation is often revealed in the very songs they sang. So, for instance, if in the beginning the songs were telling of a woman scorned and defeated, by the end they were telling of that same woman empowered to take action, be it revenge or simply leaving. One sees this, for instance, in Lucille Bogan's song "Tired As I Can Be." In this song she sings of a woman who tolerated a man taking her money and leaving her with not even enough to pay her rent. In the end, the woman proclaims that she is tired of this treatment and is going to return South, "to my used to be." Chippie Hill sings of a similar empowering reclamation of self in "Trouble in Mind Blues." In the end of this blues, after talking about how low a woman's spirit has sunk under the weight of her troubles, the woman pronounces, "You can't keep a good woman down." The power of these songs is found in the women's ability to claim the power in who they are as both black and female. It is as if they no longer permitted who they were to be used against them, thus setting them against their very selves. They did not allow their female identity to be treated as a weakness, thus leaving them vulnerable to male disrespect. They lived out of the power of being black female bodies, thus claiming their voice and perhaps recognizing the possibility for a better relationship.

A crossroads theology recognizes the crossroads as a space of infinite possibility. Such a theology views the crossroads not as a liminal space, that is, as an in-between and undefined space of various realms of reality and identity. Rather, it sees the crossroads as a stable and definite space that reflects the fullness of divine and human existence. A crossroads theology thus considers boundary lines of different realms, such as the human and divine, or spheres of identity, such as blackness and femaleness, as lines of possibility. Where all these lines enter into one space is a crossroads location, be it a social or existential space. Personal, social, and spiritual strands of life come together in the crossroads. The boundary lines can be treated as lines of division or lines of connection, depending upon one's standpoint on the line. To settle on any one line, as if to hold onto the privilege of that line, surrenders the power found by entering into the space where the various lines come together. The place of connection, the intersect of identities, for instance, is a place of power. A crossroads theology therefore affirms the transforming energy that is found in these strands intersecting as a whole. At the same time, this theology challenges the destructive forces that prevent these intersections. It laments the energy that is wasted when these strands of difference are set apart and placed in opposition to one another. It is in the separation that chaos and confusion ensue and evil forces prevail. It is in the intersections that harmony is achieved and forces for good triumph. In a crossroads theology, therefore, preferential option is given to the crossroad locations of human and divine existence. To repeat, it is in these crossroads that both human and divine transformative power is revealed.

Crossroads Revelations

"The problem of the Twentieth Century," DuBois said, "is the color line."[11] As DuBois recognized it, the problem began with the fact that the color of blackness was scorned in society. To be a black body, as we have seen, was to be an unacceptable body, while a white body was the preferred body. Color was where the line of acceptability was drawn. It was the dividing line of race in society. Thus, DuBois named the color line as a problem that had to be confronted and resolved. He saw it as both a social problem and an existential crisis. In society it was the line of separation, separating white space (the American space) from black space (the African/Negro space). Inasmuch as it was a social problem, it created an existential crisis for black bodies. This was a crisis of "double-conscious," a crisis of "two warring souls." DuBois explains that such a crisis is where the black body "ever feels his twoness—an American, a Negro; two souls, two thoughts, two unreconciled strivings; two warring ideals in one dark body, whose dogged strength alone keeps it from being torn asunder... [One] simply wishes to make it possible for a [person] to be both a Negro and an American."[12] This warring twoness depicts a crisis of the black body being divided against itself. As the color line reflects multiple identities, it represents a crossroads location. This is a location of "strife" and "striving." As multiple identities enter onto one location, like the body, there is strife when they are placed in opposition to one another. The lines of identity, therefore, serve as dividing lines. Their points of intersection are not acknowledged. But there is also a certain striving as these multiple identities yearn to come together into a unified whole. The starting point for a crossroads theology is in the strife and strivings of the multiple identities that are inscribed on the blues body. This is at once a social and existential starting point.

For DuBois, writing in the twentieth century, it was the strife and striving of the line of color. For a crossroads theology in the twentieth-first century, it is the strife and strivings of numerous lines, such as color, gender, and sexuality. A crossroads theology takes seriously the pain and sufferings from the strife of these lines as they cause blues bodies to rebel against themselves. It also takes seriously the protests and hope as blues bodies strive to achieve a wholeness found in the intersecting crisscross of these lines. Therefore the task of a crossroads theology is to do as blues do: name, disrupt, and play in the crossroads so as to reveal the power of crossroads intersections.

Naming at the Crossroads

> "Lord layin' in the bed wit my face turned to the wall
> Tryin' to count these blues, so I could sing them all."[13]

Blues songs often begin by engaging in what Angela Davis associates with the African cultural ritual of nommo. Nommo is a process of naming, in this instance naming, "in myriad ways, the social and psychic afflictions and aspirations" of blues bodies.[14] As we have seen, the opening lyrics of blues often name a situation of bad love, social injustice, community, or personal disaster that is responded to throughout the song. Essentially, blues names the social and personal predicaments that beset blues bodies. Informed by a blues framework, a crossroads theology likewise begins with nommo, this ritual of naming. It therefore engages the places where blues bodies speak and name their own blues experiences. These places can be discursive or concrete, such as blues joints or juke joints. These are places where the truths of experiences are expressed. These places of truth-telling are the primary resources from which the questions and concerns of a crossroads theology are drawn.

The naming process for crossroads theology begins, therefore, in the act of listening to blues bodies name for themselves the ways in which their identities have been contested and segmented. It listens to the manner in which blues bodies have been deemed a social problem and accordingly marginalized and rejected within wider society, their communities, and their churches. A crossroads theology listens to the stories of existential crises as blues bodies have taken into themselves the social and religious narratives that invalidate their very identities and foster internal conflicts of self. The naming ritual in crossroads theology means taking note of blues bodies as they count their blues, that is, the ways in which they have become rejected bodies, rejected by others and rejected by themselves.

In this regard, crossroads theology becomes a safe naming space for blues bodies. Crossroads theology names the pain of a black gay man whose parents kicked him out of the house because he was gay. It names the spiritual crises of a black woman who was called to the ministry but was rejected by her church because she was lesbian. Crossroads theology names the hurt of a black man whose mother questioned his worthiness to be a godfather to his best friend's child because he was gay. Crossroads theology names as heterosexist evil the disharmony that afflicts the mind, body, and souls of LGBTQ bodies, because they are LGBTQ bodies. Crossroads theology is therefore a site where the stories of blues bodies are honored and received without judgment. It is a site where the stories of these bodies are heard, affirmed, and named again in the theology itself. It is a site where blues bodies are freed to tell their stories and to name their pain. In this regard, crossroads naming becomes a site of empowerment. A crossroads theology thus recognizes the power that comes in the very act of naming. The naming space is an empowering space.

Within African cultures that engage in the nommo ritual, naming is believed to have a kind of magical power.[15] Naming grants, to the one who names, some measure of control over that which is named. To name something is to call it out on one's own terms, much in the way blues women called out the violent abuse of their bodies. To name something is to bring it into the open where it can be confronted. Not to name destructive forces does not mean these forces do not exist or that they will go away. It only means that they are allowed to function without resistance, or talk back. Naming is the beginning of resistance, it is a way of claiming ones voice and talking back to oppressing power. Silence is an act of commission and participation in one's own destruction. For it is a refusal to confront that which has created confusion and chaos in one's own body, thus giving that force authority. It allows destructive forces to have almost free reign to wreak havoc over one's existence. Essentially, silence acts as consent to the forces that disrupt social and personal wholeness. It magnifies the imposing power that such forces have over one's embodied identity. The first step of claiming control of one's self and claiming one's power is naming the demons that turn bodies against themselves. This makes it even more important for crossroads theology to name. Perhaps, in telling the stories and naming the demons of oppression, a crossroads theology can empower other bodies to begin the naming process themselves.

The process of naming becomes important for another reason. It enables people to recognize their complicity in the strife of blues bodies. Every body is shaped by multiple identities, be they racial, gender, sexual, class, religious, or some other life-defining characteristic. Multiple identities suggest multiple lines of entry into the crossroad space. The issue then becomes how one locates oneself on any particular line. At any given time, a line of identity can serve as a dividing or intersecting line on the same black body. It depends on where a person stands in the crossroads space as they define themselves in relation to other bodies, or to other identities carried by their body. Thus, one can stand on a line of identity in such a way as to maintain a distance between other lines, or one can stand in the nexus of intersect where lines come together. For instance, a black person may contest color as a dividing line and thus affirm the intersect where various lines of color come together and witness the unity of humanity. In this regard, a black person denies the color line's divisive power. The black person fights against systems and narratives that sustain racist power and racialized ways of defining the world. Yet, at the same time, this very black person may stand on the line of heterosexual identity, denying the right of other lines of sexual identity to be in the crossroads, and thus refusing to step into the point of intersect. This denial results in supporting and maintaining heterosexist narratives and systems. One's particular standpoint clearly has social and existential consequences in terms of the way in which bodies are separated one from another and from themselves. The way one locates oneself on any particular line of identity is a matter of claiming privilege or affirming connection. Claiming privilege invariably results in the subjugation of another. Privilege is, as Patricia Hill Collins notes, always defined in relation to others.[16] It is about the authority to define and dominate a space, be it a political, social, cultural, or even discursive space of knowledge. The naming process essentially calls people into crossroads locations and calls them to acknowledge their standpoint on the lines of crossroads as a point of privilege or connection. It summons people to recognize their relationship to multiple lines of identities—thus, to own their location in the crossroads as an oppressed or oppressor location. These are not fixed locations. The location can change depending on how one stands and, thus, how one sees oneself in relation to particular lines of identity. The point of the matter is that a body that is oppressed is a body that can also oppress, at different times or at the same time. It is in this way that the naming becomes a process of recognition, calling people to recognize their relationship to various blues bodies and hence the ways in which they claim privilege.

As naming calls people to recognize where they stand in relation to others, it is the process through which a blues bond can be forged, for the nexus of crossroads locations is the reality of a blues bond. It is where various bodies come together even in their differences and recognize that at any given time, depending upon the circumstances, the one who is privileged can easily become the one who is oppressed. The crossroads location offers the possibility for people to recognize how lines of power actually intersect and, thus, also the relationships between the forms of oppression as they impose themselves upon various bodies. For instance, a crossroads location reveals the way in which racist and heterosexist agenda's rely on each other. Thus, as was pointed out in the previous chapter, to support heterosexist narratives is to support the very narratives that also demonize black bodies. It is an awareness of the intersections between various forms of oppression that informs a blues bond. To forge a blues bond is to understand that whatever happens to the least of a blues body is a measure of what can happen to any blues body. This is so because the least is where multiple systems, structures, and narratives of oppression intersect, revealing their power in the intersect, but also their relationship. Put plainly, the plight of the LGBTQ body signals the plight of other blues bodies, whether or not they are LGBTQ. Thus, it is from out of the recognition of the nexus of dominating power that a blues bond can be forged.

At the same time that a blues bond exposes the similarities between forms of oppression, it does not ignore differences. Neither does it ignore the particular, if not unique, ways in which bodies are oppressed. To be black is not the same as being LGBTQ. The experience of racism is not the same as heterosexist oppression. The similarities and intersections between bodies do not blot out the differences. Nevertheless, in order to disrupt the power that divides and separates bodies from one another and segments multiple identities, those who are different need to come together, because they are all victimized from a manifestation of dualistic othering and negation. As Audre Lorde suggests, a blues bond is about coming together in "our differences and making them our strength."[17]

In the end, the process of naming is about "keeping it real." It gives expression to the "raw facts" of blues bodies. It particularizes the social, psychic, and spiritual ways in which these bodies are hurt and made to suffer. Naming undermines any efforts to mystify oppression. Forms of oppression are specified. Thus, one cannot avoid the reality of heterosexist systems and narratives as they impact black LGBTQ bodies. It is not about theory, it is about real systems and structures of oppression. The demons are concrete realities that belittle and denigrate various identities. By naming, the pain and sufferings of those bodies are made real. At the same time, naming makes it difficult to avoid the ways in which we may participate in the pain and suffering of others. That which we often fail to see, naming makes us see, that is, the ways in which we comply with heterosexist values, narratives, and systems. It confronts us with the fact that being an oppressed body does not make us immune from also being an oppressor and thus acting in ways that support the marginalization and subordination of others. Moreover, naming further concretizes the hopes and dreams of blues bodies. It undercuts efforts to render the aspirations of blues bodies as utopian ideas about a coming kingdom. It reveals the urgency of transforming society and communities so that various bodies are not bullied, bashed, or psychically and physically wounded for who they are. It makes clear what a just and affirming society and community would look like. Naming essentially calls people to attend to immediate and particular situations of strife and strivings. It is in this way that crossroads theology encourages people to sing blues and loudly name the ways in which oppressing power has wreaked havoc on, and within, their bodies.

For crossroads theology, the ritual of naming is indispensable. It prevents this theology from becoming an abstract discourse about disembodied oppression. Naming fosters embodied discourse. It holds crossroads theology accountable to the hurts and hopes of particular bodies. The act of naming keeps crossroads theology real, that is, relevant to blues bodies. But crossroads theology must do more than just name to stay relevant. It is compelled to also disrupt.

In the crossroad music of blues, naming serves as a call to which the listening audience responds. And it is the same in a crossroads theology. Naming is a call to respond. For a crossroads theology, this response is disruptive.

Disruption at the Crossroads

> "Once upon a time I stood for all he did
> Those days are gone"[18]

In who they were and in the songs they sang, blues women contested the narratives that imposed themselves upon their black female bodies and thus kept them from living out their full identities. They made it known that the days of racist, masculinist, or heterosexist narratives having any say in their lives were gone. They contested the power that these narratives had over them. In this regard, blues served as disruptive discourse.

To be a crossroads theology is to be disruptive discourse. This means disrupting the various narratives that nurture splits within social, private, and spiritual spheres of life. It must disrupt oppositional binaries, such as sacred/secular and body/soul binaries. These are the binaries that create divided identities and foster disharmony between and within bodies. They are the binaries that spawn and sustain narratives of civility and evangelical narratives of faith. In order to disrupt these binaries, crossroads theology has to challenge the either/or perception of reality. A dualistic worldview has to be dislodged from the collective consciousness of blues people.

This is not an easy task. A dualistic view of the world has penetrated the minds and imagination of blues people as well as other human bodies influenced by Western constructions of reality. Dualistic ordering has become an almost instinctive way of engaging and seeing the world. The acceptable/unacceptable, good/bad, and either/or pattern of relating to various identities is an outgrowth of a dualistic consciousness. The first order of business for disrupting oppositional positioning of multiple identities is to disrupt a dualistic consciousness. Such a disruption begins not in the head with theories but with bodies in experience.

Because crossroads theology regards blues bodies as a source of knowledge, it recognizes that dualistic constructions of reality are not consistent with the way in which these bodies experience the world and who they are in the world. Blues women, for instance, were able to rebuff oppositional identity constructs and avoid becoming bifurcated bodies, because of the way they experienced themselves and the world. They were able, therefore, to expose the lie of the gender binary projected by the narrative of civility. This binary opposed the good domesticated woman to the evil nondomesticated woman. It was not possible, according to the narrative of civility, for a woman to be at once good and nondomesticated. Yet, blues women experienced themselves as both good and nondomesticated, and thus by trusting the truth of their experience they were able to challenge the gender binary. Likewise, they experienced themselves as both Christian women and blues women and as both same-gendered and differently gendered loving women, thus they were able to challenge narratives that placed these identities in opposition to one another. In general, it was their experiences of themselves that became the source of their truth about who they were, who they could be, and of the possibilities for the world. Essentially, blues women were able to maintain an independent consciousness that allowed them to trust their experiences. In turn, their independent consciousness was maintained through their ability to, in fact, trust their experiences.

Like blues women, crossroads theology privileges experience—particularly that of the blues bodies. To reiterate, these are bodies that experience multiple realities of oppression because of their multiple identities. Crossroads theology, therefore, encourages blues women and men to allow their own experiences to shape their consciousness of themselves and the world. Essentially, crossroads theology regards the experience of blues bodies as embodied knowledge. It privileges blues embodied knowledge. As it does so, it calls blues people to appreciate their own experiences as knowledge. Thus, if a particular knowledge claim does not ring true to one's own experience, then, in the least, that knowledge claim has to be challenged and perhaps rejected. If a body is Christian and LGTBQ, then they know that the claims suggesting the sinful nature of homoerotism are false. The point being made is that embodied blues experience is a fundamental source of knowledge, it generates truths about reality. As such, it is a criterion for determining the credibility of all other knowledge claims

To reiterate, in crossroads theology the knowledge that derives from the experience of blues bodies is the preferred knowledge. It provides the foundation from which this theology is developed. Crossroads theology affirms the validity of assessing the world from the vantage point of blues bodies. It trusts the knowledge of these bodies and it therefore urges blues people to trust their own embodied experiences. It is through claiming the knowledge value of their experiences that an individual consciousness can be born within blues people, and that such a consciousness can be sustained. To be sure, it is only when blues bodies are able to trust their embodied experiences as nonbifurcated beings that dualistic constructions can be disrupted.

In keeping it real, however, crossroads theology acknowledges the way in which blues people's relationship to their own experiences can become corrupted. DuBois described the life of blues bodies as a life behind the veil, making it nearly impossible for blues bodies to see themselves or experience themselves apart from the way in which others see them. As DuBois explains, the world will not yield the blues body "true self-consciousness, [it] only lets [the blues body] see himself[/herself] through the revelation of the other world."[19] Without an independent consciousness, it becomes hard to even recognize one's own experience, let alone trust it. As mentioned in the previous chapter, the true weapon of oppressing and dissembling power is when it gets those that it oppresses to see themselves the way in which dominant forces see them. Thus, having an independent consciousness becomes imperative. Audre Lorde says it best when she says that "the true focus of revolutionary change is never merely the oppressive situations which we seek to escape, but that piece of the oppressor which is planted deep within each of us."[20] It was that piece of the oppressor's narratives "planted deep within" that created the conflict for blues women such as Sippie Wallace, Ethel Waters, and Ma Rainey as they tried to navigate their Christian and blues identities. Thus, in order to dislodge dualistic oppositional constructs of identity and the world, it is necessary to dislodge an "oppressor's" consciousness from blues bodies. The blues body must be free of outside perceptions of themselves, so that they can claim and trust their own experiences. This freeing begins with *embodied memory*. Within crossroads theology, embodied memory is another preferred source of knowledge.

Embodied memory is the herstory and history of other blues bodies. It tells the stories of how blues women and men navigated and confronted their situations of oppression. It contains the cultural wisdom, the resources of strength, and the various means by which blues people were able to maintain their sense of self and claim their power in the face of conditions that would pervert their self-images and disrespect their bodies. These are the stories of blues women and others who not only persevered but also prevailed, despite the attacks upon their embodied identities and the many efforts to define and constrain them. Embodied memories are disruptive memories, as they testify to another way of being in the world that is not determined by a dominating power. They are stories of resistance to being defined by others. Consequently, embodied memories are typically subjugated knowledge, that is, knowledge that dominating power suppresses or at least marginalizes. For, again, it is knowledge that undermines a controlling power's view of the world. It is knowledge about resistance to a controlling and subjugating power. Embodied memories provide counter-narratives to social and religious narratives that attempt to impose construct identities on blues bodies. Thus, it is knowledge reflective of an independent consciousness. To reiterate, embodied memories are stories of blues people who claimed the truth and validity of their experience and thus found a way to preserve their stories so that they could be handed down.

Crossroads theology engages embodied memories. It lifts up the testimonies, narratives, biography, diaries, music, and any other discourse that tells the stories of blues bodies being witness to the fullness of who they were in the face of complex oppressive realities. In this way, crossroads theology becomes a traditioning space as it passes on these embodied memories so that they might become a source of empowerment to other blues bodies. Embodied memories are a resource for dislodging an oppressor's consciousness from within blues bodies.

There is another form of embodied memories. These memories are nondiscursive. They are the memories contained in blues bodies themselves. Within African cultural traditions the body has always been considered a central vehicle for communication. Gods have spoken through the movements and expressions of the body. Many African cultures consider bodies a significant source of knowledge, and so too does crossroads theology. Crossroads theology recognizes that bodies carry memories. Long after the memories of the mind fade away, memories of the body linger. The mind may not remember, for instance, the details of a particular event, but the body remembers how it felt. The memories of anxiety and hurt, or peace and satisfaction, are embodied memories, they are memories grafted upon bodies. Feelings, sensations, and instinctive responses in relation to certain situations and circumstances are the body remembering what it feels like to be torn apart or what it feels like to be whole. It is the body giving feedback at any given moment in time. Embodied memories certainly involve what Lorde identifies as "erotic power." This is, Lorde says, an "internal sense" and a "depth of feeling" that is "a source of power and information."[21] It is the body speaking.

Crossroads theology recognizes the body's ability to communicate what it feels, what it needs, what it experiences, and what it remembers. Blues women sing stories about women responding to the needs and calls of their bodies. They also sing stories of bodies that cry out to be fulfilled, like the story told of Sister Green in Bessie Smith's "Preachin' the Blues." Again, as bodies communicate their needs and desires, so too do they communicate their memories. Hence, the body itself with all of its sensations, feelings, and emotions is, as Lorde says of erotic power, a source of knowledge. The body carries its own history. While the different ways in which the body responds to various situations and contexts are beyond the scope of this discussion, what is relevant to this discussion is the recognition of the body as a source of knowledge, as a carrier of memory. Crossroads theology, therefore, emphasizes the importance of blues people being in touch with their bodies, listening to them, and trusting their feelings and responses. The body and the memories it carries are again fundamental to fostering an independent consciousness.

In the end, a crossroads theology makes clear that it is only when blues people are in touch with their own bodies and trust their own experiences that they will be able to disrupt the narratives that set them against themselves, against one another, and, most importantly, against their bodies. As a disruptive discourse, therefore, crossroads theology claims the power of embodied knowledge, which is the knowledge that comes from experience and memory. And it is embodied knowledge that has the power to disrupt dualistic social and religious narratives that sustain racist, sexist, and heterosexist oppression. For uncorrupted embodied knowledge does not sustain dualistic constructions for the simple fact that this is not the way bodies live. It is when these narratives are disrupted that a new way of being, a new world, can be imagined. Such imagining is found in play. A crossroads theology is a theology that engages in blues play.

Crossroads Play

> "Make him stay at home, wash and iron
> Tell all the neighbors he done lost his mind."[22]

Key to the signifyin' laments that blues women sang was their way of playing with stereotypes and meanings. This meant reversing various stereotypes, as in the gender reversal seen in Bessie Smith's "Safety Mama." In this song, the no-good man is made to play the role of the woman he betrayed. To further enunciate the playfulness, the betrayed woman then broadcasts to the neighbors that he lost his mind. Other blues plays with color stereotypes as they mock the "high yella" associations with purity and "deep killer brown" associations with evil. Blues women further play with meanings as especially seen in their many sexual double entendres. They play as well with religious meanings as seen in "Preachin' the Blues," which questioned the meaning of salvation, and "Moan You Moaners," which questioned the meaning of mercy. In the spirit of Esu, this blues play is with a purpose. It reveals the arbitrary nature of stereotypes and thus strips them of their power. Blues play also shows the instability of racialized, gendered, sexual roles, thus challenging their authority. Essentially, through blues play the socially constructed nature of meanings and roles are revealed. What blues women show is that by not taking these meanings and roles seriously, one can deprive them of the power and authority that they presume to have over blues bodies. At the same time, through play, blues women claim their authority to create new meanings, to reconfigure roles, and to reclaim identities. Blues play essentially lends itself to a vision of new possibilities for blues body, and thus the possibility of an alternative world.

Crossroads theology is a theology that plays. It reveals the constructed nature of meanings and roles, showing them as constructions of power. It projects new patterns of thinking, new ways of being, and new paradigms of relationship that move beyond binary/dualistic frameworks. These very crossroad projections emerge from the play of blues bodies themselves. Crossroads theology therefore regards blues play as revolutionary activity, for it upsets the meanings and authority of power. In play, a new world and a new way of being break into old patterns. In play, identities are reconstituted and relationships are reconfigured. The play of blues bodies becomes a glimpse of future possibilities. In this regard, the places where blues bodies play become proleptic sites, for these are sites where blues bodies *act as if* they are free, that is, free from all that would encumber their bodies and dissemble their identities. Crossroads theology engages, therefore, in the play of blues bodies.

One of the ways in which crossroads theology engages in blues play is in projecting new ways of thinking about sexuality. As pointed out above, blues women played with sexual meanings as well as with sexual identities. For blues women, sexual play became the primary window through which they challenged oppressive narratives. In so doing, blues women were, as remarked upon before, doing more than being lewd. By foregrounding sexuality, they were showing their astute awareness of the centrality of sexuality to being human. No doubt drawing upon their own experiences as sexual beings, they recognized its very importance to the way men and women interact with themselves and the world. As ethicist James Nelson has pointed out, while sexuality is not the whole of who humans are, it is basic to being human. It is about the embodied self. It involves the way in which women and men relate to their own bodies and to the bodies of others. Sexuality is what propels human beings into relationships with themselves, one another, and even with god. According to Nelson, sexuality is a "sign, a symbol, and a means of our call to communication and communion." In short, sexuality involves embodied self-understanding, a way of relating to others and of relating to god.[23] It is thus the cauldron out of which identity is formed. Given the primacy of sexuality to the ways in which humans see themselves and interact with others—human and divine—reinterpreting the meaning of sexuality is imperative for projecting a new way of being with others and with oneself in the world.

In this regard, a crossroads theology reinforces the meaning of sexuality found in blues play. It affirms its role in human lives. Sexuality is valued, not demonized. It is appreciated as the source for human connections and harmony as opposed to being scorned as the root of all disharmony and chaos. Indeed, crossroads theology makes clear that it is when one is alienated from one's sexuality that chaos ensues. The denial of sexuality paves the way for evil relationality. Thus, as narratives of civility and those of evangelical faith advocate the denial of sexuality, they nurture chaos in human relationships and thus foster personal, social, and even spiritual evil. A denial of sexuality invariably leads to humans being alienated from themselves, from others, and from god.

In valuing sexuality, crossroads theology also disrupts the dualistic approach to sexuality projected by the evangelical faith narrative. To reiterate, this narrative sees only two purposes for intimate sexual expression: procreative purposes, which is deemed good; or non-procreative purposes, which is deemed evil. Crossroads theology recognizes the loving purpose of sexuality. It values the role of sexual intimacy in nurturing loving relationships, that is, in fostering harmony between bodies, whether or not that intimacy is procreative. Moreover, a crossroads theology rejects procreation as a measure of right and good sexual expression. Within crossroads theology, re-creation becomes the measure by which sexuality is valued. As long as sexuality is expressed in such a way that bodies are re-created, whether or not it is procreative, then it is good. It is only when sexuality is expressed or manipulated in such a way to diminish, abuse, and harm other bodies that it becomes bad. When expressed in this way, the goodness of sexuality is perverted as it creates disharmony and hence fosters evil. Essentially, as blues women play with sexuality, so too does crossroads theology. This theology repositions sexuality as central to what it means to be human, and it reinterprets sexuality as a primary source of good. It is in this way that crossroads theology empowers people to sing blues, and to proudly claim who they are as sexual beings.

Meeting at the Crossroads

In the end, crossroads theology is a blues theology. It speaks the truth about the power in the crossroads. It exposes the ways in which racist, sexist, and heterosexist power has intersected on blues bodies. It reveals the ways in which this imposing power has attempted to define blues bodies and constrict their freedom. Crossroads theology also proclaims the oppositional power of blues bodies. It tells the story of how blues bodies have achieved self-definition and wholeness, despite it all. It laments the ways in which racist, sexist, and heterosexist narratives have infiltrated the black community and prevailed in the black church. It affirms the ways in which blues bodies maintain the integrity of the black community and keep the faith of the black church. And so, like blues, it is into the nexus of the crossroads that crossroads theology must go. For it is there that it meets naming, disrupting, and playing power. This is the wild, wicked, sensuous power of the blues body: This is the power that turns right side up that which was turned upside down. This is the power that brings back together again that which has been torn apart. It is the harmonious power of good that triumphs over the disharmonious power of evil that is in the crossroads. It is this power that reconciles blues bodies to themselves and to one another. Most importantly, it is this power that calls the black church back to a faith that values and stands up for blues bodies. For blues, it is the power of an African religious heritage. It is the power of an African trickter god, Esu. For crossroads theology is the power of a black Christian faith. It is the power of the god that is Jesus Christ.

Me and the Crossroads

> "I went down to the crossroads, fell down on my knees."[24]

To listen to blues is to be called out. Blues has called me out. It has called me out into the crossroads. It has called me to recognize where I stand in the crossroads. It calls me to the uncomfortable, hard location that I stand in the crossroads. This is not the location where racist, sexist, and heterosexist power impose themselves upon my body. This is an easy place for me to be because it is the location where I name those demons of power and claim my power to disrupt and play to deprive them of their power over me. It is the location where I boldly claim my voice. When I listen to blues, I am not called to this location. Blues calls me to the location where it is hard for me to stand, even though I sometimes stand there quite easily. It is the place where I conspire in the oppression of other bodies. It is the place where I hold my line of class privilege or different-gender-loving privilege. It is the place where I sometimes loose my voice that blues calls me to.

Blues is honest. It is honest about the lives of blues bodies. And it is music that keeps those who listen to it honest. Blues keeps me honest about who I am. It keeps me honest about my own paradoxes and contradictions. We all have our own paradoxes and contradictions, even if we don't all own up about them. Blues confronts me with mine. Blues lets me know that just as I am an oppressed body, I am sometimes an oppressing body. Blues keeps me honest about the ways in which my thoughts and actions may indeed support and make it difficult for others to be whole.

Growing up, I was always clear about where I stood in the crossroads; at least I thought I was clear. Because I was often taunted and ridiculed for not fitting in, for not being girlish enough, or not being white enough, I stood with other outsider bodies. I always made friends with the kids who were teased and bullied for who they were or for who they were not. I hung out with the poor black kids who were bused into my middle-class black elementary school in order to achieve class diversity. I made friends with the boys who were called "sissies" because they were not as rough and tough as the other boys. I ate lunch with the kids who got "spitballs' thrown at them and were told to "jump back" because their skin was too "black." It seemed easy then. I stood in the crossroads at the point of connection with the other blues bodies, the ones that were teased, scorned, and rejected. But really, it wasn't so easy. I still wanted to fit in. So, while I did not tell the jokes or throw the spitballs, I did stand silent when the jokes were told and the spitballs were thrown. I hung out with the rejected, but I did not stand up for them when I was not with them. I did not always claim my voice. I did not always protect their bodies. I was not a good steward over all of god's gift of diverse human identities.

Blues calls me to claim by blues voice. It calls me to name, disrupt, and play with those dimensions of power, discursive and systemic, that perpetuate the denigration and dehumanization of blues bodies. It calls me to do these things when it is not easy. Blues calls me to confront the ways in which I have taken into myself the social and religious narratives that compromise the value of all embodied identities. Every day I listen to blues. One day I may listen to Bessie singing how she wants to "convert my soul," or another day to Ma singing that the world has turned its back on her and she's got the "broken soul blues." I listen to one of the women singing blues every day, because as these women sing the stories of blues bodies, they call me back to my better self, they call me back to my faith, they call me to the crossroads.

When Tommy and Robert went to the crossroads, they met the one who gave them the power to be the best of who they were, the guardian of the crossroads. They met an African god. They met Esu. When I go to the crossroads I meet the one who gives me the power to be the best of who I can be. I meet a crossroads god. I meet the god of Jesus Christ. This is the god about whom a crossroads theology speaks. This is the god of black faith. This is the god to whom we will now turn.

6

A Crossroads God

The God at Crossroads

"Nobody knows my troubles but the good Lord and me"[1]
"Oh Lord, send me a man."[2]

One thing is for certain, it was not easy for blues singers to claim their identities as both blues singers and church people. As important as their churches were to them, they just could not part from blues. No one demonstrated this more than Sippie Wallace. She knew since she was a little girl that blues was considered the devil's music. She knew that as a blues singer she would be scorned, if not rejected, by her church. Her church meant a lot to her, but so did blues. Try as she might, she simply could not stop singing blues. Blues enabled her to get through life as much as her faith did. In talking with Wallace, Daphne Harrison was sure that "Wallace could not stop singing the blues and live."[3] There was something about blues that compelled Wallace and others to sing them, regardless of what the good church people thought about the music. Even if they could not quite articulate it, or fully understand it, there was something about blues that was like the spirituals to them, that made it, as Hunter says, "almost sacred."[4] Bluesman Henry Townsend was clear that something they told was the truth. "Even if the blues is of evil" he said, "if I sing the blues and tell the truth, what have I done?"[5]

There is a truth about blues. It is a truth about the strife and strivings of blues bodies. But it is also more than that. It is a truth about black faith. Even as blues people confessed to a sense of apprehension, if not guilt, about singing blues, the songs they sang testified to a god that was present in their blues lives. Their sung testimony was about a god who knew, like nobody else did, all of their troubles. This was the god to whom they could ask to send them a man. Such a god was present in the crossroad intersects of their living. What they perhaps did not fully appreciate was that they were singing a truth that the black church needed to hear. Blues told the truth about a crossroads god. And this god is the god of a radical black faith.

The god of black faith is a god who is present in human history. This is the god revealed in the Exodus story—a story central to the black faith tradition since its beginnings in the "invisible institution" during slavery. It is the god of Moses, the god who led the Israelites out of slavery into freedom. It is the god that the enslaved black bodies believed would likewise lead them into freedom. This god is also the god of Jesus Christ. This is the god known in black faith as "Lord of Lords and King of Kings" and "a rock in a weary land." It is the god who was revealed on the cross as one who knew the pains and sufferings of blues bodies. This god of Moses, this god of Jesus, is a god whose spirit is infused in blues. The blues songs are virtually sung testimony about this god. Through blues, one can understand the meaning of god's revelation for blues bodies and the significance of god for the black church. Through a blues framework, this god of Moses, Jesus, and black faith comes to light. For, again, this god is a crossroads god.

The very revelation of god itself is a crossroads reality. When we state that god reveals, it means that god has entered into human history. Divine revelation therefore reflects two spheres of existence coming together, the divine and the human. The very fact of the revelation signals the intrinsic connection between these two spheres. It shows that the difference between divine and human realms does not signal an insurmountable gulf between the two. The revelation contests any attempts to project divine and human existence as antagonistic forces.

It is no wonder that enslaved Africans were attracted to the Exodus god. Undoubtedly, god's liberating acts on behalf of the Israelites ignited their theological imaginations and affirmed their beliefs that god did not create them to be slaves, but to be free. Yet, there was probably something just as significant that attracted the Africans to the Exodus god. This god was compatible with their African worldview. To reiterate, this was a worldview that affirmed a "holistic tenacity." There was simply not a sacred/secular divide within African understandings of the universe. African traditions projected a unified cosmos. As such, African worldviews typically asserted an ongoing divine presence in human lives. The story of a god engaged in a people's history as that people moved toward freedom would not have been jarring to African understandings. Such a story was certainly consistent with a unified perspective on the world.

The revelation of god undercuts ways of ordering the world based on unyielding sacred/secular binaries. God's revelation discloses this to be a fallacious binary and corrupt way of interacting with the world. Divine revelation is nothing less than god speaking truth to divisive and subjugating power. It is a divine push back to narratives that create disharmony between different ways of being. God's revelation defies social and religious narratives that create either/or and good/bad categories of difference. The revelation of god affirms the power that is found in the crossroads nexus of multiple identities and ways of being. It is in this nexus that human and divine energies come together to disrupt dualistic oppositions, along with the social and existential interactions that are generated from such oppositions. The revelation of god in Jesus, who is the embodied reality of the divine/human intersect, reveals the power of the crossroads. Blues provides insight into the meaning and power of this crossroads god. Through blues we are able to recognize what it means for this god to be wild, wicked, and sensuous.

The Wild Revelation of Jesus

"You'd better change your way an' get real wild," sang Ida Cox. For blues women to be wild was for them to be nondomesticated bodies. As we have seen, these women refused to be tamed by codes of respectability that tried to claim their individuality and deny their autonomy. Through their lives and in their songs, blues women disrupted narratives that threatened to interfere with their sense of self and thus to turn them against their very embodied identities. It is in this way that they provide insight into to the very "wild" revelation that was Jesus Christ.

It is virtually an undisputed fact that the Jesus of the Gospel narratives was not domesticated. This is the story of one who certainly did not conform to the political, social, or cultural norms of his day. The Gospels tell of one who upsets and overturns certain ways of relating and ordering the world. The story of Jesus is in this regard a blues story. Like blues people, Jesus was put upon, ridiculed, denounced, and, of course, suffered the ultimate rejection of crucifixion—all of this because he refused to be domesticated. He did not conform. He disrupted prevailing power. It is in this way that he exhibited the wild quality of blues women. Who Jesus was as a disruptive force is made clear from the very beginning of his Gospel story.

The announcement of Jesus's birth foreshadows what will be the character of his ministry. The Lukan narrative says that an Angel of the Lord appears to a Virgin bride to be, Mary. This angel tells her that she is about to give birth to a son whom she will name Jesus. This announcement immediately challenges the order of things. It displaces her future husband, Joseph. His male rights to Mary's body have been summarily usurped. Through the angelic announcement that Mary is pregnant, the male prerogative over female bodies, which is at times a physically abusive prerogative, is seized. The angel has the last word, much the same way that blues women had the last word as they sung about male abuse of their bodies. Joseph speaks no word. He has no voice in the story. The rule of men, patriarchal rule, has been upset. The line of the patriarchal fathers has been disrupted. It is no longer about Abraham, Isaac, Jacob, and all of the other men, it is about a lowly virgin woman. While women were marginalized in the patriarchal narratives of the Hebrew Testament, a woman is central to the Jesus story. In fact, according to Luke, it is two women who are key to this story as Elizabeth gives birth to the one who will herald Jesus's coming, Jesus's cousin John.

In the story of Elizabeth, patriarchal power is also supplanted. Her husband, Zechariah, is literally rendered silent because of his disbelief concerning Elizabeth's pregnancy. Zechariah's disbelief reveals his resistance to give up his male prerogative over her body. It is not until he concedes his patriarchal privilege that his tongue becomes loose and he can speak again. This occurs after he agrees to name his newborn son John and not to follow the patriarchal custom by naming him after himself. In both these stories that portend Jesus's birth, the ones that were marginalized, that were "othered" by patriarchal imperatives, now come to the center, and those marginalized ones are all women. Even as the story is told within the Matthean Gospel, the centrality of women remains.

Matthew's narrative recounts that the Angel of god came not to Mary but to Joseph. However, the result is the same. The angel instructs Joseph not to follow through with his plans to divorce Mary even though she was carrying a child that clearly was not his. In this angelic visit, Joseph is essentially being told to get on board with a new order, a new way of being. He is called to give up his male privilege and to enter into the rejected and marginalized space with Mary. For the reality of the situation is that by not divorcing or dealing even more harshly with Mary (in this world, Mary could have been put to death), not only did Joseph disregard the code of his day but he also made himself vulnerable to ridicule, if not worse, from other men. That he married Mary regardless of her pregnant state and apparent betrayal of him was for Joseph to surrender his male prerogatives. In so doing, he effectively joined the ranks of women. He became like the man ridiculed for staying home to wash and iron clothes in Smith's song "Safety Mama."

When read through a blues lens, the signifyin' nature of these annunciation stories comes to light. In these stories a reversal of power takes place. Mockery is made of patriarchal rule and male entitlement to women's bodies. Divine power is proclaimed as coming through those who are weak, marginalized, and displaced, in this instance, women. The power of god is not associated with the strong. The strong, which are men, are revealed as powerless as they have no voice in the story. Mary's virginity, in this regard, is not a statement about the sinfulness of human sexuality, rather it is a renunciation of patriarchal rule. Since there is no male involvement in the conception of Jesus, it is clear that the way of patriarchal order is not the way of god. And so, to reiterate, it is not human sexuality that is being rejected in the fact of the Virgin birth. Sexuality is not projected as a threat to the presence of god, as suggested by evangelical narratives of faith. Rather, it is patriarchal ordering that is rejected and placed at odds with the rule of god. The narrative of Jesus's birth continues to signify on patriarchal ordering and to expand on the meaning of Jesus as a wild revelation of god.

As has been pointed out many times before, Jesus's manger birth indicates his bond with those on the outside of power. Black preachers often affirm this in a homiletic refrain, "He was born in a manger with the lowly and meek, not in Herod's palace with the high and mighty." As meaningful as this is, Jesus's manger birth reveals even more than the fact that he was not born in a house of power. For, not only was he not born in Herod's palace, he was not born in a house at all. Jesus's birth does not take place in a domesticated space. It takes place in a space symbolically outside of the rule of men. The birth took place in a barn, in a manger, amongst the animals. This, in effect, is a wild space, thus again establishing the nondomesticated revelation of Jesus. It is in this way that Jesus's birth foreshadows his ministry.

Before moving on to Jesus's ministry, it is worth recapping the revelatory importance of events surrounding his birth, especially as seen from within a blues framework. The birth narrative of Jesus asserts the power found in a blues bond. When Joseph is called out of his place of male privilege, he is called to enter into the crossroads nexus with Mary. Given the social and religious narratives of the time, this nexus is an oppressive location inasmuch as it is one defined by Mary's reality as an unwed pregnant woman. It is a reality where the female body is at the will of men. It is a subjugated and abused body. When Joseph steps into this space with Mary, as indicated by his refusing to follow the patriarchal custom that would have allowed him to abandon her and seek her punishment, he makes himself vulnerable to the social and religious penalties inflicted upon those outside of male power. He makes himself one of the weak. He renders himself as if a woman. At the same time, however, to step into this nexus is for him to step into the space where god is most fully present, as symbolized by Mary being pregnant with Jesus. When Joseph enters the female space, leaving behind his location of privilege, he enters into the intersect where divine and human power come together. To be with Mary, the weak, and lowly is to be with god. In this regard, a blues bond is a mark of a bond with god. Joseph forged a blues bond with Mary, and in so doing he forged a bond with god. God is in the intersect with blues people. Inasmuch as Jesus's birth narratives portend the revelation of Jesus as wild, they also establish a divine blues bond. God's entrance into the world is through the marginalized and lowly, it is through the blues body of a woman. The meaning of god's revelation is inextricably connected to this blues bond. This is reinforced throughout Jesus's ministry. There is no story that better illustrates the significance of the blues bond in illuminating the meaning of divine revelation than the story of the Samaritan woman at the well, as told in the Johannine Gospel.[6]

This story shows Jesus repudiating the sexist and ethnocentric social, cultural, and religious narratives of his day. Specifically, Jesus disputes the construction of Samaritan women as disreputable human beings. In the socialreligious context of Jesus's time, there was a long history of conflict between Jews and Samaritans. Jews came to consider Samaritans ritually impure people, with women considered as the most impure of them. Multiple lines of oppression intersected on the bodies of Samaritan women—ethnic, gender, and cultural lines. In this regard, Jewish men and Samaritan women represented the extremes of an oppositional binary. Jewish men were pure and Samaritan women were impure. It was violation enough, therefore, for Jesus to ask the woman for a drink of water, let alone to engage her in a long conversation. But he did both. The woman was rightly confused that Jesus would speak to her, and she was most shocked that he would dare to share a drinking vessel with her. The story says that Jesus and the woman engaged in a conversation mired in "double-speak," at least in regard to the matter of water. The women did not at first understand the nature of the water that Jesus was offering to her. His was the water of eternal life. In the end, however, the woman did come to understand that Jesus was different. He was not like other men. She gains this insight after he reveals his knowledge of her five husbands and the fact that she is living with another man. No doubt, what is striking to this woman is not simply the fact that he knew her situation, but that he stated it without judgment. Possessing this knowledge did not prevent him from interacting with her and granting her salvation—as signaled by the water. At this point of Jesus telling the woman about herself, she says that he must be a Prophet and places him in the line of the Messiah who is to come. Jesus responds to her pronouncement by telling her that he is the coming Messiah. "I know that the Messiah is coming," the woman says. Jesus responds, "I am he, the one who is speaking to you." Through this story the meaning of the Messiah as a wild divine presence becomes even clearer, as does the importance of a blues bond.

Jesus's presence in Samaria is the first point of revelatory significance. Jesus did not have to pass through Samaria on his journey from Judea to Galilee. By most accounts, this was a circuitous route. It was also considered a very dangerous route, given the enmity between Samaritans and Jews. However, that which was not a geographical necessity was perhaps a revelatory necessity. By going to Samaria, Jesus placed himself in the midst of those who were outcast and marginalized in the Jewish world. He ignored the prevailing caricature of them as unclean and dangerous people. He flagrantly dismissed the established protocols regarding Samaritans by going out of his way to be where they were. In so doing, he has stepped out of his ethnic and religious place of privilege into the intersection with the castigated and oppressed. At the same time, he does away with the binary that sets him in opposition to Samaritans. His circuitous journey suggests the importance of a divine blues bond. It is not by accident of birth or by necessity of travel that this blues bond is formed. It is by divine intention, thus suggesting that the context of divine revelation, that is a blues location, is itself revelatory. In this regard, that Jesus enters into these contexts of marginalized and outcast bodies reveals something about god and about these blues contexts. In short, the contexts of blues bodies are revealed as the best standpoint from which to understand and gain insight into the revelation of god. This is made even more obvious as the story of Jesus and the Samaritan woman moves forward. Jesus continues, as noted above, to forfeit even more of his privilege by engaging in a public discussion with a Samaritan woman. It is this discussion that results in his disclosure as the Messiah. Thus, as John presents this story, it becomes about more than Jesus's surrender of gendered socialcultural privilege. That John records this conversation as the context for the first time that Jesus reveals his identity as the Messiah is significant. Even more significant is the fact that this Messianic disclosure is set in motion by a discussion concerning the Samaritan woman's five husbands and current relationship, perhaps the point of most shame for this woman. Furthermore, it is in this moment when Jesus names the woman's "shame" that she claims her power and goes forward to become an evangelist. The woman who came to the well at noon, the hottest period of the day, presumably to avoid the stares and ridicule of people, leaves the well and goes into the midst of the people without shame. Again, this transformation takes place when Jesus names her afflictions and thus tells her story, without judgment. In this act, he provides an opportunity for the woman to claim her story, which is her power. In so doing, she becomes the first person in John's Gospel to spread the news about Jesus. It is telling as well that when she spreads the news about Jesus she tells also her story of five husbands. For she says that it was when Jesus revealed his knowledge of her five husbands that her eyes were opened to who he was. That which society had deemed a weakness, Jesus helped her to see as a strength. Her experience of being shamed and rejected by others gave her insight into god's revelation in Jesus. Again, it is through the strife of blues bodies that most insight is gained into the revelation of god. The blues perspective is the preferential perspective for the crossroads god of Jesus. This story once again underscores the signifyin' reversal of power associated with Jesus, as weakness is turned into strength. To reiterate, it was the point at which the woman was the weakest that the power of Jesus as Messiah was revealed to her and subsequently to others. Her weakness was therefore not cast as a sin, but as a gateway to god. Her weakness provided revelatory insight.

In short, the story of the Samaritan woman at the well serves to reinforce the notion that power is found in the intersecting realities of blues bodies. To be sure, the Samaritan woman is a blues body. Ethnicity, gender, and multiple husbands have intersected on her body to render her an impure, unclean, woman of ill-repute. Yet, because of who she is, she has great insights into Jesus. This woman is, for all intents and purposes, a first-century blues woman. Like the classic blues singers, she takes her personal story to tell as a story that calls others to respond and claim their own story, at least as it regards their experience with Jesus. "It is no longer because of your words that we believe," her audience said, "but we have heard for ourselves, and we know that this is indeed the Savior of the world." In spreading the news about Jesus, the Samaritan woman with many husbands was doing nothing less than singing blues. Her testimony was her blues song.

Finally, it must be said that in his interactions with the Samaritan woman, Jesus was living in what it meant to be an embodied reality of the divine/human intersect. For in this interaction with the Samaritan woman, he defied all dualistic opposition. He crossed boundary lines of ethnicity, religion, gender, and more. He revealed the falseness of those lines the moment he stepped into Samaritan territory. If indeed the geographical boundaries were to be lines of separation, Jesus showed how superficial they were and transformed them into lines of connection. Once again, it was in stepping off the line of privilege and entering into a blues location that the power of god was revealed. This story is yet another example of divine push back to dualistic constructions of the world. As such, it reasserts the blues image of divine revelation as wild.

There are, no doubt, many other revelatory insights that can be drawn from this story; like the blues songs, there are layers of meaning to it. There are also numerous other stories about Jesus that suggests the blues significance of his revelation. I was especially drawn to this story, however, because it is to me a story of a wild first-century blues singing woman revealing the Messiah as a wild revelation of god. It was blues women that drew me to this story and expanded my insights into it. It will be through the story of another first-century blues woman that the wicked side of god's revelation is seen.

The Wicked Revelation of Jesus

"Now, I am all , confused," Edith Wilson sang, " 'cause I got the wicked blues." One of the ways in which blues women were "wicked" is that they were not afraid to name and call out the evil that afflicted their bodies and that was present within the black community. They, therefore, named the realities of domestic violence, colorism, heterosexism, and other manifestations of evil perpetuated by black women and men. To have the "wicked blues" in this respect was to name those very things that created blues realities. To engage the story of Jesus through a blues lens is to recognize that Jesus too had the wicked blues.

Jesus boldly named the various manifestations of evil in his own time. He, for instance, called the Pharisees to account for their hypocrisy, much like the way blues women called black church people to account for their "back-bitin' " hypocrisy. He called the money changers out for their greed and desecrating the temple, much like the way blues women called out rich people for their mansion living. Jesus also called his disciples out for their claims to power, much like the way in which blues women called black people out for imitating the ways of white folks. The point of the matter is that Jesus was wicked in much the same manner that blues women were wicked. He, like them, named the wickedness that was in the world. It is through the "wicked ways" of Jesus that we are able to gain even more insight into god's response to the "wicked ways" of others as well as god's regard for blues bodies. It is through the story of another blues woman that such insight is gained; it is the story of the adulterous woman.[7]

As John tells the story, a group of scribes and Pharisees brings an adulterous woman to Jesus. As suggested in the discussion of Joseph and Mary, such an act of adultery was an affront to male privilege, punishable by death. In this case, it is to be death by stoning. The Scribes and Pharisees, men who were faithful to Jewish law, ask Jesus if they should stone the woman. Of course, their question is about more than whether the woman should be stoned. As men of the law, the Scribes and Pharisees are not really in doubt as to what they should do. Rather, they ask the question to test Jesus. They want to determine if he has respect for the Laws of Moses, as any faithful Jew should. They want to see if he will join the woman in disregarding their laws. Jesus turns the situation to his favor. Those who came to convict Jesus end up being convicted. Jesus responds to these men by saying, "He that is without sin among you, let him cast the first stone." The story continues with the scribes and Pharisees being "convicted by their own conscience" and departing from the scene, having done nothing to the woman and leaving her alone with Jesus. With the departure of the last man, Jesus turns to the woman and tells her that he does not condemn her, so "go and sin no more."

In his response to the condemning men, Jesus did as blues women did when they dared to sing about the ways of black folks. Like these women, he reveals that there is a wicked side to everybody. The person who is at once good can at the same time be evil. There is no one who is without sin. Just as blues women refused to give credence to civility and religious narratives that attempted to draw lines between respectable and disreputable black bodies, Jesus refused to give credence to any laws that might draw a rigid line between good and evil persons and, consequently, condemn a person to death for his or her sins. It was for this reason that Jesus remained silent when the Scribes and Pharisees asked him what he thought about the Law of Moses. In this instance, Jesus's silence should be read not as consent but as an effort to disclaim the way in which these men were using the law. Reflecting a first-century blues spirit of signifyin' lament, Jesus brings the Scribes and Pharisees to the point of owning their wicked side. In the end, Jesus was able to bring these men to a point of realizing what they had in common with the adulterous woman. They were all humans, each capable of sometimes doing wrong. The line that these men had constructed to separate them from the woman became a line of connection.

When the men departed humbled by their own sense of sin, Jesus tells the woman that just as the men in the end did not condemn her, neither does he. He then directs the woman to go and to sin no more. In this proclamation, Jesus frees the woman from seeing herself through the eyes of a patriarchal world and measuring herself by condemning narratives. He frees her to claim her identity as someone valued by god. He helps her to distinguish who she is as a person, free from her sin. Her sin does not become her identity. This story makes clear that even as a body can, from time to time, manifest a wicked side, that body is not, in and of itself, wicked. This story of Jesus and the adulterous woman essentially refutes narratives that imply that certain human bodies are by nature evil/sinful bodies. It undermines dualistic oppositional relationships that set saved/pure bodies against unsaved/impure bodies. Jesus reveals that responses to what is perceived as sin should not be a castigation or rejection of certain bodies, they should simply be a repudiation of the sin itself. At the same time, there should be recognition of what it means for all persons to be vulnerable to sin—that is, the "wicked" side of us all. Essentially, in naming the wicked realities of the world, Jesus makes a clear distinction between wicked constructions and wicked people. He shows how social and religious narratives can construct wicked bodies but cautions people not to live in them. The many stories of Jesus's confrontation with demons further elaborate on this revelation. Perhaps the one story most illustrative of this point is that of the Gerasene demoniac.[8]

This particular story again shows Jesus crossing lines that nurture opposition between peoples. The story opens with Jesus going into Gentile territory. By doing so Jesus transgresses the boundary line that separates Jews from Gentiles, the clean from the unclean, in this instance a lake. When he gets across the lake he is confronted by a man who has been sent to the tombs to live. This man has been completely cut off from human civilization because the people in the region have deemed him to be a madman. Given this man's uncontrollable behavior, he was considered more beast than human. But Jesus recognizes the man's humanity and the fact that demons have possessed him. Jesus orders the demons to come out of the man. With this, the demons leave the man. The man is made whole once again. He is restored to himself, to his family, and to his community. Made clear yet again is the false distinction between bad behaviors and good people. The goodness of the man's humanness remained intact despite the fact that he was possessed by demons. Jesus cast out the demons not the man. As a result, the man was able to go forward and spread the message of Jesus. Once more, it is through one who has been marginalized and rejected that god's revelation in Jesus is made known. This man was not the only person to be possessed in such a way. There were other occasions when Jesus reportedly cast out demons from all manner of people. When read through a blues lens, these stories reiterate the wicked side of all persons. They make clear there is no line to be drawn between wicked bodies and nonwicked bodies, between the righteous and the unrighteous. By implication, these stories continue to contest evangelical faith narratives that suggest certain bodies themselves are wicked bodies, that certain creations are wicked creations, while others are good. They show the vulnerability of all bodies to be possessed by evil, while also affirming the inherent goodness of all bodies. Essentially, these stories in which Jesus names the evil that has afflicted certain bodies, cast out that evil, and returns the afflicted ones to live whole lives repudiate the social and religious constructions of sinful bodies. In this regard, the revelation of Jesus disavows the way in which social narratives construct evil bodies, such as LGBTQ bodies, and then legitimates these constructions with a religious narrative, suggesting that social constructions of embodied evil are divine creations. Such a disavowal is consistent with the claim of faith often repeated in the black church that "God is good all of the time." Among other things, this claim means that all that comes from god, all that god creates, is good. Inconsistent, therefore, is any suggestion that any part of god's creation is in and of itself bad, that is, wicked. Put simply, there can be no bad creations, no bodies that are created are sinful bodies. So, in naming the wickedness of the world, even as it may be manifests by humans, Jesus affirms the goodness of all human bodies. This affirmation suggests further the salvific meaning of Jesus's revelation. This meaning is best revealed in Jesus's response to the sin of his disciple Peter.

The Gospels report that at the time of Jesus being led to his crucifixion, Peter denied knowing him. Yet, Jesus designated Peter to be "the rock" of his church.[9] As he was with others, Jesus was with Peter—he did not judge him by his sin. Subsequently, Jesus restores him to community and provides him with the opportunity for a new life. This is the meaning of salvation, a restoration to life with god. As if to make this clear, Jesus responds to Peter's threefold denial with a threefold commission to "Feed [his] sheep."[10] Peter's identity was not defined by his wicked deed. Jesus thus saved him from his sin by calling him to serve, that is, he freed Peter from living a life defined by sin. That Peter sinned did not make him any less worthy to serve god.

And so, once again, Jesus undermines religious narratives that demonize people because of their perceived sin. Read through a blues lens, Jesus's salvific response to Peter suggests Jesus's opposition to the kind of narratives that not only errantly label blues as the devil's music, but also label blues singers as the devil's own. Notwithstanding the fact that blues is not devils music, inasmuch as there were blues singers who believed that it was and that they were wicked for singing it, they needed to know that, if a sin, they were not condemned by it. Jesus's salvific response to wickedness in his own time contests the demonization of bodies in any time. It affirms that there is no body that is ever outside the care of god, there is no sin from which salvation cannot be offered.

Just as it all comes together at the crossroads in terms of blues realities, it all comes together in the crossroads of the crucifixion-resurrection event when it comes to the revelation of Jesus as both a wild and wicked body. In fact, understanding the cross-resurrection through a blues lens perhaps provides a unique appreciation for its significance in black faith.

Before exploring the blues meaning of the cross-resurrection event, it is important to point out the nature of this exploration. This discussion is not meant to be a thoroughgoing theological analysis of the meaning of the crucifixion and resurrection, especially on matters that involve atonement theories and related issues of redemptive suffering. I have provided a fuller discussion of this in other places.[11] The point of this discussion is to engage the cross-resurrection event with a "blues slant" and thus to show once again the way in which blues witnesses a radical black faith. To be sure, the events of the cross are central to black faith, for they affirm once and for all a divine blues bond.

When viewing the cross with a blues slant, the signifyin' meaning of the cross stands out. In many respects, the cross is a signifyin' symbol in much the same way that the jug is a signifyin' symbol in "Down Hearted Blues." As remarked upon earlier, the political and religious powers that Jesus protested and repudiated were the very ones that came together to crucify him with the support of the crowd, some of whom were no doubt once his followers. That Jesus was crucified reflects the extent to which he identified with blues bodies, it thus reveals the depth of god's blues bond. It is important to recall what I and others have pointed out in other places. In Jesus's first centuryRoman world, crucifixion was reserved for slaves, enemy soldiers, and those held in highest contempt and with lowest regard in society. To be crucified was for the most part an indication of how worthless and devalued by established power an individual was. It also indicated how much of a threat that person was believed to be to the order of things. There was a decided crucified class of people. These were essentially blues people, the castigated and demonized, as well as the ones who defied the status quo of power. It is in this respect that Jesus's crucifixion affirms his identification with the marginalized and outcasts. So complete is this identification that he becomes, in fact, a blues body. For on the cross he fully divests himself of all pretensions to power and anything that would compromise his blues bond. The reality of the cross affirms the profundity of god's blues bond. At the same time, the cross represents the height of human wickedness. It is at this point that its signifyin' significance becomes clear.

It is on the cross that the impotence of human evil, that is, divisive and destructive power—that which would destroy bodies—is revealed. This is revealed in several ways. First, Jesus takes on all of this evil, yet he is not destroyed by it. The first indication that evil has no power over Jesus is seen in his response to the jeering and taunts from the crowd throughout his crucifixion. As he is spat upon and ridiculed for not being able to save himself, Jesus does not respond in kind, neither does he try to prove himself by conforming to the demands of the people to come down from the cross. Most striking is the fact that he does not condemn the crucifying crowd. Instead, he asks for their forgiveness. It is in this respect that Jesus refuses to allow evil to destroy who he is and thus to become somebody that he is not. He does not succumb to narratives outside of himself, namely, narratives of power. Most importantly, he does not allow them to compromise his blues bond. At this point it is beginning to become clear that divisive and destructive human power at its height is impotent in relationship to the power found in the intersect of divine and human realities. This was the power of Jesus, and this was the power of the cross.

Like the jug in "Down Hearted Blues," the cross points to a power that is not defined by historical circumstances or social status. It represents a power to set things straight in the world, and thus to subvert and subdue evil. It, like the jug, witnesses to a force greater than human authority. As the jug serves as a vehicle for "corking evil" and making right that which was wrong, so too does the cross. Again, though Jesus was crucified to the cross, and hence subjected to the worst of evil human power, he was not conquered by it. The cross shows that evil at its mightiest simply cannot prevail against the power found in the intersect of divine and human goodness that is Jesus. Ironically, the power that attempts to destroy Jesus on the cross is itself destroyed by the cross.

There is a final irony in the fact of Jesus's crucifixion. That Jesus had to be crucified actually reveals his power. If he were not a threat to the dominating political and religious forces of the day, then they would have summarily dismissed him. That he was a threat, that he was powerful, meant that they had to crucify him. Thus, that which is to be a sign of Jesus's weakness—the crucifixion—actually reveals his power. In this sense, Jesus's words, "Forgive them Lord, for they know not what they are doing," takes on a new layer of meaning. They signify on the pretensions of power. On the cross, god has used the weak to confound the power of the strong. The resurrection makes this unequivocally clear.

The resurrection is god's definitive triumph over crucifying evil power. Power that denigrates human bodies and destroys life is revealed as actually illusory and certainly no match for god. The resurrection shows that evil has no stable existence. In the end, the one that was crucified was restored to life. Thus, a mockery was made of prevailing political and religious forces. It is in this way that the signifyin' jug points back to this cross-resurrection event, even as the cross and resurrection suggest the power that black cultural tradition saw in the jug. The crucifixion and resurrection of Jesus witness a force that restores harmony to the universe. It is a force that repudiates and virtually makes a joke of crucifying power. The meaning of the cross as a signifyin' symbol is obvious. For, on the cross, god plays with power. Just when power seemingly prevails, its defeat is at hand. The resurrection of Jesus is god's last laugh. The ultimate reversal of power has occurred. The life force of god has reversed the power of death. The realities of death are defeated. In defying death itself, god showed the very futility of life-negating, dehumanizing power, and thus the transitory character of evil constructs. In the final analysis, the cross-resurrection event reflects what blues testified to as a blues hope.

As mentioned in chapter 1, a blues hope is not naïve. Rather, it is a hope that takes seriously the body-destroying and death-dealing facts of black life. It does not belittle or romanticize the pains and sufferings of blues bodies. Yet, it does not give into the hardship. While blues often tell of despair, they rarely end in despair. Blues stories do not give in to hard times and ill-fortune. Blues are not testimonies of defeat. As blue as life gets, blues affirm life's possibilities. They refuse to believe that the forces that would destroy black bodies will have the last word. Blues often resolve in a blues hope. This is the hope that Ma Rainey testified to when she sang, "the sun is going to shine in my back door someday." This is the hope that is expressed through the cross-resurrection event. Blues hope is nothing less than a reflection of resurrection hope. The hope of blues people is therefore vindicated through the resurrection of Jesus. It shows that suffering does not have the last word. There is real life after suffering. The meaning of divine revelation as wicked now becomes clear.

Reflecting the spirit of a wicked blues body, Jesus entered into the midst of evil realities. He named it, called it out, took it on, and defeated it. He essentially revealed a god that can be found in the midst of the places where evil power is most manifest, that is, with blues bodies where various lines of oppressing power intersect. This god is one who takes on this evil and defeats it, not allowing it to destroy the lives of blues bodies. It is this god that blues women witnessed in their own lives and in their music, as they too were unafraid to take on the wicked realities of their lives, name it, resist it, and not be defeated by it. To claim the god of the crossroads as wicked is to recognize this god's presence and power in the most wicked realities of human living. It is also to recognize the ways in which god takes on narratives that construct wicked bodies and shows the fragility of condemning and castigating wicked power. Through the wicked revelation of god, the futility of the wicked ways of power is revealed.

There is yet another way in which god can be seen as wicked. It is in this way that the god of Jesus shares something in common with another crossroads god, Esu. Esu, as we have seen, was a trickster. Esu often created chaos to bring about a desired end or to teach a particular lesson. Because of these trickster ways, some have suggested that Esu sometimes committed evil deeds. And perhaps Esu did. Maybe Esu did have a decidedly evil side. To be sure, the god of Jesus did not have an evil side, but this god did have a wicked side. In this way, god was like Esu, a trickster. The tricks of Esu were the play of god. This god, like Esu, did use chaos to bring about a new order. This was the god of Moses who sent plagues upon the Egyptians in order to free the Israelites. This was the god of Jesus who overturned the tables in the temple in order to reclaim it as a place of god. And, of course, this was the god of the crucifixion-resurrection who used crucifying realities to reveal the power of good. As Esu played with the way things were, played with peoples perceptions of the world and even themselves, so did the god of Jesus. The god of Jesus liked to play. Esu and god meet at the crossroads in play.

To reiterate, god's play was a blues play. Like blues, the play of god subverts oppression, affirms the humanity and sanctity of all human bodies, and divests evil of its power. It is a play that turns evil on its head. It is in this regard that the play of god reaffirms the "wickedness" of god. God's play is the "wicked play" of blues. Through blues, another aspect of the crossroad revelation of god is made clear, and that is its sensuous meaning.

The Sensuous Revelation of Jesus

"I'm a one-hour mama," Ida Cox sang, "so no one minute papa... for me."[12] Blues women were not afraid of their bodies. With plenty of double-talk and sexual innuendo, blues women gave voice to their body's needs. They were in touch with their bodies. The way they sang blues reflected the passion and desires of their bodies. Blues women embraced and valued their bodies. They saw their bodies as a virtue and not a vice. This is what it meant for them to be sensuous women. It is in this way that they witnessed the sensuous revelation of Jesus.

The incarnation itself reveals the god of Jesus as a sensuous god. In taking a human body, god literally makes clear the sacred relevance of the human body. Once again, the body is seen as a vehicle for divine possibilities, not as an inexorable cause of sin. The body is not a human burden, it is a divine blessing. Moreover, the body is affirmed as essential for all interactions, human and divine. That the incarnational reality of god in Jesus does not stop with the mere fact of this embodied reality makes this clear. The story of Jesus does not end with his birth in a manger. It continues through the embodied ministry of Jesus. Through Jesus, god's active presence in human history is made real. That god cares and is concerned for human bodies become more than simply an abstract confession of faith, it becomes fact. Jesus takes the bodies of others seriously and responds to the needs of those bodies. He feeds them when they are hungry and he heals them when they are sick. Moreover, he is not repulsed by any human body. Thus, he touches and heals the lepers. At the same time, Jesus is in touch with the needs of his own body, as perhaps demonstrated by his permitting a woman to anoint his feet and then wipe them with her hair.[13] The theological significance of this act notwithstanding, it, in the least, shows Jesus allowing another to touch and care for his body in an intimate fashion. The point of the matter is that Jesus shows that the incarnation of god is an affirmation of the human body. It affirms the body as "a temple" for god's presence. Jesus's ministry makes clear once and for all that the body has sacred regard. It is the vehicle through which the care and compassion of god can be made known. It is through the body that divine and human interaction is possible. And it is through the body that the hope of god is made real. As Jesus touches lepers, reaches out to women, and heals other rejected bodies, he provides an opportunity for these rejected bodies to realize their own divine worth and recognize, while opening to them, new life possibilities. This can be seen in the resurrection of Jesus.

The Gospel reports of Jesus's resurrection leave little doubt that it was a bodily resurrection. Jesus was not resurrected in some disembodied, ethereal form. As if to enunciate this point, the Gospel reports him as showing his crucifying scars to the disciples, as well as sharing a meal with them. The Gospel of John records Jesus inviting Thomas to touch the crucifying wounds on his hands. Made clear is that the body that was nailed to the cross and pierced in the side was the one that was resurrected. The resurrection, therefore, verifies what Jesus's ministry demonstrated, the sacredness of life in the body. In addition, it refutes any claims that salvation requires some kind of outer body experience. One does not have to deny the body, with all of its scars and brokenness, in order to be "saved." Once again, any notions of soul/body splits are undermined. Religious narratives that assert that a denial of the body, that is, chaste and abstemious living, is a requirement for salvation are invalidated. The bodily resurrection of Jesus shows that god does not regard the body as an impediment to salvation or a barrier to a divine relationship. The body is more than simply a means to navigate an earthly existence. The body is the source for a relationship with god. Moreover, the resurrection reveals that the hope of resurrection is not disembodied. It is about real bodies being freed from real pain and suffering. It cannot be said enough that salvation is not a disembodied reality. It is not an abstract notion of spiritual freedom. The resurrection reveals that salvation is inextricably linked to an actual change in conditions for oppressed bodies. Salvation means freedom; it means wholeness for bodies, not just for souls. In this respect, Jesus's healing and caring for broken and oppressed bodies foreshadows the meaning of the resurrection. The one who was resurrected resurrects. He restored broken and put-upon bodies to life in much the same way his own body would be restored. There are, of course, no greater testimonies to the resurrecting Jesus than his restoring the daughter of Lazarus and Jairus to life after death. The point of the matter is that the resurrection is about real bodies being restored to life again in the face of conditions that would portend their death. It is about those who have been made to feel ashamed of the embodied identities being able to reclaim their embodied selves. It is about LGBT Q people beaten down by social and religious narratives that sometimes literally seek to destroy their bodies being re-created to live fully as who they are. The resurrection is about nothing less than the defeat of all the forces of racist, sexist, and heterosexist power that dares to deny and destroy human bodies.

Inasmuch as blues re-create bodies, as explained in chapter 3, they witness the power and meaning of the resurrection. The re-creation power of blues is nothing less than the resurrection power of god. It is, again, the power to bring bodies that have been destroyed by the harsh facts of life back to life. It is about this resurrection power that blues singers testified to when they explained that they sang blues to live. Blues keep alive a resurrection faith.

A resurrection faith, then, is a faith in a sensuous god. Just as the revelation of god in Jesus is an embodied reality, so too is the resurrection hope of god. The resurrection reinforces what the incarnation reveals, that the body is important to god. The god revealed in Jesus values the human body. The body is the vessel through which god chooses to be present in human history. It is through regard for the body that god's freeing, caring, and loving reality is made real. The resurrection thus becomes the last word when it comes to god. To know the god revealed through the ministry and resurrection of Jesus is to know a sensuous god. The crossroads god is a sensuous god.

It is important to note that a sensuous god is compatible with an African religious heritage. This heritage has affirmed the sacredness of the body. It recognized the possibility of various gods entering into particular bodies as a means of communication. The fact of Jesus as an embodied revelation of god would not have been disconcerting to the enslaved Africans. One thing is for sure, it is because of the sensuousness of god that the enslaved could testify that god took care of their every need. Essentially, the black faith tradition, as it was shaped in slavery and informed by an African worldview, was able to recognize that god's embodiment was critical to any understanding of god's meaning in black lives. This tradition makes clear that it is only through their bodies that humans can reach out to god and that god can reach out to them. Black faith witnessed the sacredness of the human body. This is the faith that pulsates through the sung testimony of the enslaved found in the spirituals. As we know, the spirituals signified as did blues. They used hidden/coded language to pass on messages and to talk about freedom. It was through this hidden/coded language that they made a connection between heavenly salvation and earthly freedom. In this way, enslaved men and women testified in song to the fact that soul salvation meant nothing less than bodily freedom, the two were inextricably connected. So, while spirituals may not have been sexual discourse as was blues, they were sensual discourse, as they took the body seriously. The connection between the spirituals and blues becomes even more intricate as they both testify to the truth of an incarnate faith—the truth of the god of Jesus. It is a sensuous faith, and it is a sensuous god. And so, in the end, what is the meaning of a crossroads god? Who is the god at the crossroads of blues bodies?

The God at the Crossroads

> "I'm down with the blues, just as blue as I can be"[14]

A crossroads god is one that is wild, wicked, and sensuous. This god names, disrupts, and plays with the multiple realities of oppression that intersect upon blues bodies. This is what we have demonstrated above. But how then are we to identity this god? In what crossroads are we to find this god? What is the meaning of this god for black people? What is the significance of this god for the black church? The answer to these questions is captured by the affirmation that god is blue. A crossroads god, the god embodied in Jesus Christ, is blue. The god at the crossroads of divine and human realities is a blues god.

To call god blue is first to affirm the blues bond established through the birth, ministry, and crucifixion of Jesus. God enters history in the strife and strivings of bodies. These are bodies that are impacted by multiple intersecting realities of oppression, and, thus, bodies that find themselves on the underside even of outside communities. These are bodies that suffer from the social and religious constructions of "warring identities." These are bodies such as black LGBTQ bodies, for which narratives of civility make it virtually impossible to be both black and LGBTQ, while religious narratives proclaim it impossible to be both Christian and LGBTQ. A blues god enters into the fray of the strife and strivings of these bodies as they strive to live freely in the fullness of who they are. This god reconciles that which has been torn asunder by these oppressive narratives. To be as frank as this god is bold, a blues god makes clear that a LGBTQ body is as sacred as any other body and can be at once Christian and LGBTQ. The narratives that say otherwise are not simply fallacious but are against the god of Jesus Christ. For these are narratives that demonize the body even of an incarnate god.

This means that a blues god at once affirms and renounces. God affirms a people inasmuch as they foster wholeness and freedom. God renounces a people inasmuch as they impede wholeness and freedom. That which god chooses is freedom and wholeness. To be a chosen people, therefore, is to be a people of freedom. In this regard, chosenness is not a static category. It is not a designation of privileged status. Rather, it is a call to embody and embrace freedom. It is a challenge to make the choice to be where god is: in the intersections where people are striving to be free. A people who are chosen by god can betray what it means to be chosen. A people who were at one time working with god can find themselves at cross-purposes with god the moment they step out of the nexus where freedom and wholeness are being sought. As earlier stated, being an oppressed body does not mean that one cannot become an oppressing body and, thus, find oneself alienated from god. A blues god is indeed on the side of the oppressed, but only as long as those who are oppressed remain on the side of freedom and wholeness for all bodies.

There is no getting around it. A blues god values bodies. This means that god calls people to be in touch with their bodies and to recognize the rich possibilities of embodied life. This god calls people to live in concert with their bodies and thus to respond to its needs, desires, and passions. In order for people to encounter themselves, one another, and god, they must do so through their bodies, not apart from their bodies. Women and men cannot avoid the gendered, sexual nature of the bodies. It is for this reason that a blues god rebuffs any efforts to overcome the body, and at the same time challenges people to embrace their body and those of others in an affirming manner. It cannot be said enough that a blues god stands in opposition to constructions that render the body bad, as well as any actions that denigrate or humiliate the body. There is no form of body-denying or body-denigrating behavior or discourse that a blues god tolerates. A blues god therefore calls people to account for the ways in which they participate in the oppression of other bodies. This god does not make choices between saved and unsaved bodies. Instead, a blues god recognizes the sacredness of all bodies and, thus, contests all ways in which that sacredness is violated. A blues god, therefore, does not renounce or reject bodies. Rather, this god renounces that which disrespects bodies and, thus, rejects body-harming activity. This means that a blues god does not oppose that which re-creates bodies, only that which does not. As suggested earlier, as long as expressions of sexuality re-create bodies and foster harmonious relationships, then they are not an affront to god. At the same time, a blues god contests any narratives that do not allow for the re-creation of bodies. This god therefore contests narratives of civility and evangelical faith narratives because they deprive people from fully living in the possibilities of bodily interactions and re-creation and turn people against their own embodied identities. Any narrative, regardless of how religious it pretends to be, that diminishes the sacred importance of the body, or demonizes any embodied identity, is not true to the god that was incarnate in Jesus Christ. These narratives are simply wrong. They perpetuate perhaps the most insidious form of evil; they turn people against their own bodies. They turn "people inside out."[15] They create existential disharmony for those who have been told that their embodied ways of being are sinful ways of being. For the god of Jesus is indeed a blues god.

As the Gospel narratives tell the story of Jesus, they tell a blues story. The Gospel narratives are blues discourse. They tell a story of one who was wild and wicked, but most of all of one who was sensual. Just as sensuality is a defining characteristic of blues, it is a distinctive characteristic of the Gospels. For the Gospel story is all about the sensual revelation of god, Jesus Christ. It is Jesus Christ that is distinctive to Christianity. And so it is that the Christian faith, therefore, is a sensual faith, just as blues is a sensual music.

It is interesting that when many of the blues singers left blues, reacting to narratives that suggested it as the devil's music, they went on to sing Gospel music. It is no accident that Gospel emerged from blues. Because of its blues rhythms, this music was also banned for a time in the black church. Yet, this music is, with its blues form, perhaps the best reflection of what the Gospel narratives really are.

When Sippie Wallace returned to the church and made up her mind that she was going to give up blues, she admitted that it was still hard for her not to play blues, even when she did not intend to. She said it was easy for her blues to become Gospel, and her Gospel to become blues. Harrison said that this disturbed her "because [Wallace] thought that there must be some distinction between what she composed as blues and what she composed as a church song"[16] What Wallace did not understand was that in her confusion was the truth. The confusion, the going back and forth between "churchy songs," as she said, and blues reflected the nexus of a crossroads god.[17] It confirmed the false separation between sacred and divine realities, but most of all it witnessed the fact that the Gospels are blues. The story the Gospel tells is a blues story, and the story that blues tell is a Gospel story. They, each in their own way, tell the story of a wild, wicked, sensuous god.

Ma Rainey sang that as she was more and more down with blues she could hear the angels sing "Nearer My God to thee." Indeed it is the case, to sing and appreciate blues is to be brought nearer to god. Blues is faithful testimony to the god of Jesus Christ. And so while blues women may not have had much in common with the black church, they did have much in common with Jesus. They, in their own way, revealed the god that was born in a manger, was crucified, and was resurrected. Blues women kept this god alive. Blues keeps alive the god that has brought black people a mighty long way. Blues bears faithful witness to a radical black faith tradition. It reveals the god that crossed the middle passage and that the enslaved came to know in the "invisible institution" of slavery. For the black church to stay true to itself, it must be down with blues.

My Gospel Blues

"Jesus loves me yes, I know."

My mother taught my sisters, brother, and me the song, "Jesus loves me this I know, because the Bible tells me so." She would sing this song to us all the time. She wanted it to become a part of our consciousness. She wanted us to be able to sing it whenever we needed to. This was important to her because she knew the world we were growing up in would not always treat us in a loving way. She knew that, because our bodies were black, her children would be treated with disdain and with hate. She wanted us to know that no matter how others treated us, Jesus loved us—and that was all that mattered.

I will never forget the day that a friend and I were walking from our high school to the bus stop. I went to a mostly white high school. It was in the middle of a working-class white neighborhood. In order to get home from school I had to take public transportation—this was before busing and before school buses were provided for kids who chose to go to schools out of their district. I had to walk through the white neighborhood to catch the city bus. This was often a perilous walk. On this particular day, a couple of young neighborhood boys decided to throw rocks at my friend and me. There was no doubt in our minds that it was our black bodies that warranted the rocks. Just as we were picking up speed to get out of the range of fire, a woman stuck her head out the door to come to our rescue. She shouted at the boys, "Stop throwing rocks, leave them niggers alone." "Jesus loves me yes I know."

I remember another time when we were visiting my grandparents in Granville, Ohio. At the time, they were the only black people living in this small college village. One day while visiting, my younger sister came in from play. She was very upset by a question that a little girl at the school yard asked her. Upon seeing my sister, the girl asked, "Are you Mexican or something, why are you so dirty?" "Jesus loves me, yes I know."

I remember trying for a long time to figure out why it was that white people treated black people so badly. One day, it came to me, so I raced to tell my dad. I announced, "Daddy, I finally figured it out," as if he knew what it was I was trying to figure out. He asked, "What did you figure out?" I said, "I figured out why white people treat us so badly." He said, "Oh, why?" I said, "For no reason, they just do. There is nothing wrong with us." My dad smiled. I was happy. It was because I knew that Jesus loved me, that I was alright, and those white people were all wrong.

When I was little, I remember laying in bed on the night before Christmas, singing, "Away in a manger, no room for a crib, the little Lord Jesus lay down his sweet head." I used to cry when I sang this song because I never could understand why Jesus was treated so badly. I remember praying to Jesus, if I were living then I would have shared my bed with you. I loved Jesus because I knew how much Jesus loved me.

I simply cannot imagine growing up not knowing that Jesus loved me. I was born before the 1960s and grew up during the civil rights and black power movements. My sense of self was shaped during a time when having black a body was seen as a curse, not a blessing. I know that if it was not for the love of Jesus, I would have never been able to find a way to love my black self. "Jesus loves me, yes I know" was my blues song. Like Sippie, if I could not have sung that song, I could not have lived.

Just as it made me cry to think of Jesus being born in a manger, it makes me cry today to think of people who are relegated to manger realities because of their embodied identities. It makes me cry to think that there are people who actually have been led to believe that Jesus does not love them for who they are.

I remember the day after I delivered a lecture on this matter of sexuality. A young black gay man came up to me. With tears in his eyes he thanked me for helping him to feel good about himself, even if just for a night. For that night, I let him know that Jesus loved him. "Jesus loves you, this I know, because the Bible tells you so." This is my blues song. It is the song that I must sing if I am going to tell the good news of a blues god. This is the song that the black church must sing, to whosever comes, if indeed it is going to be true to its radical blues faith. It is to the black church that we will now turn.

7

Black and Blues Church

Oh blues, oh, blue, oh blues[1]

A Home for Blues Bodies

Say, I wished I had a heaven of my own
I'd give all those poor girls a long old happy home[2]

Bluesman John Sellers went to what he called a "Holy Roller church," where they played "the tambourines, the guitars, and the horns." Sellers particularly liked one of the songs often sung in his church. He recalled the lyrics saying "everybody ought to pray sometime," even gamblers, liars, and all kind of persons. Sellers liked this song, not because it called out sinners, but because the lyrics spoke truth. Sellers said, "The [black] Church should take in everybody."[3]

In describing the importance of the black church to the black community, DuBois called it both a "religious center" and a "social center." E. Franklin Frazier characterized it as a "nation within a nation."[4] Both descriptions point to the pervasive role the black church has played in black life. This church has not only been the central purveyor of values for black men and women, but it has also filled in the gaps left by white racist neglect. It has met black people's personal and social needs. The black church has, therefore, been at once a political, civic, economic, educational, and spiritual resource for the black community. The magnitude of its presence in black life is a part of what makes it distinctively black. Yet, as all-encompassing as the black church has been in addressing black well-being, there is one thing that it has not been—and that is all-embracing. The black church does not "take in everybody." While it has been a religious center, a social center, and a nation within a nation, it has not been a home. If the black church is to be true to its blackness and to its faith, then it must take seriously its role as a home for black bodies. To be a home is to be a "safe space," where black men and women are able to live and grow into the fullness of their created identities. It is to be a place where black bodies can come in from the storms of living and re-create so they can face the "troublin' blues" ahead.[5] Home is for a black body to have "a little heaven of [their] own" on earth.[6] Every black body that desires to do so should be able to find a home in the black church. But, far too often, this has not been the case. Over and over again, the black church has closed its doors to certain black bodies, in the sense that they have not been made to feel welcome in the church as they are. The way a black person's body labors or loves, the way a body is colored or gendered, has frequently determined how welcomed that body is in the black church. As we have seen, at any given time, various black bodies have been virtually put to the test. How easily a comb passed through their hair, how much their skin color matched that of a brown paper bag, and how animated they were in worship determined if a particular body was locked out of the church or let inside. More recently, when it came to the LGBTQ body, the black churches have made their position of "welcome" clear, as black clergy have actively campaigned against LGBTQ rights, such as marriage. One clergyman described LGBTQ sexuality as "wicked, deviant, immoral, self-destructive, anti-human," while others have suggested that "homoerotic sexual expressions go against what God intended."[7] Such comments do not make an LGBT body feel at home in the black church.

There is a problem in the black church. It is not simply a problem with particular black bodies, it is a problem with the body itself. There is a prevailing body denying/body-phobic culture in the black church. As long as this is the case, the black church will not be a reliable home for every black body, and both its blackness and faith will be compromised.

White Gaze/Blues Bodies

Listen to my story, and everything'll come out true.[8]

This body-denying/body-phobic culture in large measure points to the impact of a "white gaze" upon the black church community. As black people tried to gain acceptance within white society by changing the black image in the white mind, they adopted white cultural standards of "respectability." In the main, these standards reflected Western dualistic perspectives that did not respect the body. Within this perspective, the body and the soul were placed in an antagonistic relationship. The bad body was seen as an albatross to the good soul. The body had to be overcome. The way in which to do this was by living a chaste and pure life that did not cater to the needs or desires of the body. In general, white culture was itself a body-denying/body-phobic culture. White cultural disregard and fear for the body was most often played out on nonwhite bodies. As if to avoid becoming "body people," that is, a people controlled by passion and not reason, white people attacked nonwhite bodies. Of course, the body that came under the most attack was the one that contrasted most with whiteness, that being the black body. In the white collective consciousness the black body represented all that had to be overcome, it was a body fueled with passions and desire—it was a body out of control. As we have seen, in an effort to escape the caricature of being an out-of-control body people, the black community fostered a body denying/body phobic narrative of civility to match that of white culture. This narrative represents a Faustian pact with white society—in order to survive, black people deny the needs and vibrant richness of their own bodies. The black church adopted this narrative, essentially making the same pact. This is the most obvious way in which the body-denying/body-phobic culture in the black church reflects a white gaze. There is, however, a more subtle way.

The narrative of civility and the values it promotes is a reaction to whiteness. The measure of what black people do or avoid doing, the barometer of black values and ways, is that of white acceptability. In effect, to avoid the stereotype as body people, the narrative of civility urges black people to live against their bodies. In doing so, this narrative has fostered hyper-restrictive attitudes toward the body and sexuality.[9]

Whether or not black people are living according to a stereotype or living against it, they are still living in relationship to it, especially when it becomes the reason for the choices they make. The way in which white people view black people still controls the way in which black people view their bodies and themselves when it comes to the narrative of civility. Essentially, inasmuch as a white stereotype of blackness influences—wittingly or unwittingly—the black psyche, black people are still relating to themselves through the lens of a white gaze. This is the aforementioned life behind a veil of whiteness, as described by DuBois. This is a life where there is "no true self-consciousness."[10] The narrative of civility with its body-denying/body-phobic values is a veil of whiteness. It virtually serves to extend white control over black bodies. It suggests a certain black minstrelsy of whiteness. It is a tool of white discursive power. The price of the Faustian pact thus becomes more insidious because blackness itself is forfeited for acceptance in the white mainstream. The black church's body-denying/body-phobic culture reflects such a Faustian pact. An evangelical faith narrative makes this pact even more formidable.

Born from the same soil of white culture, yet overlaid with Protestant puritan values, this religious narrative casts into the cosmos white body-negating values. With an evangelical faith narrative, Protestant Puritan culture projects onto god the body-denying attitude of white culture. By adopting an evangelical faith narrative the black church has done the same. Within the black church, disdain for the body receives religious legitimacy. It is important to keep in mind throughout this discussion the basic fact that the evangelical narrative provides sacred justification for the narrative of civility. The narrative of civility thus becomes a sanctified narrative. This sacralizing of the narrative of civility lends itself to the most disturbing distortion of the black faith tradition, for, as mentioned before, it implies the whiteness of god. That the black church effectively promotes a white god is perhaps the ultimate irony. The reality of this white god is evident as black people sing of "get[ting] their souls washed white in order to be saved."[11] It is then no wonder that Bishop Henry McNeil Turner, who stressed the importance of black people being able to see god as black, railed against black people singing the evangelical hymn calling for being washed "as white as snow." He knew that a white soul equated to a white god, at least a god that disdained blackness. Either way, the song did not suggest a god that affirmed the goodness of the black body. That black church people sing this song without pause is a sign of how ingrained the sanctified narrative of civility is in the black church, which is nothing less than the looming presence of a sanctified white gaze. What does this mean for the black church if it is ever to become a home for black bodies? It means that the black church must find a way back to itself. It must find a way back to its own black faith tradition, one unsullied by whiteness. This way back has been paved by blues women.

The songs that blues women sang reflected their independence from narratives that attempted to constrain or control their bodies.

These were women who recognized that it really did not matter what they did or did not do because folks, black and white, were going to criticize them anyway. So, they simply decided not to react to others, but to act as themselves. They believed it was nobody's "bizness" but theirs how they acted.[12] Their way of life and sense of self flowed organically from within. Personal contradictions notwithstanding, in the main, blues women lived life in response to the needs of their own bodies, not in reaction to the prejudices of others about their bodies. They lived in a self-regarding, not other-regarding, manner. In so doing, while they were often rejected by the black church, they were actually reflecting the radical spirit of the black church.

As established earlier, when the black church emerged as an "invisible institution," in the "hush harbors" of slavery, it did so in response to the needs and cries of the black body. Black embodied experiences and black embodied memory were the crucial sources for understanding god. It was because they knew what god did for, and through, their bodies and how their bodies felt in the presence of god that the enslaved crafters of the black church were sure that the god about whom their white enslavers spoke was no god at all. They realized that the god of white Christianity reflected the limitations and biases of white people, not the care and love of the gods of their African heritage, or the god they experienced in slavery, and certainly not that of the god of Moses and Jesus. The church of the enslaved, inasmuch as it was invisible to white eyes, was free from a white gaze. The god of this institution was defined, therefore, by blackness, not whiteness. The god in the "hush harbor" faith of slavery was a god that valued black bodies, this was a black god. In fact, this hush harbor faith carried forth the very spirit of Jesus.

As demonstrated in the previous chapter, Jesus simply did things his own way. From his birth to resurrection, Jesus was not controlled by narratives and values outside of himself. He went about his business as the incarnate revelation of god, with a first-century blues spirit. He was doing just what he wanted to do anyway. If the black church is to get back to itself, to reclaim is own black faith tradition, it must follow the way of blues women, which is the way of the "hush harbor" church and the way of Jesus. And this is the way of a sensuous god.

Once again, the sanctified body-phobic/body denying culture of the black church is a betrayal of both the blackness and faith of this church. It is therefore not the body that the black church must overcome, but rather the sanctified narrative of civility. The practical consequences of not doing so are great.

As a de facto discourse of white power, the sanctified civility narrative functions as it is supposed to function, it harms and destroys black bodies. Just as white culture targeted black bodies as most offensive to whiteness, the sanctified black civility narrative has also targeted various bodies as being offensive to blackness, as that blackness is understood behind the veil of respectable whiteness. Today, the LGBTQ body has perhaps become the most targeted body. As such, black LGBTQ people are considered body people within the collective consciousness of the black church. Virtually the same way in which white cultural narratives caricatured black people, the sanctified narrative of the black church caricatures LGBTQ people. They are people considered driven by the lustful passions of their bodies. They are seen as lewdly out of control. Hence, these are bodies that have been shunned and ignored by the black church. The result is not only the inner conflict and turmoil it creates for LGBTQ peoples, but also the way it literally kills these black bodies.

The disregard for the LGBTQ body has meant indifference and at times outright antipathy toward issues that particularly affect LGBTQ people. This indifference was seen in the way in which the black church addressed the spread of HIV/AIDS. Unfortunately, within the black church community, initially this disease was erroneously considered a "gay" disease. Consequently, the disease went unchecked within the black community. The one institution that traditionally took the lead when addressing concerns of black bodies remained conspicuously on the sidelines when it came to HIV/AIDS. The result has been deadly for the black community.

To date, over 230,000 black people have died of AIDS. This staggering statistic accounts for almost 40 percent of the total deaths due to AIDS in the United States. Moreover, of the more than 1 million people who are living with AIDS in the United States, more than 50 percent are black. The black population is also leading the way in the HIV infection rate. In 2009, black people made up 44 percent of all new HIV infections in the United States, even though they only constituted 14 percent of the overall population. Black women account for 30 percent of those new cases. The rate of HIV infections for black women is 15 times as high as the rate for white women and 3 times as high as that for Latina women. There was also a 48 percent increase of infection in the 13–29 age group of black men who have sex with other men.[13] Socioeconomic conditions such as poverty, lack of health care, and other forms of racial discrimination are a significant factor in the disproportionate impact of HIV/AIDS on the black community.

Just as significant, however, are the attitudes about sexuality and the body that are prevalent in the black community, especially as perpetuated in the black church. Pernessa Seale, founder of an organization that works to educate and mobilize black churches around HIV/AIDS issues, says, "There is no doubt that the link between HIV/AIDS, drug abuse and sexual activity has been a stumbling block for churches who feel that such behavior is contrary to their tenets."[14] The black churches' body-denying/body-phobic culture has prevented it from being responsive to the health needs of black bodies. In this regard, it has not only failed at being a home, but also a social center and nation in a nation. Moreover, as long as the black church harbors such anti-body narratives, it will not be able to provide a home, a safe-space, for those who perhaps need it most—black youth struggling with their sexual identities. The statistics in terms of youth suicidality amongst the black LGBTQ population have grown more and more alarming. There are far too many stories of African American teens who have resorted to suicide rather than face the condemnation of their families and community regarding their sexuality.[15] The urgency of the problem is clear, the sanctified narrative of civility helps to destroy black bodies. The black church must free itself of this narrative. This, however, is easier said than done.

Breaking patterns of the way people think about and view the world is difficult to do, especially when these patterns reflect sanctified perspectives that have ostensibly served one well. There is little doubt that the casting of the body as a source of sin, and the demonizing of certain bodily behaviors, has saved many a black body from succumbing to numerous destructive activities. It has no doubt prevented or rescued black people from unhealthy lives of drink, drugs, or even sexual promiscuity. This does not, however, mitigate the fact that body-denying/body-phobic narratives betray both black bodies and black faith. How then are we to dislodge these narratives from the black church? The answer is, again, suggested by blues.

Blues emerged from the raw facts of black living. They were not songs that started in the head, but songs that came forth from black bodies. These songs spoke about practical realities of black life; they were not theoretical abstractions about that life. Embodied experiences were the starting point for blues narratives. Such must be the case when it comes to the black church. The response to the narrative of civility must be a practical one. It must begin with the way in which the black church engages black bodies. The first step in dislodging the sanctified narrative of civility from the collective consciousness of the black church community is for the black church to change the way it acts in regard to black bodies. The black church in this regard must become a "proleptic" community, that is, a community that acts as if the sanctified narrative of civility does not exist. It must act in accordance with its collective imagination of a different world, that is, of god's world. This is, of course, what blues women did through their blues play. They acted as if the various narratives that tried to control their lives did not exist. They lived in a reality that allowed them to be freely themselves, warts and all. They sang about a "heaven of their own" right down here on earth. Once again, in doing this they were keeping the spirit of Jesus alive. In his revelatory play, Jesus acted as if the time of god was already consummated and all bodies were accepted as worthy and equal bodies. The black church must engage in blues play, it must play like Jesus played. To play, to act as if, is an act of imagination that also requires an act of remembering.

To remember first and foremost means mining the "taken for granted" embodied knowledge of the past. It is perhaps what ethicist Stacey Floyd-Thomas refers to as "mining the motherlode."[16] The point is to remember the ways in which past black bodies contested the narratives that dehumanized and denigrated them. Most significantly, it is remembering the knowledge that undermined dualistic perspectives on the world. This is "oppositional knowledge." It is knowledge that "fosters [black] self-definition and self-determination."[17] This is knowledge that emerges through the lens of a black African-influenced gaze, not knowledge that emerges from a white gaze. For the black church, such knowledge can be found in its very songs of worship, the spirituals. As pointed out before, the spirituals were nothing less than songs of protest against white religious narratives that repudiated the body, especially the black body. There was no bifurcation of the body and soul in the spirituals. Soul salvation meant body freedom. Even if there are black churches that still find themselves unable to embrace blues, at least in really listening to and learning from spirituals they will capture the sensuous blues spirit—this is a spirit that maintains a "holistic tenacity" and values black bodies. Spirituals, like blues, are counter-narratives to the sanctified civility narrative that projects the body-denying/body-phobic white gaze; and so too are the Gospel narratives.

It cannot be stressed enough that the Gospels are sensuous narratives that witness a Jesus who played with the very narratives, political and religious systems that created insider/outsider bodies in his own time. The fact of god's incarnation in Jesus made clear the importance of the body to divine revelation and salvation. Jesus's ministry reinforced the importance of all bodies and stressed the significance of the rejected bodies to understanding the very revelation of god. The "good news" of the Gospels was the play of Jesus that overturned the either/or disembodied views of the world and ways of relating. Such play empowered the outcasts and the marginalized and dethroned the outcasting and marginalizing powerfuls. The embodied revelation of god through Jesus lets it be known in no uncertain terms that the way of god is a way that takes the bodies of all people seriously. The ministry of Jesus discloses that it is through the "strife and strivings" of blues bodies, that is, the rejected bodies, that the way of god is most manifest. Essentially, the god of Christian faith makes clear the necessity of a blues bond for those who would follow this god. If the black church is ever to get back to itself, if it is to be true to its black faith tradition, then it must remember the center of its embodied faith, Jesus.

The act of remembering involves embodied memory in another way, this is the way in which Jesus called his followers to remember, that is, through the body. During what has come to be known as the Last Supper, Jesus said, "Do this in remembrance of me." We are instructed by the Greek word for "remembrance" used in this text. This word is "anamnesis." This particular word means more than simply a mental recollection of events. It suggests an embodied kind of recall. It means to bring the past into the present through one's own embodied actions. Anamnesis is perhaps best understood as the reenactment of past events. During the Last Supper, Jesus was calling his disciples to remember him through their bodies—that is, to act in their present as he had acted. To do so would mean caring for the bodies of others, especially blues bodies, the way in which he had cared for them. It would require treating other bodies as if the time of god would come when all bodies are respected, when all embodied identities are celebrated as reflecting the image of god.

For the black church to remember, as Jesus called his followers to remember, is for the black church to develop an *embodied blues ethic*. A former enslaved person gave voice to this ethic when she said, "Ole white preacher used to talk wid dey tongues widdout sayin' nothin', but Jesus told us slaves to talk wid our hearts."[18] An embodied blues ethic is one that talks with the heart, it is one that flows from the body of people, not simply from the heads. An embodied blues ethic involves listening to one's own body concerning the right and wrong way to treat other bodies. Put simply, it is doing for other bodies what your body would want done for it, and not doing to other bodies what your body would not want done to it. This seems like a simple "Golden Rule," but as simple as it sounds and as familiar as black church people are with it, it is not easy to follow. For, the head usually interferes with the heart, the reasons of the mind too often overcome the feelings of the body. That is to say, one rationalizes why they should or should not respond to the needs of another body. Such rationalization surely has taken place when it comes to the black church response to LGBTQ bodies. Instead of following the call of black bodies, the black church has followed the dictates of sanctified narratives of civility.

Jesus says, remember me. For the black church to get back to its own black faith is for it to remember the way Jesus "told the slaves" to remember—with their hearts, with their bodies. It is the hearts and bodies of people that must inform the thoughts and beliefs. This kind of remembering is about nothing less than putting black bodies first. It is about listening to the memories carried in black bodies. It is about an embodied blues ethic. It is about a blues bond. It is simply hard for me to imagine that a body that remembers what it is like to be enchained, whipped, lynched, destroyed, and otherwise discarded could ever do the same to another body. In her song, "Blue, Blue," Bessie Smith said, "Listen to my story, and everything'll come out true."[19] The story that Smith was urging her audience to listen to was the "tale" of a blues body. Indeed, blues bodies carry a truth of black faith. It is to these bodies that the black church must listen, it is the memories of these bodies that must govern the black church's interactions with other bodies. Retrieving embodied memories is the only way in which the black church can begin to free itself from the disruptive power of a white gaze. To be sure, embodied memories are essential if the black church is ever to be a home for all black bodies, especially LGBTQ bodies.

It must be said that while the LGBTQ body has become the most visibly targeted body when it comes to the black church's sanctified narrative of civility, in large measure because of the eruption of the LGBTQ voice in rightfully asserting its right to be free and whole, this does not mean that other bodies are no longer targeted within the black church community, such as the black female body. This body has long been subjugated and oppressed. Multiple lines of oppression have consistently intersected on it. As discussed fully in previous chapters, the black female body has routinely shouldered the brunt of black oppression and the responsibility for black "well-being."

Even as black women have been considered the "moral centers" of the black community, their bodies have likewise been abused and disrespected. The black female body has been viewed through the lens of a sexualized white male gaze, even within the black community. In this regard, the way blues women have been viewed within the black community is representative of how black women in general have been viewed. Black women have been viewed as temptresses within their own churches. The sanctified narrative of civility has fostered an atmosphere in which the black female body is feared and disrespected. One overt indication of this fear is the practice of black women having to cover their legs so as not to tempt the men, especially those in the pulpit. However, there is no issue that shows the disrespect for black women's bodies and thus the lack of attention to issues that affect their bodies more than intimate (domestic) violence.

Blues women have named this issue, yet it still remains a neglected if not taboo subject for the black community. The fact of the matter is that black women are victimized by domestic violence at a rate higher than other women. Black women reportedly experience "intimate violence" at a rate 35 percent higher than that experienced by white women and 22 percent higher than experienced by women of other races. The number one killer of black women between the ages of 15 and 34 is intimate violence.[20] Numerous social economic factors contribute to the higher incidence of intimate violence within the black community. The very pressures of black life, about which blues women sang, that trouble black relationships are the same ones that lead to a higher incidence of intimate violence. While a thorough examination of intimate violence within the black community certainly goes beyond the scope of this discussion, it is important to name it as an evil and to recognize its prevalence within the black community. More to the point, it is to be named to make clear that this is an issue that inflicts black bodies. "Victims *and* perpetrators of domestic violence are sitting in every church in the United States every Sunday morning—including the Black Church."[21] Unfortunately, even as black women are more gravely victimized by intimate violence than other women, they are less likely to report it. The reasons for this are numerous, not the least of which is the black women's responsibility of carrying the aforementioned burden of black progress. In this regard, the reaction of black women to the way in which black males are treated by a racialized criminal justice system and their effort at protecting the image of black people—particularly black males—have meant that black women have suffered in silence. Domestic violence has become virtually a taboo issue within the black community. The black church has complied with this silence. Concerned black women have observed, " 'The yoke of silence'—in the name of racial solidarity—also weighs upon the Black Church Community."[22]

While there are certainly black churches aggressively engaged in addressing the problem of intimate violence, the prevailing ethos of the black church is one of silence.[23] The sanctified civility narrative that governs black church responses to LGBT bodies is the same one that governs black church responses to intimate violence. The black female body is a discarded body inasmuch as black women are seen as bodied people—as mentioned above, that is, as temptresses. In this regard, they are practically blamed for the attacks on their bodies. In the least, black women are compelled to "sit in silence" regarding their abuse, since they are very aware that they will not be fairly heard.

It is perhaps no accident that it would be female and LGBTQ bodies that are most targeted when it comes to the narrative of civility. Because this narrative sustains heterosexist and sexist values, it reflects not only the very values of white mainstream society, but also the inextricable relationship between heterosexism and sexism. Both of these patriarchal systems of oppression are sustained by an ideology that constructs masculinity in opposition to femininity. Masculinity is seen as good/rational/strong while femininity is seen as bad/passionate/weak. Not only is the "nonmasculine" considered inferior, it is not tolerated and therefore harshly rejected. This invariably leads to a disregard for the female and LGBTQ body. The female body is, of course, the degraded opposite of the male. As for LGBTQ bodies, lesbian women are seen as usurping male prerogatives to female bodies and declaring themselves independent of male control, while gay males are viewed as rejecting masculinity and taking on the ways of the inferior gender, the female. Both undermine views of masculinity and masculine superiority, and, thus, they along with women become targeted "othered" bodies. As the narrative of civility functions within the black church community, it is an extension of this heterosexist/sexist patriarchal othering of certain bodies.

It cannot be said enough that the sanctified civility narrative is lethal, it destroys black bodies. The black church must do as blues women have done, name the evil and then act in such a way that does not foster this evil. It is only in acting another way—the way suggested by embodied memories—that the sanctified narrative that ultimately destroys black bodies can effectively be disrupted.

This is not to suggest that the black church does not need to begin to think in another way that reflects a cultural perspective and view of the world, of others, and of themselves more in keeping with heir own African religious heritage. This is a perspective that, of course, does not tolerate pernicious splits between sacred and secular dimensions of living. What this focus on the actions of the black church does suggest, however, is that discursive power is maintained from below. To change the web of interactions from below, that is, the way in which bodies relate to one another on the ground, will disrupt the discourses from above, such as sanctified narratives of civility that attempt to control and govern those interactions in ways that perpetuate disharmony—which, to be reminded, is nothing less than evil. Actions themselves can contest and protest, and they can change the way people come to see the world, see themselves, see others, and most certainly change the way people see god. This is, perhaps, what god was banking on when god became an embodied reality in Jesus. It was as Jesus walked the earth and touched, healed, and resurrected human bodies that those who witnessed his ministry and were touched by it began to view divine and human realities differently. Jesus did not engage the Samaritan woman at the well in a discourse on faith, he offered her water and he talked without judgment about her life. This led her to see both herself and Jesus in a new way. Likewise, Jesus did not discuss the way in which the Scribes and Pharisees should view the law or the limitations of binaries that led to a condemning judgments of the adulterous woman, rather he showed them how to be. This caused them to see themselves, the adulterous woman, and Jesus in a new light. To repeat, it was in this way that Jesus showed himself to be the revelation of a sensuous god. This was a god who, through the absolute care and concern for bodies, changed the way the world was perceived. Because of Jesus, people were able to see the world the way it could be, beyond the binaries and, thus, one that would reflect the nexus of the divine/human encounter. It is this spirit of a sensuous god that blues women carried forth in song and in life. They did not invest their energy in debating the various narratives of power that tried to circumscribe their lives. They simply lived differently and treated their bodies differently, urging those who listened to their blues to do the same. The way of blues women, the way of Jesus, must become the way of the black church. This church simply must act differently when it comes to blues bodies. It must touch, heal, and re-create these bodies without judgment, regardless. To do anything less is a betrayal of its faith.

Even as the black church engages blues bodies, it must rethink its very notions of sin. If sins are those acts that alienate one from god, then at least one thing becomes clear when considering sin. Narratives that call for people to live against their bodies, deny their bodies, or lead to attacks on various bodies are acts of sin. For, again, the god of Jesus Christ is an embodied god. To deny the body is to deny god. To attack the body is to attack god. Furthermore, it cannot be stressed enough that a denial of sexuality is to deny a means through which one can be in human and divine relationships. Right expressions of sexuality—expressions that lead to the re-creation of bodies—is a divine activity. Denying persons the ability to express their sexuality is a sinful activity.

A Prophetic God

Ah, you hear me talkin' to you.[24]

Blues suggests another way in which the black church must recapture its radical faith tradition. Blues women sang signifyin' laments. Through blues, black men and women were called to account for the ways in which they contributed to the strife of black bodies. It is in this way that blues reflects the signifyin' nature of god. The god of the Exodus tradition was indeed one that signified. This was most evident through the messages of the prophets. Like blues, the prophetic message was a message spoken to their own community, the Israelites. Inasmuch as the Israelites had abandoned their faith, the covenant they had made with the god that led them out of slavery, they were called to repent. The prophets urged the Israelites to change course and act in a different way. It is the prophetic voice of god that the black church must hear. It is a divine blues lament calling the black church to live in its very faith—the faith that emerged from the "harsh harbors" in response to the needs of black bodies. The black church has often been prophetic in its responses to the way in which others have treated black bodies, particularly when it comes to racial matters. What the black church must recognize, however, is that through the prophets god spoke to those whom god had freed. The prophetic voice of god is an inwardly directed voice. It is "talkin' " to the black community. It is the voice of Jesus calling those who would condemn and critique others to "first take the log out of the own eye and then you will see clearly to take the speck out of your brother's eye."[25] This is what the black church must do. It must take the log out of its own eye. It must repent for the way in which it has treated blues bodies. Again, it must simply stop all the talking and justifying, and act differently.

There are numerous ways in which the black church has not been a home to blues bodies. Various bodies have not been able to freely live in the fullness of who they are, to enjoy loving relationships, and to re-create themselves because of an irrepressible sanctified narrative of civility that governs the actions of black church people. One thing is certain when it comes to this sanctified narrative of civility, it has compromised the very blackness and faith of the black church. This narrative is defined by a white gaze. This fact alone places it in opposition to blackness. That it invariably lends itself to the harm and disregard of black bodies only reinforces its threat to the church's black identity. The moment a black body cannot be at home in the black church, this churches' blackness is jeopardized. Moreover, there is no getting around the fact that the narrative of civility is a body-denying/body-phobic narrative. As such, it is a blasphemous narrative when viewed in the light of the black faith tradition. The defining character of Christianity is the incarnate revelation of god, Jesus Christ. It was this incarnate god that, no doubt, attracted the enslaved Africans to Christianity. For the black church to adopt and sustain a narrative of civility is to renege on its embodied faith. It is to betray the crossroads god of Jesus.

In the final analysis, the black church must come to terms with the fact that its faith is an incarnate faith. Christianity is defined by a god who came though a human body to reveal god's care and hope for the world. Not only that, god continued to uphold the value of human bodies through Jesus's own very ministry to wounded, rejected, and put-upon bodies. The body is not extraneous to the revelation, it is essential to it. And, of course, the "othered" bodies are the ones through which the meaning of god's revelation is most clear. This means that the black church must not only refrain from oppressing and rejecting various black bodies, but it must also join on the side of other bodies, black or not, that are striving to be whole. It must forge blues bonds. It is in the crossroads of the "strife and strivings" of marginalized, rejected, and oppressed bodies that the power of god's revelation is made most manifest. In short, to disregard, dismiss, or denigrate the body in any way and thus to participate in the oppression of any body is not only for the black church to compromise its blackness and its black faith tradition, but to, in fact, reject the very embodied revelation of god. Jesus said, "Foxes have holes, and the birds of the air have nests, but the Son of Man has nowhere to lay his head."[26] As long as the black church maintains a body-denying/body-phobic narrative, then one of the blues bodies that will not be able to find a home in the black church is that of Jesus. To reject LGBTQ bodies is to reject the incarnate god.

Pulitzer Prize winning journalist Eugene Robinson says that black America has become disintegrated. He argues that in a post-civil rights era of desegregation, affirmative action, and black immigration, four black America's have developed. He identifies a mainstream middle class, an elite transcendent class, a black immigrant class, and a large abandoned class. The abandoned class comprises the poor black bodies left with little or no hope of getting out of their impoverished conditions. They have been abandoned to their poverty with all of the concomitant social problems. Most disturbing is that this class has been "left adrift" not just by white society but also by blacks in the mainstream middle and transcendent elite classes. "But look how you behave. Look how you really are. *You deserve [your plight in life]*"[27] This is the "black" logic that Robinson says justifies the abandonment of these poor abandoned black bodies. This logic is reminiscent of that which civility-minded churches during the Great Migration resorted to in their rejection of southern black migrants. This is the logic of white racist narratives in regard to black bodies. It is the logic of a narrative of civility. Such logic signals the disintegration of black America. For, as Robinson argues, it can no longer be assumed that there is a unified "black agenda" or a "solidarity" of black commitment to all black bodies. With this being the case, the disintegration of black America, Robinson says, has left many wondering "what it means to be black."[28] In many respects the black church community is a reflection of this disintegration. It has abandoned far too many black bodies. It has left them without a place to call home. There is a problem in the black church.

The black church has recently been riddled with various high profile "scandals" regarding its leadership. These scandals have involved matters of sexual abuse and domestic abuse. As they surfaced, many in the black church community were in a quandary concerning how these could have happened. Unfortunately, the black church fosters an atmosphere that is ripe for sexual abuse and domestic violence. As long as the black church is uncomfortable dealing with issues involving the body, then it will be unable to effectively address the ways in which bodies are abused. Moreover, it will lend itself to surreptitious behaviors that ultimately harm all bodies involved. There is a problem in the black church.

What is the problem in the church? It is a body problem. And, to have a body problem is to have a crisis of identity. As long as the body remains a problem for the black church, then this church is nothing more than a "disinte-grated" collection of "incidentally black" churches.[29] And perhaps worse yet, they are churches that are only nominally Christian. This is what it means for the black church to be "de-radicalized," for it has betrayed its core identity and its core faith.

Bluesman Willie Thomas said that god gave black people blues.[30] I believe Thomas is right. Blues challenges the black church to remain true to its own crossroads black faith tradition. This is a tradition with a crossroads god. This is a tradition that rejects either/or narratives that foster a rejected blues class of people. Essentially, blues challenges the black church to remain true to its own crossroads religious heritage. Blues carries forth the legacy of black faith. It carries forth the spirit of a crossroads god.

In her song "Preachin' the Blues," Smith ends by imploring her audience to sing the blues songs and to convert their souls. If the black church is to become more reliably black and more authentically Christian, then its soul must be converted from white to blue. "Blues, Oh blues," Ma Rainey sang. If the black church is to find its way back to itself, it must become blue, oh blue.

A Blues Church and Me

"Now, I've got the crazy blues."

I love the black church. Even when voices were telling me that I was not a member of the black church, I still loved the black church. This is the church that my grandmothers' loved. This is the church that they never failed to attend on Sunday mornings, and sometimes during the week. This is the church that re-created their black female bodies to face the storms of living in a post-reconstruction-era white world. This is the church they turned to when they migrated from the South, one from Georgia and the other from Kentucky, up to the Ohio North. My love for the black church was instilled in my heart and soul way before I was born.

I know what the black church has been to black bodies, because I know what it was for my grandmothers. I know what the black church can be, because I know what it has been. And so I am disappointed when I see what it has become. Because I love it, my heart is broken and my soul is hurt when it acts unlike itself.

My cousin and best friend was a gay black male. He was a godfather to my son. He was a very faithful person. He grew up in the black church. He loved his church. But his church did not love him back. Far too often he was subjected to sermons that told him how much of a sinner he was. He did not believe it. But many close to him did. Because his black church could not affirm his very embodied identity, it disrupted his relationships with those closest to him.

Over and over again, I watch people dear to me struggle with their LGBTQ identities because of their churches. They are convinced that they simply cannot be LGBTQ and Christian at the same time. They live over and against themselves, some to their own peril. By the grace of god, I am sometimes able to get them to see that the problem is with their church, not with them.

When I think of my cousin, when I witness people in struggle, I realize that the black church has a problem. It is a body problem, it is a problem of blackness, it is a problem of faith, and it is a problem of love. The black church far too often hurts and destroys people who love it, because it cannot love them back. It cannot love them the way the god of Jesus Christ loves them—body and all. And so I have the crazy blues. Blues are about bodies; they are about Jesus; they are about the church I love. I sing blues for the black church to help it find its way back to loving blues bodies the way blues bodies are loved by god.

Blues Coda: Back to the Crossroads

I went to the crossroad
fell down on my knees[1]

I returned to where Route 61 and Route 49 cross in Clarksdale, Mississippi. I took the route that Bessie Smith supposedly took the night she died en route from Memphis to Mississippi. I don't know what I expected to find in going back. It was just a sign with a guitar and a plaque beneath that talked about Clarksdale. There was nothing about Robert Johnson and pacts with the devil. There was no sign that I saw on the way down pointing you to the crossroads. You had to look up to find it. There were no signs telling you where Bessie Smith had her accident. Yet, I was very aware of what took place on that road. And I was very aware of what took place at the crossroads. Driving down Route 61 and getting to the crossroads, I came to appreciate its significance in perhaps a different way. It is not about blues and Robert Johnson, it is about the pacts that people make with themselves and their god(s). When I stood at the crossroads, I did not think of Johnson, I thought about the god of my faith, the god of the Exodus, the god of Jesus. It is this god that calls me back to the crossroads every day. These are crossroads in my living. These are the places where blues bodies are hurting and struggling to live and be whole. These are the places where I am called upon to be accountable. These are the places where the power of god is most present.

The crossroads is a place of making pacts. I am not sure who Robert Johnson met at his crossroads. What I do know is who I meet at my crossroads daily, I meet my god. I am not sure if Robert Johnson traded his soul to become a bluesman. But this I know, even though I cannot sing blues as Bessie, Ma Rainey, Sippie, Alberta, Ida, Victoria, and all the blues women who sang them, if I don't stand up for blues bodies to live and be whole, then it is I who has traded away my soul.

When I stood at the crossroads, I made a pact with the god I met there. I made a pact to do my best, as imperfect and flawed as I may be, to sing blues for the blues bodies with every crossroads opportunity I get. I made a pact to be with god at the crossroads of my living. And so I offer this book. This is my blues song.

Notes

Introduction

1. Ma Rainey, "Ma Rainey's Mystery Record," 1923. Reissued, *Ma Rainey: Complete Recorded Works in Chronological Order* volume 1, Document Records, DOCD-5581, 1998.
2. The Reverend Dr. Jeremiah Wright, The National Press Club, Washington, DC (April 28, 2008).
3. Ibid.
4. Ma Rainey's Mystery Record.
5. Ma Rainey, " Blues, Oh Blues," "Ma Rainey Mother of the Blues, 1927." Reissued, JSP Records, 2007. JSP7793D.
6. Rod Gruver, "The Blues as a Secular Religion," in *Write Me A Few of Your Lines*, ed. Steven C. Tracy (Amherst: University of Massachusetts Press, 1999), 224.
7. Ibid., 224.
8. James Cone, *Spirituals and the Blues: An Interpretation* (New York: The Seabury Press, 1972), 111.
9. Ibid., 112, 109.
10. Garon, *Blues and the Poetic Spirit* (San Francisco: City Lights, 1975 and 1996), 148.
11. Ibid., 148.
12. Jon Michael Spencer, *Blues and Evil* (Knoxville: University of Tennessee Press, 1993), 69.
13. Charles Keil, *Urban Blues* (Chicago: University of Chicago Press, 1966), 148.
14. Ibid., 147.
15. Shawn Copeland, "Theology at the Crossroads: A Meditation on the Blues," in *Uncommon Faithfulness: The Black Catholic Experience*, ed. M. Shawn Copeland, with LaReine-Marie Mosley and Albert Raboteau (Maryknoll, NY: Orbis Books, 2009).
16. Bessie Smith, "Blue, Blue." Reissued,1993 Bessie Smith The Complete Recordings, Vol. 4, Columbia/Legacy 52838.
17. Bluesman J. D. Miller spoke of a "blues slant." Quoted in Paul Oliver, ed., *Conversations with the Blues* (Cambridge: Cambridge University Press, 1965), 125.

18. Quoted in Paul Oliver, *Conversations with the Blues*, 176.
19. W. C. Handy, *Father of the Blues: An Autobiography* (Cambridge, MA: Da Capo Press, 1941), 74.
20. Angela Davis, *Blues Legacies and Black Feminism* (New York: Pantheon Books, 1998), 128.
21. Handy, quoted in Nat Shapiro and Nat Hentoff, eds, *Hear Me Talkin' to Ya: The Story of Jazz as Told by the Men Who Made It* (New York: Dover Publications, Inc., 1955), 252.
22. Quoted in Robert Palmer, *Deep Blues* (New York: Penguin books, 1981), 59–60.

Chapter 1

1. Maime Smith, *Complete Recorded Works* volume 1, Document Records, DOCD-5357, 1995.
2. Perry Bradford, *Born with the Blues* (New York: Oak Publications Inc., 1965), 125.
3. Bradford, *Born with the Blues*, 116, 119
4. Ibid 125 .
5. Hunter, quoted in Chris Albertson, *Bessie*, revised and expanded ed. (New Haven: Yale University Press, 2003), 24.
6. Spivey, quoted in Giles Oakley, *The Devil's Music: A History of the Blues*, 2nd ed., updated (London: Da Capo Press, 1997), 84.
7. Bradford, *Born with the Blues*, 118.
8. Lawrence Levine notes how "phenomenal" these record sales were, given the black population at the time. *Black Culture and Black Consciousness Afro-American Folk Thought from Slavery to Freedom*, 30th anniversary ed. (New York: Oxford University Press, 2007), 225.
9. Richard Wright, *12 Million Black Voices* (New York: Thunder's Mouth Press, 1941), 128.
10. Quoted in Paul Oliver, *Conversation with the Blues* (Cambridge: Cambridge University Press, 1965), 20.
11. Quoted in Oliver, *Conversation with the Blues*, 20.
12. Levine, *Black Culture and Black Consciousness*, 157.
13. From this point forward, when I speak of Africa I am referring to West African traditions, unless otherwise noted.
14. Samuel A. Floyd Jr., *The Power of Black Music: Interpreting Its History from Africa to the United States* (New York: Oxford University Press, 1995), 32.
15. Giles Oakely, *Devils Music, 136.*
16. Wright, *12 Million Black Voices*, 100.
17. Ida Cox, "Pink Slip Blues," Vocalian 05258, 1939.
18. Big Bill Broonzy, "The Young Big Bill Broonzy 1928-1935," Shananchie Entertainment, 2005
19. Bertha, "Chippie"; Hill, "Trouble in Mind," Circle J1003A, c. 1946.
20. Big Bill Broonzy, "Trouble in Mind," version 2.
21. Paul Oliver, *The Story of the Blues* (Boston: Northeastern University Press, 1969), 3.

22. Leon F. Litwack, *Trouble in Mind: Black Southerners in the Age of Jim Crow* (New York: Alfred A. Knopf, 1998), 436.
23. This manual would later become a fuller text entitled, "the Negro in Etiquette."
24. Victoria W. Wolcott, *Remaking Respectability: African American Women in Interwar Detroit* (Chapel Hill: University of North Carolina Press, 2001), 16.
25. Litwack, *Trouble in Mind*, 436.
26. Johnson, quoted in Giles Oakely, *The Devil's Music*, 197.
27. Otis Harris, "Waking Blues," quoted in Paul Oliver, *Blues Fell This Morning: Meaning in the Blues* (Cambridge: Cambridge University Press, 1960), 284.
28. Samuel A. Floyd Jr., *The Power of Black Music*, 77.
29. Stephen Henderson, *Understanding the New Black Poetry: Black Speech and Black Music as Poetic References* (New York: Morrow, 1973), 44.
30. Levine, *Black Culture and black Consciousness*, 297.
31. Bessie Smith, "Downhearted Blues"; Columbia A3844-D, 1923. Remastered, "Bessie Smith: Queen of the Blues," JSP Records JSP929A, 2006.
32. Patricia Hill Collins, *Black Feminist Thought: Knowledge, Consciousness, and the Politics of Empowerment*, 2nd ed. (New York: Routledge Press, 2000), 34.
33. Henry Louis Gates Jr., *The Signifying Monkey: A Theory of African-American Literary Criticism* (New York: Oxford University Press, 1988), xxiv. Description of signifying as a trope is informed by Gates's complete discussion in this text.
34. Samuel A. Floyd Jr., *The Power of Black Music*, 8.
35. Ibid., 78.
36. Frank Walker, quoted in Nat Shapiro and Nat Hentoff, eds, *Hear Me Talkin' to Ya: The Story of Jazz as Told by the Men Who Made It* (New York: Dover Publications Inc., 1955), 240.
37. Newbell Niles Puckett, *Folk Beliefs of the Southern Negro* (Kissinger Publishing's Rare Reprints, Whitefish MT, 1925), 243.
38. Chris Albertson, *Bessie*, 38.
39. Zora Neale Hurston, Their Eyes *Were Watching God* (New York: Perennial Classics, 1990 originally published by J.P. Lippincott, Inc. 1937), 104.
40. In John F. Callahan, ed., *The Collected Essays of Ralph Ellison* (New York: The Modern Library, 2003), 155–188.
41. Smith, "Moan You Moaners," Columbia 14538-D, 1930. Reissued on *The World's Greatest Blues Singer*, Columbia CG 33, 1972.
42. This analysis of laments draws upon that of Emilie Townes, as found in the chapter "The Formfulness of Communal Lament," in *Breaking the Fine Raine of Death:African American Health Issues and a Womanist Ethic of CareI (New York: Continuum, 1998)*.
43. Charles Keil, *Urban Blues*, 114–142.
44. T-Bone Walker, quoted in Shapiro and Hentoff, *Hear Me Talkin' to Ya*, 250–251.
45. Carl Van Vechten, quoted in Levine, *Black Culture and Black Consciousness*, 235.
46. Baker, quoted in Shapiro and Hentoff, *Hear Me Talkin' to Ya*, 243.

47. Rainey, "Toad Frog Blues," Paramount 12242, 1924. Reissued on *Ma Rainey: Mother of the Blues*, JSP Records, 2007 JSP7793B, 2007.
48. Hunter, quoted in Shapiro and Hentoff, *Hear Me Talkn' to Ya*, 246.
49. Hooker, quoted in Oliver, *Conversation with the Blues*, 171, 180.
50. Handy, quoted in *Shapiro and Hentoff, Hear Me Talkn' to Ya*,, 252.
51. Angela Davis, *Blues Legacies and Black Feminism*, 8.
52. James Cone, *Spirituals and the Blues*, 112. Cone says he is indebted to C. E. Lincoln for this phrase. n9, 152.
53. Lawrence Levine, Black Culture and Black Consciousness, 237.
54. Jon Michael Spencer, *Blues and Evil*, xxvi.
55. Ibid.
56. Trixie Smith, "Praying Blues," Paramount Records.
57. Ma Rainey, "Ma Rainey's Mystery Record."
58. Julio Finn, *The Bluesman: The Musical Heritage of Black Men and Women in the Americas* (New York: Interlink Books, 1992), 6.
59. Spencer refers to the"shadow side of blues." *Blues and Evil*, 72, 74.
60. Julio Finn, *The Bluesman*, 6.
61. Smith, *Red Mountain Blues*, Columbia, 1925. Reissued JSP Records, JSP929D, 2006.
62. Rainey, "Lawd Send Me A Man Blues," Paramount 12227, 1924. Reissued *Ma Rainey Mother of the Blues*, JSP Records, JSP7793A, 2007.
63. Ma Rainey, "Ma Rainey's Mystery Record."

Chapter 2

1. Sterling Brown, "Ma Rainey," in *Blues Poems*, ed. by Kevin Young (New York: Albert A. Knopf, Everyman's Library, 2003), 33.
2. Ida Cox, "Wild Women Don't Have the Blues," Paramount, 1924. Reissued Ida Cox Complete Recorded Works 1923–1938, Volume 2, 1924–1925. Document Records DOCD-5323, 1995.
3. Shapiro and Hentoff, *Hear Me Talkin' to Ya*, 249.
4. Giles Oakley, *The Devil's Music: A History of the Blues* (London: Da Capo Press, 1997), 103.
5. Sterling Brown, *Ma Rainey*, 33.
6. See Hazel V. Carby's discussion in "They Put a Spell on You," in Carby, *Cultures in Babylon: Black Britain and African America* (New York: Verso, 1999), 52.
7. Shapiro and Hentoff, *Hear Me Talkin' to Ya*, 214.
8. Ibid., 247.
9. Anna Julia Cooper, *A Voice from the South*, with an introduction by Mary Helen Washington (New York: Oxford University Press, 1988; originally printed 1892), 27.
10. In 1900, only 2 percent of the black population lived outside of the South. By the end of the Great Migrations, six decades later, 6 million southern black people had migrated to the North, which meant that 47 percent of black America now lived outside of the South.

11. Quoted in Victoria Wolcott, *Remaking Respectability: African American Women in Interwar Detroit* (Chapel Hill: University of North Carolina Press, 2001), 15.
12. I take this term "moral panic" from Hazel V. Carby in her discussion of the northern black "bourgeois" culture that emerged during the time of the Great Migrations. See Carby, "Policing the Black Woman's Body in an Urban Context," in *Cultures in Babylon: Black Britain and African America* (New York: Verso, 1999), 22.
13. Virginia W. Broughton, "The Social Status of the Colored Women and Its Betterment," in *The United Negro: His Problems and His Progress*, ed. I. Garland Penn and J. W. E. Bowen (Atlanta: D. E. Luther Publishing, 1902), 450.
14. Wolcott, *Remaking Respectability*, 54.
15. See *The Memphis Diary of Ida B. Wells: An Intimate Portrait of the Activist as A Young Woman*, ed. Miriam DeCosta-Wills (Boston: Beacon Press, 1995), see particularly her letter written under the pen name Iola.
16. Anna Julia Cooper, *A Voice from the South*, 31.
17. Hazel. V. Carby, "Policing the black Woman's Body in an Urban Context," 28.
18. Quoted in Virginia Wolcott, *Remaking Respectability*, 56.
19. Ibid., 57.
20. Ida Cox, "Wild Women Don't Have the Blues." Paramount, 1924. Reissued Ida Cox Complete Recorded Works 1923-1938.Volume.2 1924–1925. Document Records DOCD-5323, 1995.
21. Daphne Duval Harrison, *Black Pearls: Blues Queens of the 1920s* (New Brunswick, NJ: Rutgers University Press, 1988), 111.
22. Ibid., 9.
23. Quote taken from Daphne Duval Harrison, *Black Pearls*, 114.
24. Quoted in Paul Oliver, *Conversations with the Blues*, 53.
25. For a comprehensive discussion on this topic of domestic service as well as the club woman's movement, see Deborah Gray White, *Too Heavy a Load: Black Women in Defense of Themselves, 1894–1994* (New York: W. W. Norton & Company, 1999). For this particular discussion of domestic training schools, see 130.
26. Victoria W. Wolcott, *Remaking Respectability*, 85.
27. Daphne Duval Harrison, *Black Pearls*, 114.
28. Ibid., 21.
29. For discussions on Smith's contracts and earnings, see Chris Albertson, *Bessie* (New Haven: Yale University Press, 2003); Jessie Carney Smith ed., *Encyclopedia of African American Popular Culture*, volume 1 (Santa Barbara, CA: Greenwood, 2010), 1301.
30. See, for instance, Chris Albertson, *Bessie* (New Haven: Yale University Press, 2003), 67.
31. Other women like Alberta Hunter, who took care of her mother, also took care of their families from the income received from the blues industry.
32. See Victoria W. Wolcott's discussion in *Remaking Respectability: African American Women in Interwar Detroit*, 100.

33. Quoted in Debora Gray White, *Too Heavy a Load: Black Women in Defense of Themselves 1894–1994* (New York: W. W. Norton & Company, 1999), 129.
34. Victoria W. Wolcott, *Remaking Respectability*, 100.
35. Daphne Duval Harrison, *Black Pearls: Blues Queens of the 1920s.,129.*
36. Quoted in Ibid., 114.
37. Ibid.
38. TOBA, also known as TOBY Time, was the Theatre Owner's Booking Association established in 1909. This association organized and scheduled appearances of black vaudeville and tent shows throughout the South and Midwest. Many of the blues women gained their start on the TOBA circuit, including Ma Rainey and Bessie Smith. To many of the black entertainers, TOBA stood for Tough on Black Asses, because the conditions under which they performed and traveled, as well as their wages, were all but good.
39. I agree with Angela Davis' interpretation of this song as social commentary on the conditions that condemned black women into domestic service. See Davis, *Blues Legacies and Black Feminism* (New York: Pantheon Books, 1998), 98.
40. Quoted in Frank C. Taylor with Gerald Cook, *Alberta Hunter: A Celebration in Blues* (New York: McGraw-Hill Book Company, 1987), 43.
41. Quoted in Taylor with Cook, *Alberta Hunter*, 43.
42. Quoted in Taylor with Cook, *Alberta Hunter*, 43.
43. Hear Bessie Smith's "Safety Mama Blues," which sings of this "gender reversal."
44. Angela Davis, *Blues Legacies and Black Feminism*, 72.
45. See Ida Cox, "Wild Women Don't Have the Blues."
46. Ibid.
47. Edith Wilson, "Wicked Blues," Columbia A-3558, January 21, 1922.
48. Ibid.
49. See Chris Albertson, *Bessie* (New Haven: Yale University Press, 2003), 133–134.
50. Ibid., 94–96.
51. Ibid., 174–175.
52. Ibid., 123.
53. Sara Martin, "Mistreating Man Blues," Paramount 14025, 1928; Victoria Spivey, "Blood Hound Blues," RCA Victor V-39570, October 1929. Reissued by Victor on *Women of Blues*, LP534, 1966.
54. Alberta Hunter, "A Good Man is Hard to Find,"
55. Ma Rainey, "Sweet Rough Man," Paramount 1928. Reissued on Document Records DOCD, 5156, 1993.
56. Sandra Lieb, *Mother of the Blues: A Study of Ma Rainey* (Massachusetts: The University of Massachusetts Press, 1981), 120.
57. Ibid., 121.
58. Ibid., 120.
59. Ibid.
60. Angela Davis, *Blues Legacies and Black Feminism*, 26.

61. Bessie Smith, "*Yes Indeed He Do*," Columbia 1928. Reissued, *Bessie Smith the Complete Recordings*, volume 4. Columbia Legacy, 1993.
62. Bessie Smith, "Tain't Nobody's Bizness if I Do, Columbia 1923." Reissued, *The Essential Bessie Smith*, Columbia Legacy Sony Music, 1997.
63. Daphne Duval Harrison, *Black Pears: Blues Queens of the 1920s*, 111.
64. Smith, *I've Been Mistreated and I Don't Like It*. Reissued, *Bessie Smith*, volume I JSP Records JSP929D, 2006.
65. Angela Davis, *Blues Legacies and Black Feminism*, 33.
66. Bessie Smith, "Need A Little Sugar in My Bowl," 1927. Reissued, *The Essential Bessie Smith*.
67. Montgomery and Dorsey, quoted in Giles Oakley, *The Devil's Music: A History of the Blues* (Da Capo Press, 1997), 91.
68. Oakely, *The Devil's Music: A History of the Blues*, 91.
69. Remark reported in Sandra Lieb, *Mother of the Blues: A Study of Ma Rainey*, 36.
70. Story recalled in Chris Albertson, *Bessie* (New Haven: Yale University Press, 2003), 114.
71. Quoted in Ibid.
72. Alberta Hunter, "My Man is Such a Handy Man," Jazz at the Smithsonian.
73. Ida Cox, "One Hour Mama," 1939. Reissued, *Ida Cox Complete Recorded Works in Chronological Order*, volume 5, October 31 to December 29, 1940. Document Records DOCD-5651, 1999.
74. Quoted in Chris Albertson, *Bessie* (New Haven: Yale University Press, 2003), 170.
75. Ibid., 170–171.
76. Daphne Duval Harrison, *Black Pearls*, 111.
77. Zora Neale Hurston, *Their Eyes Were Watching God* (New York: Harper & Row, 1990), 16.
78. Bessie Smith, "Taint Nobody's Bizness if I Do."

Chapter 3

1. Bessie Smith, "Devil's Gonna Get You," Reisssued, *Bessie Smith Sings Them Dirty Blues* Mp3 Album Download Gramercy Records.
2. Goodson interviewed in *Wild Women Don't Have the Blues*, produced by Carole van Falkenburg and Christine Dahl, 1989.
3. Paul Oliver, ed. *Conversations with the Blues* (United Kingdom: Cambridge University Press, 1965), 178.
4. Quoted in Daphne Duval Harrison, *Black Pearls: Blues Queens of the 1920s*, 138.
5. Quoted in Paul Oliver, ed. *Conversations with the Blues* (United Kingdom: Cambridge University Press, 1985),177.
6. Quoted in Paul Oliver, ed. *Conversations with the Blues* (United Kingdom: Cambridge University Press, 1985), 177.
7. Angela Davis, *Blues Legacies and Black Feminism*, 123; Sandra Lieb, *Mother of the Blues: A Study of Ma Rainey*, 47f.

8. See Lil Son Johnson's discussion of the two sides of the road and blues singing being on the wrong side in Oliver, *Conversations with the Blues*, 177.
9. Jon Michael Spencer, *Blues and Evil* (Knoxville: The University of Tennessee Press, 1993), 63ff.
10. Ma Rainey, "Slave to the Blues," Paramount, 12332, 1927. Reissued, *Ma Rainey: Mother of the Blues*, JSP Records, 2007.
11. See my discussion of this morally active commitment in *Black Bodies/White Souls* (Maryknoll, NY: Orbis Books, 2006).
12. "The Negro Church [Essay]" originally published in *The Crisis* in 1912 reprinted in *DuBois on Religion*, ed. Phil Zuckerman (Walnut Creek, CA: Alta Mira Press, 2000), 45.
13. Milton C. Sernett, *Bound For the Promised Land* (Durham: Duke University Press, 1997), 87.
14. Ibid., 103.
15. Ibid.
16. Quoted in Evelyn Brooks Higginbotham, *Righteous Discontent: The Women's Movement in the Black Baptist Church, 1880–1920* (Cambridge: Harvard University Press, 1993), 176.
17. The Charleston Messenger, October 11, 1919 quoted in Milton C. Sernett, *Bound For the Promised Land*, 129.
18. Mary McCleod Bethune quoted in Milton C. Sernett, *Bound for the Promised Land*, 130.
19. Gayraud Wilmore, *Black Religon and Black Radicalism: An Interpretation of the Religious Hisoty of African Americans*, 3rd edition (Maryknoll: Orbis, 1998), 170.
20. *My Southern Home: or The South and Its People* (Boston: A.G. Brown & Co. Publishers, 1880) Electronic Edition made available by University of North Carolina at Chapel Hill, 2000, docsouth.uncedu/neh/brown80/brown80.html, 188.
21. William Wells Brown, *My Southern Home*, 193.
22. *Reflections of Seventy Years: By Bishop Daniel Alexander Payne, D.D., LL.D., Senior Bishop of the African Methodist Episcopal Church* with an introduction by Rev. F. J. Grimke, A.M.D.D. (Nashville, TN: Publishing House of the A.M.E. Sunday School Union, 1888), Electronic Edition made available by University of North Carolina Chapel Hill, 2001, docsouth.unc.edu/church/payne70/payne, 253.
23. Ibid., 253–254.
24. Ibid., 254.
25. Ibid., 256.
26. Ibid., 255.
27. Ibid., 257.
28. W. E. B. DuBois, ed. *The Negro Church, Report of a Social Study Made under the Direction of Atlanta University; Together with the Proceedings of the Eight Conference for the Study of the Negro Problems, held at Atlanta University, May 26th, 1903*. Electronic Edition made available by University of North Carolina at Chapel Hill, 2001, docsouth.unc.edu/church/negrochurch/DuBois.html, *202, 208*.

29. All quoted in Deborah Gray White, *Too Heavy a Load: Black Women in Defense of Themselves 1894–1994*, (New York: W. W. Norton & Company, 1999), 72.
30. Member of Philadelphia's "old guard" quoted in Milton C. Sernett, *Bound for the Promised Land,* 41.
31. Quoted in Milton C. Sernett, *Bound for the Promised Land*, 162.
32. See discussion of this blues in chapter 1.
33. Richard Wright, *12 Million Black Voices* (New York: Thunders Mouth Press, 1941), 135.
34. See especially Milton C. Sernett's discussion, "A Heaven All their Own," in *Bound for the Promised Land.*
35. Richard Wright, *12 Million Black Voices*, 131.
36. Benjamin E. Mays, *Born to Rebel: An Autobiography* (Athens, GA: University Gcorgia Press 2003, original copyright 1971), 13.
37. Richard Wright, *12 Million Black Voices*, 126.
38. Ma Rainey, "*Ya Da Do*" Paramount, 1924. Reissued *Ma Rainey: Mother of the Blues.* JSP Records, 2007.
39. Quoted in Paul Oliver, ed. *Conversations with the Blues*, 20.
40. Ma Rainey, "Blues the World Forgot, Part 2"1928. Reissued *Ma Rainey Mother of the Blues,* JSP Records, JSP7793D, 2007.
41. Quoted in Daphne Duval Harrison, *Black Pearls: Blues Queens of the 1920s*, 117.
42. Davis, *Blues Legacies and Black Feminism*, 123, 124.
43. Quoted in Jon Michael Spencer, *Blues and Evil*, 63.
44. Quoted in Bruce Cook, *Listen to the Blues* (New York: Scribner, 1975), 204.
45. Chris Albertson, *Bessie*, 154.
46. "Blues Spirit Blues, 1929. Reissued Columbia Records, The Complete Recording of Bessie Smith, Vol. 4, 1993.
47. Ma Rainey, "The Blues the World Forgot, Part 2"
48. Bessie Smith, "On Revival Day, 1930. "The Essential Bessie Smith," Columbia Legacy 2007.

Chapter 4

1. Ma Rainey, "Hear Me Talkn' To Ya," 1928. Reissued *Ma Rainey* The Complete 1928 Sessions in Chronological Order. Document Records, DOCD-5156, 1994.
2. See Chris Albertson, *Bessie.* My account of Smith's death is informed by Albertson's extended discussion of the events, which includes the Associated Press Report, 255.
3. Reference to "Yassuh an Nosuh Blues," sung by Willie Thomas, quoted in Leon F. Litwack, *Trouble in Mind: Black Southerners in the Age of Jim Crow* (New York: Alfred A. Knopf, 1998), 37–38.
4. Chris Albertson, *Bessie*, 274.
5. Samuel Charters, *The Poetry of the Blues* (New York: Avon, 1963), 98.

6. Paul Oliver, *Blues Fell This Morning: Meaning in the Blues* (New York: Cambridge University Press, 1960), 272–273. Angela Davis offers an incisive critique of these comments as well as those of Charters in *Blues Legacies and Black Feminism*, 92–94.
7. Paul Oliver, *Blues Fell This Morning: Meaning in the Blues*, 270.
8. Maud Smith and Ruby Walker give an account of this incident in Chris Albertson, *Bessie*, 156–157.
9. Angela Davis, *Blues Legacies and Black Feminism*, 110.
10. Ma Rainey, "Chain Gang Blues," Paramount 12338, 1925. Reissued on *Ma Rainey, Complete Recorded Works in Chronological Order*, volume 3, Document Records DOCD-5583, 1998.
11. Sandra Lieb, *Mother of the Blues: A Story of Ma Rainey*, 153. "hanging crime" references the actual lyrics of the song.
12. Davis, *Blues Legacies and Black Feminism*, 94.
13. Bessie Smith, "Young Woman's Blues," Columbia 14179-D, 1926. Reissued on *Bessie Smith: The Complete Recordings*, vol. 3 *Roots N' Blues.*
14. Story recounted in Chris Albertson, *Bessie*, 14.
15. Story recounted and Ruby Walker quoted in Chris Albertson, *Bessie*, 238.
16. Sandra Lieb, *Mother of the Blues: A Study of Ma Rainey*, 8.
17. E. Franklin Frazier, *The Black Bourgeoisie* (New York: Free Press Paperbacks, 1957), 135.
18. Gray White, *Too Heavy a Load*, 79.
19. For a discussion of many of these issues and a comprehensive discussion of "colorism," see Kathy Russell, Midge Wilson, and Ronald Hall, *The Color Complex: The Politics of Skin Color Among African Americans* (New York: Anchor Books, 1992).
20. See White's discussion of this in *Too Heavy a Load*, 79.
21. E. Franklin Frazier, *The Black Bourgeoisie*, 114.
22. Such rituals are reported in Russell et al. *The Color Complex*, see especially Chapter 2, "The Color Gap in Power and Privilege."
23. Although I am focusing on blues women, it should be noted that many of the blues songs sung by black men also spoke to this issue of color. Hear, for instance, Barbeque Bob, "Brownskin Woman"; or Sonny Boy Williamson, "My Black Name."
24. Smith, "Young Woman's Blues."
25. Lillian Glinn, "Brown Skin Blues," 1927. Reissued Lillian Glinn: Complete Recorded Works in Chronological Order 1927-1929, Document Records, DOCD-5184.
26. Sara Martin, "Mean Tight Mama," 1928 Reissued Sara Martin: Complete Recorded Works in Chronological Order, volume 4, (1925-1928) Document Records, DOCD 5398
27. Roger Bastide, "Color, Racism and Christianity," in *Daedalus*, vol. 96, no. 2, "Color and Race" (Spring, 1967), 312–327, Published by The MIT Press on behalf of American Academy of Arts and Sciences. Article stable URL:http//www.jstor.org/stable/20027040. Accessed January 25, 2012, 321. This discussion of color symbolism in Christianity is largely informed by Bastide's article.
28. Quoted in Leon Litwack, *Trouble in Mind*, 392.

29. See Job: 3:3.
30. Harriet Wilson, *Our Nig; or Sketches from the Life of a Free Black*, 1859. Reprint, with an introduction by Henry Louis Gates (New York: Vintage Books, 1983), 84.
31. James Baldwin, "My Dungeon Shook: Letter to My Nephew on the One-Hundredth Anniversary of the Emancipation," in *Fire Next Time* (1963 reprint; New York: Vintage Books, 1993), 4.
32. Baldwin, "My Dungeon Shook: Letter to My Nephew," 4.
33. Much has been written on the persistence of the color code within the black community. See, for instance, Marita Golden, *Don't Play in the Sun: One Woman's Journey through the Color Complex* (New York: Anchor Books, 2004); See also the documentary film *Dark Girls: The Story of Color, Gender and Race* (Urban Winter Entertainment and Duke Media Production, 2011), Directors Bill Duke and D. Channisin Berry. For evidence of color continuing to play a factor in white responses to black people, see the then senator Joe Biden's and Senate Majority Leader Harry Reid's comments concerning the then presidential candidate Barack Obama's attraction to white people during the 2008 presidential campaign.
34. For a discussion of how the idea of a corrupt creation was explained in light of a god who pronounced all creation as good, and for the discussion of religious racism in it, see Kelly Brown Douglas, *What's Faith Got to Do with It? Black Bodies/Christian Souls* (Maryknoll: Orbis, 2005), Chapter 4. A fuller discussion of this will be taken up in this book in regard to heterosexist bias in the black church.
35. Ma Rainey, "Prove it On Me Blues," Paramount 12668, 1928. Reissued on *Ma Rainey, Ma Rainey Mother of the Blues* JSP Records, 2007.
36. Recounted in Chris Alberston, *Bessie*, 116. Also referred to in Sandra Lieb, *Mother of the Blues: A Study of Ma Rainey*, 17.
37. Recounted in Chris Albertson, *Bessie,* 132–133, 134–136.
38. See a reprint of this advertisement in Sandra Lieb, *Mother of the Blues*, 127.
39. Hazel Carby, "The Sexual Politics of Women's Blues," in *Cultures in Babylon: Black Britain and African America* (New York: Verso, 1999), 17.
40. Ma Rainey, *Sissy Blues* 1928, Paramount 12384. Reissued *Ma Rainey: Mother of the Blues.*
41. Bessie Smith, "Preachin' the Blues" *Bessie Smith; The Complete Recordings, I volume 3* Roots N Blues, Sony 1992.
42. Hunter, quoted in Nat Shapiro and Nat Hentoff, *Hear Me Talkin' to Ya*, 247
43. St Louis Jimmy, quoted in Paul Oliver, *Conversations with the Blues*, 107.
44. Patricia Hill Collins, *Black Feminist Thought: Knowledge, Consciousness and the Politics of Empowerment* (New York: Routledge, 1990), 11.
45. Mississippi Shieks, 1932.
46. Hambone Willie Newbern, 1929.
47. Gayraud Wilmore, *Black Religion and Black Radicalism* Third Edition (Maryknoll: Orbis Books, 1998).
48. Ma Rainey, "Countin' The Blues," Paramount 12237, 1925. *Ma Rainey: Mother of the Blues.*

Chapter 5

1. Robert Johnson, "Cross Road Blues," 1936, "The Complete Recordings," Columbia C2K46222.
2. See this description in Robert Palmer, *Deep Blues* (New York: Penguin Books, 1981), 113.
3. Ledell Johnson recalled this story to researcher David Evans. Quoted in Robert Palmer, *Deep Blues*, 60.
4. Newbell Niles Puckett, *Folk Beliefs of the Southern Negro*, 554.
5. As I did earlier, I will refer to this god as Esu. As I do so, I am informed by the analysis of Henry Louis Gates Jr. in *The Signifying Monkey: A Theory of African American Literary Criticism* (New York: Oxford, 1988).
6. Cited in Erik Davis's figments. "Trickster At The Crossroads: West Africa's God of Messages, Sex, and Deceit," *figments*, www.levity.com/figment/trisckster.html.
7. This story is repeated in numerous collections of African American folktales. A version of it is also repeated by Erik Davis in *Trickster at the Crossroads.*
8. Robert Pelton, *The Trickster in West Africa: A Study of Mythic Irony and Sacred Delight* (Berkeley: University of California Press, 1980), 138.
9. Hunter, quoted in Shapiro and Hentoff, *Hear Me Talkin' to Ya*, 247.
10. Quoted in Daphne Duvall Harrison, *Black Pearls*, 66.
11. DuBois, *The Souls of Black Folks* (New York: New American Library, 1969), 5.
12. Ibid., 9.
13. Ma Rainey, "Countin the Blues," Paramount 12237, 1925.
14. Davis, *Blues Legacies and Black Feminism*, 33.
15. In Dogon cosmology, Nommo are ancestral spirits that play a major role in Dogon creation mythology. In the end, various nommo are associated with the power of the word and speech. See Robert Pelton, *The Trickster in West Africa*, especially 163.
16. Patricia Hill Collins, *Black Feminist Thought*, 225.
17. Audre Lorde, *Sister Outsider* (New York: Crossing Press, 1984), 112.
18. Bessie Smith, "I've Been Mistreated and I Don't Like It," 1925. Reissued *Bessie Smith: The Complete Recordings, I vol. 2 Columbia 1991.*
19. DuBois, *Souls of Black Folks*, 9..
20. Audre Lorde, *Sister Outsider* (New York: The Crossing Press, 1984), 123.
21. Lorde, *Sister Outsider*, 54.
22. Bessie Smith, "Safety Mama," Columbia, 1931. Bessie Smith, Columbia Sony Music, *The Complete Recordings, Vol. 5-The Final Chapter*, 1996
23. James B. Nelson, *Embodiment: An Approach to Sexuality and Christian Theology* (Minneapolis: Augsburg, 1978), 117–118.
24. Robert Johnson, *Crossroads Blues*, 1936.

Chapter 6

1. Ma Rainey, "Ma Rainey's Mystery Record."
2. Ma Rainey, "Lawd, Send Me a Man Blues," Paramount 12227-B, 1924.

3. Harrison, *Black Pearls*, 139.
4. Hunter, quoted in Shapiro and Hentoff, *Hear Me Talkin' to Ya*, 246–247.
5. Henry Townsend, quoted in Paul Oliver, *Conversation with the Blues*, 181.
6. John 4:1–26.
7. John 8:1–11.
8. Mark 5:1–20.
9. Matthew 16:18.
10. John 21:15–19.
11. See my discussion of this in *What's Faith Got to Do with It? Black Bodies/ Christian Souls* (Maryknoll, NY: Orbis Books, 2005).
12. Ida Cox, One Hour Mama, 1939. Reissued, Ida Cox's complete Recorded Works, Document Records, volume 5 DOCD-5651
13. John 11:55–57.
14. Ma Rainey, "Ma Rainey's Mystery Record."
15. Bessie Smith, "Moan You Mourners."
16. Harrison, *Black Pearls*, 141.
17. Wallace, quoted in Harrison, *Black Pearls*, 141.

Chapter 7

1. Ma Rainey, "Blues, Oh Blues," *Ma Rainey: Mother of the Blues.*
2. Bessie Smith, "Work House Blues," 1924. Reissued, *Bessie Smith the Complete Recordings Vol. 2.* Root N'Blues, Sony Columbia, 1992.
3. Quoted in Paul Oliver, *Conversation with the Blues, 181.*
4. See DuBois, *Souls of Black Folks*; Frazier, *The Negro Church in America*, chapter 3.
5. Bessie Smith, "Woman's Troubles Blues," Reissued *Bessie Smith the Complete Recordings Vol. 2* Roots N Blues, Sony, Columbia, 1992.
6. Bessie Smith, "Work House Blues," 1924. Reissued on *Empty Bed Blues* Columbia CG 30818, 1972.
7. Pastor Patrick Wooden, quoted in Peter Cassels, "The Black-Gay Divide: A Clash of Race, Religion and Rights," in *Edge/Boston, Massachusetts* (Febraury 7, 2012), www. Edgeboston.com/politics/news/129667/the_black-gaive_divide:_a_clash_of_races,_religion_&_rights; accessed February 24, 2012. See also "The Dialogue around Gay Marriage in Black Churches," NPR (February 23, 2012), www.nr.org/2012/02/23/147295677/the-dialogue-around-gay-marriage-in-black-churches; accessed February 24, 2012.
8. Bessie Smith, "Blues, Blue."
9. For a full discussion of this notion, see Kelly Brown Douglas, *Sexuality and the Black Church* (Maryknoll, NY: Orbis Books, 2000).
10. DuBois, *Souls of Black Folks*, 9.
11. Bessie Smith, "Moan, You Mourners." Reissued *Essential Bessie Smith*, Sony, 1997.
12. Allusions are to Bessie Smith's song, "Tain't Nobody's Bizness if I Do."
13. This data concerning HIV/AIDS in the black community was provided by Center for Disease Control (CDC), www.cdc.gov/features/BlackchurchHIV/AIDSAwareness/; and Avert HIV and AIDS charity, www.avert.org/hiv-african-americans.htm (Both sites accessed on February 17, 2012).

14. Ibid.
15. For more on this, see "Youth Suicide Problems Gay/Bisexual Male Focus," www.youth-suicide.com/gay-bisexual/; Karen M. Jordan, "Substance Abuse Among Gay, Lesbian, Bisexual, Transgender, and Questioning Adolescents," *School Psychology Review* vol. 29, no. 2 (2000): 201–206, at www.nasponline.org/publications.spr/pdf/spr292substance.pdf, accessed January 18, 2012; Keith Boykin, *For Colored Boy Who Have Considered Suicide When the Rainbow is Still Not Enough" Coming of Age, Coming Out, and Coming Home*, forthcoming (Magnus Books, June 2012).
16. Stacey M. Floyd Thomas, *Mining the Motherlode: Methods in Womanist Ethics* (Cleveland: Pilgrim Press, 2006).
17. Patricia Hill Collins develops this notion of oppositional knowledge. See *Black Feminist Thought: Knowledge, Consciousness, and the Politics of Empowerment*, 2nd edition (New York: Routledge, 2000), 299.
18. Quoted in Hill Collins, *Black Feminist Thought*, 2nd edition, 262.
19. Bessie Smith, "Blue, Blue." Reissued, Bessie Smith The Complete Recordings, Vol. 4, Columbia/Legacy 52838.
20. Data taken from American Bar Association Commission on Domestic Violence and Sexual Violence, www.americanbar.org/groups/domestic_violence/resources/statistics.html, accessed 18 January 18, 2012. This site also provides links to numerous other data bases on the subject.
21. Lynne Marie Jordan, "Domestic Violence in the African American Community: The Role of the Black Church," www.hds.harvard.edu/cswr/resources/print/rhb/reports/05.Jordan.pdf. 2005, accessed January 18, 2012, 17.
22. Jordan, "Domestic Violence in the African American Community, 17.
23. See, for example, The Black Church and Domestic Violence Institute, Atlanta Georgia. For an ethical response to intimate violence from a black female scholar, see Traci West, *Disruptive Christian Ethics: When Racism and Women's Lives Matter* (New York: Westminster John Knox Press, 2006); and *Wounds of the Spirit: Women, Violence and Resistance Ethic* (New York: NYU Press, 1999).
24. Ma Rainey, "Hear Me Talkin' To You."
25. Matthew 7:6.
26. Matthew 8:20.
27. Eugene Robinson, *Disinte-gration: The Splintering of Black America* (New York: Doubleday, 2010),138.
28. Robison, *Disinte-gration*, 21.
29. This notion of "incidentally black" was suggested by my colleague Isaac Lawson in our discussions of black churches.
30. Quoted in Oliver, *Conversation with the Blues*, 22.

Blues Coda: Back to the Crossroads

1. Robert Johnson, "Cross Road Blues" 1936, "The Complete Recordings," Columbia C2K46222.

Index

CPSIA information can be obtained at www.ICGtesting.com
Printed in the USA
LVOW04s1802090615

441785LV00014B/398/P